THE
WEALTHY
WORLD

THE WEALTHY WORLD

The Growth and Implications of Global Prosperity

John C. Edmunds

*Edited by Karen Maccaro
and W. Randolph Thompson*

John Wiley & Sons, Inc.

New York • Chichester • Weinheim • Brisbane • Singapore • Toronto

Library of Congress Cataloging-in-Publication Data:

Edmunds, John C., 1947–
    The wealthy world: the growth and implications of global prosperity / John C.
Edmunds ; edited by Karen Maccaro.
        p.   cm.—(Wiley investment series)
    ISBN 0-471-39077-1 (cloth : alk. paper)
        1. Wealth.   2. Stock exchanges.   3. International business enterprises.
    4. International finance.   5. Economic history—1990–   I. Maccaro, Karen.
    II. Title.   III. Series.

HC79.W4 E35 2001
332.63'22—dc21   00-043609

Printed in the United States of America

10 9 8 7 6 5 4 3 2 1

To my mother,
who gave me my love of languages;
and to the memory of my father,
who gave me my love of the stock market.

Contents

Preface

The world made a giant step toward becoming wealthy during the 1990s. A new, more powerful wealth-creation mechanism caused this steep rise. The mechanism is so new that many parts of it were not linked effectively together before 1990. There had been rustlings and rumblings in the 1980s, because enough parts of the wealth-creation machinery had appeared that the whole assemblage would sputter to life from time to time. But the wealth-creating Leviathan in its present form did not really begin to roar until the early 1990s. Now the enormous apparatus is running fast and is giving glimpses of what it will be able to do when it gets going full blast. Already, the wealth being created every month exceeds the wealth that the old methods created during entire years. Wealth creation exceeded $2 trillion a month for several months in 1999, and the potential is for $5 trillion a month or more. World wealth has gone up by more than $10 trillion in the past 12 months, and it can go up by $20 trillion or more in the next 12 months. The rate of $5 trillion a month cannot be reached yet, because many parts of the world economy are lagging or stagnant or are still trying to use the old methods.

Despite the huge jumps in world wealth, there are many experts who deny that anything really new is happening. The decade's mammoth increase in wealth, according to these experts, is just another swing of the pendulum, or a bubble in U.S. asset prices. According to them, the world will soon revert to normal: The decade's instant millionaires will have their comeuppance, and they will tumble back into the middle class. Other experts are preachers of doom. As always, they are predicting that financial assets will become worthless overnight. According to them, there will be a cataclysmic financial meltdown, accompanied by the sounds of teeth gnashing and orphans wailing disconsolately.

This surge in wealth creation was easy to overlook or to misclassify. Every observer was trained not to see it, or to think it is something we have seen before, or to say that it is localized when it is in fact widespread. The news media did not portray the surge as an all-pervading phenomenon; on the contrary, media coverage gave the impression of a series of exceptions against the usual backdrop of poverty and suffering. The 1990s were said to be like the Roaring Twenties: People who were lucky or brilliant did especially well, better than they would have done earlier, with the same luck or brilliance. People who were mediocre did well, also—indeed, absurdly well, better than they had any right to expect. Consequently, most observers viewed the 1990s as an aberration, rather than as a fork in the road leading away from the old ways.

Longtime observers' sense of proportion was violated. The rewards to financial investments no longer seemed commensurate with the risk taken, the effort expended, or the value created. The laws of fairness—indeed, the laws of physics—appeared to have been repealed. Common sense said that the repeal had to be temporary. The visceral belief pulled what they saw back into the framework of their previous experience and training. They would repeat to themselves that what goes up has to come down.

Meanwhile, hundreds of millions of people got some of the wealth. And the masses at the bottom of the world's income distribution also gained: The per capita incomes of India and China doubled during the decade of the 1990s.

This book describes how the new surge in wealth creation happened and explains why the surge will continue. It gives an ultimate target for how much wealth will be created, and what that wealth will be based on, and who will have it. It gives a trajectory, and a timetable, and checkpoints that will have to be met along the way if the surge is to remain on track.

Many people have criticized the trajectory that the world is on. The wealth-creation machinery can be destructive, and it can create injustices as it steamrollers forward, flattening obstacles in its path. Critics express distaste for the direction in which the world economy is moving and speak of reversing the course of the wealth-creating Leviathan. They argue on many different grounds that the ultimate target cannot be reached. They also argue that the wealth-creation process will sooner or later blow up, leaving the world worse off. Future events may prove them right. But for now there is no turning back. The world is hurrying along the path of rapid wealth creation and is achieving more success as the method propagates. There will be bumps in the road, but those will not shatter the consensus to stay on the path.

·∾·

Many people have asked me how the ideas in this book came to me, and why I hold such a categorical view that world wealth can quickly vault to multiples of its current level. Most other specialists have more modest aspirations: Their hope is that a long, arduous struggle will raise world wealth up by its bootstraps. Recessions, currency crises, and political upheavals have battered their optimism and brought it into line with the "realistic" consensus that the world is doing very well if it can raise output by 3% a year, and that setbacks are inevitable. Meanwhile, my own optimism has risen. To me it seems that the stage is set for a quantum leap in world wealth, and that the leap is already underway. This unorthodox view came to me because I saw a particularly extreme contrast, like two blindingly bright colors in juxtaposition. The experience was so stark and so pivotal that it defined my position irreversibly.

What follows in the rest of this preface is a personal memoir describing this defining experience. It is a true story of economic depression in the midst of plenty. All the components of prosperity were there, but they were scattered asunder, and for most of an entire decade nobody, including myself, could get the machinery of growth started again. I have worked in many poor countries, and all of them should have been rich. In all of them the raw materials, the people, the ingenuity, and the energy were present, but poverty prevailed and lingered despite everyone's best efforts to alleviate it. In one of them, however, the contrast between reality and potential was so striking, and so galling, that it caused me acute distress. I worked frantically, talking to everyone I could find who might have an idea for a remedy, and I thought intensely for long hours, trying to discover some new permutation. The people around me felt my distress and suffered through my excesses of frustration. They consoled me, because they were wrestling with the same conundrum, and it was soothing to have their company, even if we were not making any progress.

The question we were struggling to answer was how to reactivate the economy of Costa Rica, which had fallen into a deep recession after having a banner year in 1979. The country had run out of foreign exchange and could not get any more. During the lengthy skull sessions and bull sessions I had with my colleagues and fellow-sufferers, we called Costa Rica's dilemma a foreign exchange drought.

During the 1970s I had lived and worked in Latin America and had a close affiliation with top experts in economic development and management. I had academic credentials and access to top economic policymakers. Then from 1982 to 1985 I lived and worked in Costa Rica. During that time the country was caught in a prolonged, severe recession, deep enough to be called a depression. It was frustrating to see this beautiful, peaceful, and previously prosperous country flailing so helplessly. A deep gloom hung over the economy, especially toward the beginning of my time there, and it cast a pall over most of the decade of the 1980s before starting to lift.

Costa Rica in Economic Paralysis

The depth of Costa Rica's economic crash can be chronicled by citing two statistics: In less than a year and a half its currency was devalued from 8.5 per dollar to 62 per dollar, and in one year its real output fell 10%. This profound slump was especially hard to watch because the country had been, in a modest way, well-off before economic depression hit. It was a pleasant place, with literacy approaching 100%, excellent indicators of physical quality of life, a vibrant democracy, and good public services. The expressions of bewilderment on people's faces and the sudden shattering of their middle-class lives cannot be described.

What was particularly galling to me, and to the Costa Ricans, was that only a couple of little things had gone wrong, and those things were nowhere near enough to have caused such economic devastation. The country had borrowed too much money from international banks, and the legislature had guaranteed too many of the loans. The prices of export commodities fell too low, and stayed down too long. The neighboring countries that usually bought Costa Rica's manufactured exports were not able to buy enough. And so Costa Rica ran out of foreign exchange.

Only a few remedies were considered, and most were the same trite and unimaginative remedies that other indebted countries were trying at that time. And they did not work. Like a captive tied up with rope, the country struggled but could not free itself. Costa Rica took all the conventional steps to free itself from the foreign exchange bind. It sent experts to negotiate debt-rescheduling agreements. It tried to develop new, nontraditional export industries. It tried to attract foreign investment. As the crisis went on, Costa Rica tried a few innovative remedies. It pioneered debt-for-nature swaps: Ecology-minded humanitarians bought some of Costa Rica's foreign debt, then gave it to the Costa Rican government in exchange for land that was then turned into national parks.

Costa Rica endured almost a decade of recession, depression, and gradual, painful recovery, and did not need to suffer so grievously. Its policy errors, and the external shocks it suffered, need not have caused such a prolonged slump. Recovery could have been swift, and could quickly have taken the country to new heights of prosperity, well above the level it enjoyed in its bonanza year of 1979.

Financial Gridlock

When a country's inflows of foreign exchange are below target, it can limp along, with many activities curtailed, or it can borrow to bridge the shortfall. Costa Rica borrowed, and the country maintained its growth as long as it could. Unfortunately, the foreign exchange earnings shortfall went on too long. The country then needed a huge rebound in its foreign exchange earnings to pay for normal imports, and to repay foreign borrowings. For a small country like Costa Rica, running out of foreign exchange is a serious problem. The country needs essential imports such as fuel, spare parts, pharmaceuticals, and agricultural chemicals in order to keep operating. Its national currency is not well known in other countries, and foreigners were not willing to accept it, unless they could immediately convert it to dollars. So there was a crisis.

The country tried floating the exchange rate, thinking that if the Costa Rican currency were a little cheaper, foreigners would buy more of the country's exports, and that would ease the shortage of foreign exchange. The strategy backfired catastrophically. The exchange rate was supposed to float from 8.5 per dollar to 12 or 14 per dollar. Instead a wave of panic selling broke out, and everyone who held Costa Rican currency tried to sell it and buy dollars. The exchange rate rocketed to 40, then 45, then 62 per dollar. Import prices went up sixfold in 18 months.

Currency collapses had happened before in other countries, and they happened again many times afterward—for example, in Mexico and Russia. What made this crisis particularly hard to resolve was the gridlock it caused in the Costa Rican banking system. Most of the loans that Costa Rican banks had made were dollar-linked. That is, the borrower had borrowed colóns (the local currency) and promised to repay colóns. But the repayment had an exchange-rate escalator clause, so a loan of C85,000 (colóns) taken out before the exchange rate exploded was considered a loan of $10,000; consequently, when it came time to repay, as much as C620,000 had to be repaid. And that was not all: On most loans the interest rate was variable and could be revised upward if market rates rose.

Borrowers could not repay. Some of them had been able to increase their incomes because they could charge more in colóns for their output. Inflation reached all parts of the economy to varying degrees, but not enough to bring borrowers' incomes back into line with the loan amounts. Before the crisis, the borrower who was earning C10,000 a month could have paid the C85,000 loan in three years. The interest rate before the crisis was below 15%. The monthly payment would have been C2,947 per month, or just under 30% of the borrower's income. After the crisis, the borrower's monthly income might have increased to C14,000 per month, or perhaps C18,000 per month, but either figure is obviously inadequate to repay C620,000. Interest rates rose to 30%, or 50% in some cases. So the interest alone would exceed the borrower's total monthly income.

The banks all went into suspended animation. All the loans they had made were suddenly uncollectable. They had borrowed dollars from banks in London and New York and were unable to repay these borrowings.

There were no runs on Costa Rican banks. Depositors had no difficulty withdrawing their local currency savings. The banks were all government-owned, so all the deposits were guaranteed. The government deposited newly printed banknotes in the banks, and the banks always had enough local currency on hand to pay depositors.

And there the banks sat—ostensibly open for business, willing to accept deposits, but unable to make new loans to local borrowers, and unable to pay their dollar liabilities to banks abroad. Construction projects were halted, because the banks did not have enough cash to fund their loan commitments. The cash was supposed to come from depositors, from collections of loans that had been given earlier, or from foreign borrowing. But depositors kept their money in their pockets, because they needed it to buy groceries, or because they were buying things they hoped would retain their value, such as imported consumer durable goods. Loan collections stopped coming in, and foreign banks stopped lending, so there were many buildings that remained half-finished for years.

Financial Intermediation Sputters, 1983 to 1985

There was no political will to close or liquidate banks. Bank employees had permanent status as government employees, so it would have been very messy and expensive to lay them off. And there was always hope for swift recovery—a commodities boom would have done nicely, but none came. Nor was there political will to get tough with borrowers. Borrowers were working hard and making their best efforts to repay. There were a few whispered grumblings about money that some borrowers had taken out of the country, but most borrowers were honest, hard-working people who had been dealt a hard knock by fate. They were not hated, and they did not steal money from their businesses. Instead, they were widely believed to have lost it fair and square, in investments that should have paid off. Borrowers were wealthy Costa Ricans, separated from ordinary citizens only by their wealth. They were not members of an ethnic minority, and among themselves they spoke the same Spanish as everyone else, so they were not demonized or isolated. They were not appealing targets for politicians.

In hindsight, one obvious remedy would have been to liquidate the banks, and then encourage new banks to be created. Liquidating the banks would have involved paying off all local currency deposits, selling the loans in a series of well-advertised auctions, and then selling the banks' computers, desks, and office buildings. The banks' dollar liabilities would have been replaced with Costa Rican government dollar bonds.

Not enough new Costa Rican banks would have come into existence, so the policy would have included allowing foreign banks to come in and operate. Removing restrictions on convertibility of the colón would have been part of this policy. Costa Ricans would have been allowed to hold foreign bank accounts and would have been allowed to convert colóns to dollars.

Privately owned banks would quickly have replaced the state-owned banks that were the only ones allowed to operate from 1948 to 1982. This would have meant that young people who entered their prime earning years from 1982 to 1989 would have gotten loans. These loans would have included business loans, home mortgages, car loans, and credit cards.

Saving via the financial system would have been encouraged. Many of the half-finished buildings would have been finished, as risk-takers would have bid for the buildings when they were auctioned. These risk-takers would then have rented or sold the buildings to new buyers. Tax revenues to the Costa Rican government would have risen, and the government would then have had more resources.

Instead, a dual financial system emerged. There was the official system, consisting of the paralyzed state-owned banks, the government bond market, the regulated foreign exchange market, and the stock exchange. There also emerged a parallel financial system, which operated outside the Costa Rican legal framework. It consisted of unregulated currency dealers and unregulated bankers. These underground bankers had dollar accounts in Miami and Panama. They accepted deposits, both dollars and local currency, and paid high interest rates to depositors. They made loans secured by physical collateral, and they made mortgage loans. When they made loans secured by raw materials, they kept the collateral in warehouses that the bank controlled and released the collateral as the borrower needed it. Mortgage loans were arranged in a circuitous way. The owner of a piece of real estate sold the real estate to a Panama corporation and then placed the shares of the corporation in escrow in Panama. The underground bank could take the shares and sell them if the loan were not repaid. When the mortgage loan was repaid, the escrow agent in Panama would release the shares back to the owner who had borrowed from the bank.

The unregulated currency exchange process was simple. Local currency was exchanged for dollars in the street. Dollar checks and traveler's checks were sent to Miami for collection. Pilots of the national airline and people with diplomatic passports carried the checks to Miami and Panama for collection. They were used as couriers because their luggage was not opened when they went through customs.

These ingenious methods worked, but they were not a complete substitute for full reform of the official banking system. Any real estate or collateral that had already been pledged to one of the official banks was outside the reach of these underground bankers, who had the fetching nickname of "coyotes." The reason was that the official banks would not release the property until they were paid in full, so a large portion of the assets in Costa Rica were immobilized. Consequently, new economic activity had to work around many of the existing assets. Some existing assets could be brought into use, but only in ways that did not lead to new demands for repayment of the immense amounts that were owed.

The parallel financial system had several obvious drawbacks. Most obviously, depositors had no legal protection. Several underground bankers found it expedient to abscond, and depositors also pulled off spectacular swindles. Counterfeit money, bad checks, and holdups at gunpoint were a constant threat to this fragile system. The underground bankers were unable to use wire transfers, except outside Costa Rica. Because of the risks and high costs, depositors demanded high interest rates, and borrowers had to pay even more. Interest rates were quoted in terms of monthly interest—for example, 3% a month for a well-secured loan in dollars.

There were also no lenders of last resort, no audits, and no guarantees of solvency. There was also no protection against Ponzi schemes. Consequently, depositors were wary and rarely put more than a few thousand dollars at risk. Each underground banker had to take utmost care to maintain a reputation. Consequently, the amount of business that each banker could do was severely limited, because a delay in collection could put a banker in a liquidity crisis. Underground bankers always had to maintain liquid reserves large enough to pay deposits when they fell due, regardless of any delays in collection the bankers might have suffered.

Because of these limitations, the parallel financial system was small compared to the size of the economy and the amount of growth opportunities that existed. Many worthy projects did not get financed.

A side effect was that Costa Rican government statistics did not describe all the economic activity that went on. Much of the economy went off the books. The Costa Rican government did not collect tax revenue on this underground activity, and it also lost control of monetary aggregates, so its monetary and fiscal policies lost much of their potential efficacy. The monetary authorities were well trained, and they knew what was happening, but they could not do much about it. They knew that economic activity could revive if there was some way to bring the full benefits of financial intermediation back into operation. But they could not make that happen, so they tried to muddle through.

Measuring the Lost Growth

Costa Rica had all the conditions for rapid growth that are hard to create: a highly educated population; excellent telecommunications; good roads, ports, and airports; abundant, cheap electricity; a reasonably clear set of rules about land titles and ownership rights; an excellent location; and a moderate, popularly elected government, with good transparency and accountability. Costa Rica gave favorable treatment to foreign investors and welcomed immigrants who had money to invest or professional qualifications. For these reasons, real economic growth of 9% should have been possible from 1980 to 1989.

Costa Rica also had impediments to growth that could easily have been set aside. Some of these were left in place because they were part of the social contract that Costa Ricans forged following their revolution of 1948. Others were in place for reasons that were accidental or misguided, and they were left in place because the Costa Ricans did not see how much damage they were doing.

What follows is a calculation of how much growth was lost during the period from 1980 to 1989. The calculation cannot be verified with statistics, both because it includes the underground economy and because it compares what did happen to what might have happened.

Suppose that in 1979 the value of output was 100. This is 70 in the official economy and 30 in the parallel economy. If progrowth policies had been in place for the years from 1980 to 1989, and if 9% real growth had been achieved, and if the portion of economic activity in the parallel economy had remained at 30%, then by 1989 the value of output would have been $100 \times 1.09^{10} = 237$. This would have consisted of 166 in the official economy and 71 in the parallel economy. Instead, only the parallel economy grew. The official economy shrank, then revived. For simplicity, assume that output in the official economy remained at 70 every year. With these assumptions, the cumulative loss of growth for the 1980 to 1989 period was 459! This is four and a half years of output at the 1979 rate, and more than six years of output for the official economy at the 1979 rate.

No wonder the 1980s were the Lost Decade for Latin America.

Performance Could Have Been Better

As the stagnation and financial gridlock were happening, I was racking my brain to find a solution. Conventional theories did not offer any relief because they were all targeting ways of increasing production. Raising output and exports were the objectives. Exports in particular had to rise to bring in more foreign exchange. Everybody knew that foreign exchange was the constraint. Producing more for the local market would not work because people would use any increase in their local currency income to buy goods, and some of the goods would be imports, so production could not grow unless there was more foreign exchange. Producing more would also require more financing. Factories needed to have raw materials on hand, and they needed to borrow the money to pay for those materials.

These hard realities buzzed around in my head and kept me awake at night. Endlessly I debated with other foreign experts, local experts, business people, radicals, and reactionaries to find a way to cut Costa Rica free from the straitjacket it was in.

The answer was lying all around me, and little by little I was able to see it. The country is so beautiful, so pleasant, and so peaceful that the idea gradually formed in my mind that the country had to be valuable. The valuable assets that I could see all around me had to be worth much more money than the amount needed to jump-start the economy.

The idea formed in my mind of figuring out what Costa Rica's assets would be worth if the foreign exchange crisis had not existed. I wanted to value them as if they were in any other pleasant, well-organized country. I wanted to value them not for producing exports, but for other purposes, such as providing a pleasant place to live. Costa Rica's assets were not worth much for exporting commodities. As an exporting country, Costa Rica had no special advantages. Its coffee, sugar, and bananas were just commodities, and commodity prices happened to be depressed. Costa Rica was barely able to produce and sell $1 billion a year of traditional commodity exports, so if the country were a farm, it would not have been worth much more than $10 billion dollars—or perhaps less.

This paltry amount was obviously much too low. Houses in the U.S. at that time cost about $100,000 each. If the $10 billion figure were correct, a mere 100,000 houses in the United States would have been worth as much as the whole country of Costa Rica, with its highly educated population of 2 million people.

The disparity in the dollar amounts convinced me that the prices of buildings and land in Costa Rica were much too low compared to how nice they were and how good life could be there. People talked of selling their houses in Miami and moving to Costa Rica and living on the interest from their savings. They sold a couple of hundred dollars every week and lived very well.

Meanwhile, an even smaller figure—$4 billion—was the nail in the country's knee. That was the face amount of the dollar-denominated foreign debt. The figure was not large except in comparison to the country's annual exports: It was equal to about four years' worth of exports. At the time it looked enormous and insurmountable, but the amount that lenders would have accepted was much less. Costa Rican government-guaranteed debt paper was trading at 20% of face value. There were banks in Europe and the United States that would sell their loan receivables for that price instead of waiting to get paid in full, so the real amount needed to clear the country's foreign debt was much less than $4 billion.

The full answer to Costa Rica's economic stagnation in the 1980s came to me piece by piece. I published the first bits in 1988, but I did not formulate the answer in the form that I am expressing it here until later. The answer was to ignore production and to ignore exports. The Costa Rican government should have turned all its attention to raising the market value of the productive assets in the country. The market value of all the income-producing assets in the country was terribly low in the first half of the 1980s, and it rose too slowly in the second half of the 1980s.

In 1982, the market price for all the houses, farms, factories, motor vehicles, and machinery in the country was probably no higher than $3 billion. This figure is distorted because it is based on only a few transactions. If buyers had begun showing up in large numbers and had begun buying, prices would have jumped quickly. But cash was so scarce, and financing was so hard to obtain, that there were not very many transactions.

The market for assets was more paralyzed than the market for goods and services. A small improvement would have made a big difference. If the government had put its attention and resources into stimulating the asset market, Costa Rica might have recovered faster and sooner.

THE
WEALTHY
WORLD

Chapter 1

The Trajectory and
the Potential

Most people in the world traditionally knew where they stood in the hierarchy of wealth. They knew from childhood whether they were wealthy or poor. They did not need a wide range of categories to bracket themselves. A few pigeonholes covered the possibilities. Most people could also resign themselves to staying down if they were not in one of the higher categories. Their hope—and for most it was a slim hope—was that their children would move up.

Now it takes more categories to classify people, and there are more people moving up, and people know it. They have realistic hopes of ascending the ladder of wealth during their own lifetimes. A latter-day version of Nurkse's "demonstration effect" has portrayed for many precisely what the next steps up the ladder look like. Full-motion color video and quadraphonic sound now envelop even the poorest people, and demonstrate for them much more detail than Nurkse contemplated in 1958, when battery-powered radios carried the vanguard of information propagation beyond the span of the electric power grid.

People stuck in a rut of poverty, in a chronic state of unconsummated aspiration, now know that entire communities, even entire countries, can suddenly become wealthier. They know the heretical truth, and they

1

grasp it at an instinctual level. They do not know how to make it happen, but they know perfectly well that it does happen. It happens across the world, across town, and across the street. People know it whether they live in cities or in remote areas, even in countries that try to control access to information.

This heretical, universally known truth has four premises:

- The world is much wealthier than it was 10 or 20 years ago.
- The potential for further enormous increases is at hand.
- Wealth is increasing at a faster rate each year.
- The wealthy are getting wealthier, and their wealth is growing faster and faster.

There are uncertain parts too: the questions of whether the poorest are obtaining any absolute improvement in living standards, and how to bring the benefits of increasing wealth to the entire population.

The potential world wealth today could be as high as $1 quadrillion. This figure is an estimated maximum potential market value of all productive assets on earth. These include land, buildings, machines, intellectual property, and franchises. These also include mineral resources that have already been discovered and developed, as well as commercial forests. This figure also includes the value that organizations like corporations are able to achieve in excess of the value of the assets they are managing. This figure does not assume any quantum leap in technology or resources. Explicitly, it does not assume that a clean, renewable, costless source of energy will be discovered; it does not assume any sudden increase in the educational level of the workforce; it does not assume any big jump in construction or infrastructure; and it does not assume any important new discoveries of oil or minerals.

The $1 quadrillion figure for potential wealth compares with the much lower figure that exists today. With today's market conditions, total world wealth does not exceed $130 trillion. Today's total includes more than $87 trillion worth of financial assets; other assets are not securitized, and so are not priced daily in financial markets. Those other assets would probably be appraised at about $42 trillion today.

The gap between today's puny level and the much larger potential level seems enormous, but it is due to only a few factors, and those factors are easy to identify and remedy. Moreover, the task of raising the market values up to their potential level is already underway, and the gap is being bridged very quickly.

To put the world wealth figures into per capita terms, the potential is $166,666 of assets for each of the 6 billion people on earth, compared to the approximately $20,000 that has been achieved until now. The same assets can be worth more, but presently are not. The increase in value is approximately 20 times the world average annual per capita income. Wealth increases have the potential to exceed income and have already done so for short periods of time. The steep rise of wealth can be made to continue.

Tracking the Rise

Most readers would not have guessed how high world wealth has already risen. The big increase has been recent, and most of the increase has been in the market value of financial assets. The tangible assets that most people used to think of as wealth have not increased much. There is no more land than there was before, and only slightly more gold has been extracted and refined. There may be more buildings and roads but there are probably fewer trees, and there is certainly less oil because so much of it has been extracted and burned.

So it would seem that there is not much more real, physical wealth in the world than there was at those times in the past that people think of as reference points, like 1980 or 1990. Nevertheless, the rise in market value of financial assets has been spectacular. In 1980 the value was $13 trillion. By 1990 it had reached $37 trillion. And at the end of 1998 it was $78 trillion. The annual compound growth rate for the first interval was 11%, already a remarkable rate. The growth rate for the second time interval was 9.7%. And the growth rate from 1996 to 1999 has been 14.3%, an astounding increase by any standard, so astounding as to require discussion.

The 14.3% annual rate of growth from 1996 to 1999 is not the achievement of one country; it is a world average. It is 1½ times higher than the growth rate of the previous period, and if it continues it would quickly raise world financial wealth to the $500 trillion level, and from there to the $1 quadrillion target figure. At a 14.3% annual growth rate, the year-end 1998 figure of $78 trillion compounds to $500 trillion in 14 years, or by 2012. At the slightly higher annual growth rate of 23%, it compounds to the $1 quadrillion level over the same time horizon. Financial assets grew faster than the world average in many individual countries, so they might achieve the potential level in less time.

Skeptics argue that these growth rates are aberrations, and are not sustainable. They argue that the world is in a serendipitous interlude, when conditions favor a buildup of financial wealth, but sometime soon conditions will revert to normal, and financial wealth will fall back into its normal proportions. They support their argument by scrutinizing components of total financial wealth, and then affirming that the growth in the total is accounted for by only a few of the components. They then argue that those few components are going to slow down, or go into descent. Let us consider some of the standard arguments that skeptics adduce.

First, the growth of financial assets was not entirely driven by the rise of the U.S. stock market. Taking out the U.S. stock market boom, the annual rate of increase from 1996 to 1999 was still 10.1%. Second, the growth was not entirely driven by new issuance of government bonds. Taking out the increase in Japanese and Euroland* government bonds, the annual growth rate from 1996 to 1999 was still 11.8%. Third, the growth was not caused by inflation in the prices of goods and services. Inflation was low in the United States, Euroland, and Japan during the 1996 to 1999 period. Inflation would not have caused the market value of financial assets to rise, because it is the enemy of financial assets. Financial assets are claims on future amounts of *money*, not future amounts of purchasing power. Their market prices would not rise if investors were worried about inflation. Fourth, a falling rate of inflation did not cause the rise of financial assets either. Inflation in the dollar market was high in 1980, then declined by 1982, and has been low ever since.

The high growth rates are not so easy to brush aside. They survive the piece-by-piece deconstruction. In particular, the rise is not entirely a case of collective speculative delusion. It is not simply a few million rich kids tossing a few dozen hot stocks back and forth among themselves at astronomical prices. That is just the foam on top of the wave. The wave is much more substantial than that.

To dissect the increase in financial assets, and see what it consists of, consider Table 1.1. The numbers are a consequence of several important trends.

* The countries of the European Union, which have adopted the euro as a common currency.

Table 1.1   World Financial Assets, $ Trillions

Category	1980	1990	2000 (est.)
Bank deposits and cash	5	15	24
Equities	3	8	38
Government bonds	3	9	17
Corporate bonds	2	5	9
Total	13	37	88

Note: Excludes mortgages and gold. Total for 1998 was $78 trillion.
Source: Data from the International Monetary Fund (IMF), International Finance Corporation (IFC), Bank for International Settlements, Morgan Stanley Capital Markets International (MSCI), Salomon Smith Barney, and *The Economist*.

First, banks are losing market share everywhere. Middle-class savers used to put their money into savings accounts at banks. Now they no longer do so. Instead, they put their savings into mutual funds and pension funds. Savers also buy stocks and bonds directly, and they do so in much greater numbers than they used to. They now feel confident enough to buy stocks and bonds, when previously only the intrepid and the wealthy did so. The recent performance of stocks and bonds has justified their confidence. If their confidence continues, and if the buying power they can muster is sufficient, the dollar value of financial assets can keep rising, and can keep revalidating their confidence.

Second, stocks held in tax-exempt retirement and pension accounts are gaining market share. Middle-class savers used to be cautious with the savings under their control, because their pensions and their current livelihood were both tied to the same employer. If the company they worked for went under, it would take their job and their pension down together. The Employee Retirement Income Security Act, passed in the late 1970s, gradually decoupled pension security from job security, so savers now are more risk tolerant.

Third, there are now more savings products offered to middle-class savers. These products target narrower segments of the saving public, and appeal to them at different phases of the life cycle. Savers who might not have put much into plain-vanilla financial products like savings accounts or whole life insurance policies have put money into products that combine tax exemption, downside protection, and upside potential.

In summary, the rise of financial assets has its grounding in the happy conjuncture of macroeconomic stability, favorable tax and regulatory rulings, and savers who can afford to take risks. Later chapters will show how some corporate managers and governments have done their part to spur the rise. The same illustrations will show there is still more room for growth. The rise is gathering momentum and gaining new converts and can continue.

Is $1 Quadrillion Attainable?

Starting from $78 trillion in 1998, can the market value of world financial assets reach $500 trillion or $1 quadrillion in a short time? Surely that would be a stupendous accomplishment. Those immense figures equate to 500 million or 1 billion people with financial assets of $1 million each, assuming that the rest of the people on earth have no financial assets. A vertical ascent that large would be too much of a leap. All the world's productive assets, even if they were securitized and packaged as well-designed financial assets, could hardly support such a high figure for world financial asset value.

Standard calculations show how difficult it would be for world financial asset values to attain the $500 trillion or $1 quadrillion level. World annual output for 1999 is worth $39 trillion. For a country, total market value of financial assets can hardly be expected to exceed 5 times the value of annual output. If the same multiple is applied to the world, it would seem that the maximum attainable figure for financial asset values, assuming that all assets had been securitized, would be $195 trillion. A different calculation indicates how high the target figure is, compared to annual output and savings. Suppose that world savings is 25% of output. Suppose also that all savings are invested in low-yielding investments like bank deposits or short-term government bonds. Savings would be $9.75 trillion for the year 1999, and that is only $\frac{1}{43}$ of the difference between $78 trillion and $500 trillion [(500 − 78)/9.75 = 43]. And it is only about 1% of the difference between $78 trillion and $1 quadrillion.

These standard calculations are correct, yet it is still possible for world financial assets to attain a total market valuation of $500 trillion or $1 quadrillion in less than 20 years. Three facts make this exclamatory assertion a real possibility:

- *Prices of financial assets sometimes rise sharply when only a small portion of them change hands.*   To see why, consider first an example from the world of tangible assets. Suppose that in a town there are 10,000 houses. During a normal year 500 of these come onto the market. If, in a particular year, 800 would-be buyers appear, the prices are bid up. Some owners who were not thinking of selling change their minds and put their houses on the market. This increases the supply, but the total number of houses for sale does not reach 800. Some would-be buyers give up, but others persist. So the prices keep moving up, until finally the number of houses offered equals the number purchased. If 700 houses are sold, for example at prices 20% higher than they were before, the 9,300 owners who did not sell have a gain. The gain is a paper profit, and may disappear before they are able to take advantage of it, but in the meantime they can borrow against their houses as if the new, higher valuation were real.

  Now consider a common stock. Seventy million shares of this stock have been issued, but most of them are not for sale. They are held in blocks by the group that controls the company, or by large, long-term investors. The free float of shares that are available in the market on a daily basis may be only 20 million. Daily trading may be only 1 million shares. So if buyers appear wishing to buy 2 million shares, their purchases may drive up the price. Again, the price increase is a paper profit for the holders of the 68 million shares that did not trade that day. Nevertheless, those shares can be pledged as collateral for loans, and they will be valued as if they were really worth the most recent market price.

  So a small amount of buying, much less than $9.75 trillion per year—indeed, less than $3 trillion per year—can drive up market prices of financial assets. The buying power only has to slightly exceed the selling, and only on a majority of days, not every trading day.

- *Savings are not the only source of buying power.*   Owners of tangible productive assets like farms can convert them into financial assets. At first glance this would not seem to generate any new buying power, but it can. Suppose that a person owns a farm worth $500,000. The owner mortgages the farm for $400,000, and puts the proceeds into a bank account. This creates a mortgage receivable and a bank account. The owner's net worth is the same as before. The only difference is that the owner holds more of it in the form of financial assets and less in the form of unencumbered tangible assets. Financial assets rise by $800,000—namely, bank accounts rise by $400,000 and mortgages receivable rise by $400,000. This transformation does not immediately create any new wealth. But it does add to the total amount of financial assets, and it can also increase buying power for volatile financial assets.

Suppose that the farm owner uses the $400,000 to buy common stocks that have small amounts of free float. This purchase might drive up prices of these stocks. Suppose that one of them was the stock mentioned before, and the farm owner's purchase drove up the price of the stock by $1. In that case, for one day at least, the farm owner's purchase would have raised the market value of that company's shares by $70 million.

But who had the $400,000 before, and what prevented them from using it to buy the stock? The bank that gave the farm owner the loan had the money before. The bank got it from its depositors. The depositors could have bought the stock, but they did not. They were risk averse. The farm owner took a risk. The farm owner mortgaged the farm and put the money into a volatile stock.

The risk taking in this example is an important part of its message. The farm owner could have used the $400,000 to buy Treasury bills. But Treasury bills do not jump up in value the way volatile common stocks can. If the market value of financial assets is going to reach a level as high as $500 trillion or $1 quadrillion quickly, owners of assets are going to have to take actions that historically have been considered risky. Investing in growth will give capital gains, and later some of the gains will be invested in bonds, including newly issued bonds.

- *Many new businesses produce and sell intellectual property.* For example, they invent new drugs, or they write new computer software. It is widely agreed that they create value when they do this. It is also clear that the value they create is not limited by the constraints that implicitly cap the value of financial assets. The cap of 5 times annual output can be surpassed. For an illustration, consider an island country that has two industries: farming and iron-ore mining. The total value of all claims on this economy is strictly limited. Rational investors would not pay more than 5 times the value of the annual output of the farms. This assumes that the crops are annual staples with no exceptional qualities, and that labor and purchased inputs leave only part of the value of the output to pay dividends to the owners of the farms. Rational investors would not pay more for the iron-ore mines than the present value of the ore in the ground, less the costs of extracting it. So the market value of the total capital stock of this island economy is capped.

Now suppose that a brilliant person on the island discovers a new drug that can cure malaria, tuberculosis, and AIDS. This truly remarkable compound is cheap and easy to make. In a spirit of civic generosity, the brilliant person donates the patent to the government of the island country. The cap can now obviously be exceeded. The government can now sell enormous amounts of government bonds, and the total value of financial assets supported by the country's assets will greatly exceed 5 times its annual output.

The cap on market values of productive assets comes from traditional relationships between inputs and outputs, and from traditional ranges for the distribution of the output. Seed, land, and labor produce grain. Some of the grain has to be set aside as seed, and the laborers have to eat. The landowner can keep the rest. When the landlord wants to sell a farm, the value of the land is determined by its fertility, by the price of the crop, and by the opportunity cost of capital. Since farming is an uncertain business, a buyer who pays more than 5 times the value of the annual output will probably regret it.

Many businesses now, however, do not obey these traditional relationships. The relationship between inputs and outputs does not stay within predictable ranges. Computer software is an example. The cost of writing a new program may be recouped after the first 10,000 copies of it are sold. But it may go on to sell millions more copies. For some businesses, it is apparently rational to pay 25 or more times annual revenues. If that ratio would apply to all the income-producing properties in the world, they would already be worth $975 trillion ($39 trillion world output × 25 = $975 trillion).

The question of whether the market value of world financial assets can or will reach $500 trillion or $1 quadrillion is therefore open. The possibilities for assets to increase in value are so open-ended that old rules of thumb do not cap them. The traditional 5-to-1 cap implies that for world wealth to reach $1 quadrillion, world annual output would have to reach $200 trillion. But that traditional ratio may no longer apply. So world wealth may reach $1 quadrillion before world annual output reaches $200 trillion.

Requirements for $500 Trillion of Financial Wealth

This book presents two similar scenarios for world wealth. This chapter presents the first scenario, illustrating what the annual macroeconomic aggregates would have to be for world wealth to reach a market value of $500 trillion. Chapter 12 presents another scenario, showing what those aggregates would have to be for world wealth to reach a market value of $1 quadrillion. As mentioned, the two scenarios are similar to each other; the one in Chapter 12 is just a bit more extreme. Both describe a vision of prosperity that the world can reach. Both are expressed in terms of world aggregates, and the reader may find them iconoclastic. If this book achieves its intended effect, the latter scenario will seem unremarkable and reasonable. Achieving a fivefold or tenfold increase in world wealth will seem a suitable and feasible objective.

Here is the first scenario. Suppose that world financial assets have a market value of $500 trillion. Suppose that the $500 trillion consists of bonds, bank deposits, and other fixed-income securities worth $200 trillion, and common stocks worth $300 trillion. The fixed-income securities yield 5% on average, so $10 trillion of annual output would have to be dedicated to paying interest to the holders. The common stocks are trading at 30 times earnings, so $10 trillion of corporate earnings would be needed to support the $300 trillion valuation of all common stocks.

What level of annual world output would be required to support those amounts of debt service and corporate profit? Historically, total interest payments plus corporate profits after tax have been less than 25% of annual output. On that basis it would appear that world annual output would have to be at least $80 trillion. That is slightly more than twice the 1999 level of $39 trillion. But suppose world output were $60 trillion, and $20 trillion of that were dedicated to interest payments and corporate profits. That could be done if society chose to direct those resources to those ends. In that event there would still be $40 trillion of annual output left over, after interest and corporate profits. That would leave about $6,700 a year per person for the 6 billion people on earth, well in excess of the present figure of approximately $5,500. The people who do not own financial assets could gain 22% in per capita income terms while world output increased 54%. Holders of financial wealth, including new holders, would gain more than 500% from the policy of dedicating a higher portion of the annual output to corporate profits and interest payments.

The policy would make winners of some people and would leave some others as losers, at least in relative terms. The winners would gain much more than enough to be able to compensate the losers. Here is a direct way of showing how easily the winners could afford to compensate everyone who would be worse off in any sense. Suppose the owners of financial assets give the nonowners some of their gargantuan capital gains, which would be most of the increase of $422 trillion ($500 trillion − $78 trillion = $422 trillion). If every winner gave one-tenth of his or her gain to a pool to compensate the losers, the pool's worth would equal approximately one entire year's annual output.

Another way to show that the winners could compensate the losers is to describe two growth paths. The first one prioritizes current consumption: Society pays to owners of financial assets whatever is left over after current consumption needs have been met. The second one prioritizes the value of financial wealth. On the first path, annual world output rises at 3.1% per year, and the value of financial assets grows at a slow rate, for example 7%, because payments to wealth holders are held at a low level. On the second path, annual world output grows at 3.1% per year, and the value of financial assets grows at 14.3% per year. The difference in the first year would be 7.3% (14.3% − 7% = 7.3%) of $78 trillion, or $5.7 trillion. That amount is nearly 5 times the value of the annual increase in world output of $1.2 trillion. It follows that wealth can increase much faster than output, and winners would have enough gains to compensate losers several times over. Directing more of each year's output to reward wealth holders creates a much bigger pie.

To conclude this scenario, the computations indicate that world output would have to rise only a little more than 50% to support a sextupling of world wealth, to $500 trillion. The key requirement for wealth to increase that much is to dedicate a larger portion of current output to corporate profits and interest payments. World output would have to grow at only 3.1% a year to accomplish an increase of slightly more than 50% in 14 years. World output has grown that fast during several periods in the past, and can do it again. World financial wealth would have to grow only as fast as it did in the 1996 to 1999 period to reach $500 trillion by the 2012 to 2014 time frame. It can grow that fast, and if it does, the impact on all facets of life on the planet will be unprecedented.

The scenario in Chapter 12 is only a bit more extreme. After the descriptions and numerical illustrations in the chapters that follow, it may seem obvious and attainable. Yet the scenario in Chapter 12 contemplates world wealth of $1 quadrillion, a figure more than 10 times today's level.

In conclusion, the world economy is on a trajectory of rapidly increasing financial wealth. Annual output, the daily fare of news about the economy, is growing at its usual slow and erratic pace, and government policymakers in Euroland and Japan are trying to reactivate sluggish growth. Financial wealth, meanwhile, is growing beyond all previous magnitudes. Financial wealth has always risen and fallen, and has not been at center stage. Now it has taken the starring role, and is pushing aside other measures of economic performance. Financial wealth has not yet come anywhere near reaching its potential. The magnitudes discussed here seem outlandish, but the world economy is on a trajectory to attain them. The following chapters show piece by piece the mechanisms and motors that are creating so much financial wealth.

Chapter 2

Buyers and Sellers

Buying has set the tone in financial markets most days since 1987. Buyers have channeled more and more cash into acquiring financial assets. Sellers have been able to liquidate any piece of paper, provided that it has had some claim to cash payments coming later.

Buyers Chasing Pieces of Paper
Previous generations would have been surprised how easy it has been lately to sell securities. In the past, sellers sometimes had to wait weeks or months. A quick sale used to bring a much lower price because buyers did not pop up quickly. Of course, there were always first-quality securities that could be realized quickly, without steep commissions. Now, in comparison, a much wider range of securities enjoys such instant liquidity. The criteria have broadened for entry into the top categories of blue-chip, investment-grade respectability. Even many securities that do not have a very definite claim on future cash flows are treated as first-rate most of the time. There is also room in the market for claims that are unabashedly questionable. As long as the paper is not downright fraudulent, a willing buyer will be in the market with money in hand, ready to buy. In fact several willing buyers will usually be found there, bidding for the paper.

Buyers have not been completely indiscriminate. Sometimes they do scramble to buy any security in a category that is in fashion, but they can also sometimes turn gimlet-eyed and pull back their bids while they punch buttons on their calculators. And although the great mass of investors may disdain categories that are out of favor, some buyers specialize in finding overlooked gems among out-of-favor securities that faddish buyers are shunning.

Sellers, meanwhile, have been in short supply. There has not been enough paper on sale to keep prices from rising. Some selling is random, because owners of securities face emergency needs for cash, and sell to deal with the sudden need. Sellers also calibrate value carefully, using personal gauges of risk and return. During previous market booms, sellers lost their nerve sooner as prices rose. They would reach their personal trigger points, and then start a cascade of selling that would bring prices down. During the prolonged rally of the 1990s, many owners evidently held on to their securities. One view is that instead of bringing forth more securities into the market, rising prices caused sellers to withhold.

What is particularly surprising is that issuers, seeing the demand, did not create enough new paper to satisfy the buyers. Governments issued more bonds, but not enough to keep prices of bonds from rising. Corporations acted in even more contrary fashion. They did not show any sustained willingness to take up and use the new funds that were being offered to them. They issued bonds, but sometimes only to refinance other bonds they had sold earlier. During some time periods, the total supply of corporate bonds did not increase. And corporations' issuance of common stock was even more conspicuously Lilliputian. Many corporations, especially U.S. corporations, bought their own shares in the market and then destroyed them. So during some time periods from 1982 to 1999, the total supply of common stock actually shrank.

This striking fact—that strong demand did not call forth enough new supply—flies in the face of an elementary principle of capitalist economies: If consumers want more of a product, businesses will produce more of it. In this case, there was no obvious restraint braking the increase in the supply of securities. Issuing new paper does not require any exotic raw material or secret production process. Any credible government or corporation could have done it. Many did, but in the aggregate they were evidently not issuing enough new paper. If governments and well-known corporations were not willing to issue more securities, new entities should have appeared, which would issue securities and sell them to the legions of buyers who were constantly on the lookout for new securities. The new issuers should then have invested the cash in new construction, research and development, or consumption.

Common sense and the profit motive both dictate that there should have been a steady increase in the amount of stocks and bonds, approximately in line with the increase in demand, or trailing slightly behind the increase in demand, so that prices would go up slowly. Instead, there was a chronic shortage of securities all during the period from 1980 onward, and the shortage has been particularly acute since 1991.

The herding behavior of buyers, who pile new purchases on top of their earlier ones, the reluctance of sellers, and the mystifying reluctance of issuers to allay the shortage of new securities all need to be understood. The motivations of buyers, sellers, and issuers make sense when they are examined one by one. Their behaviors have been rational, and if buyers, sellers, and issuers continue to act rationally, it is feasible that the rally in securities prices can continue for a long time. For securities prices to keep rising, there does not need to be mass hysteria nor collective delusion. Careful assessment may reveal how the rational actions of buyers, sellers, and issuers can combine in concert to produce price appreciation, windfall capital gains, and real prosperity.

Buyers Choosing Paper Wealth over Tangible Wealth

Since 1980, middle-class savers everywhere have gradually felt more comfortable with the idea of owning paper assets. Prior to that time, ordinary people in the United States, Europe, and elsewhere had been wary of having too much of their savings tied up in paper assets. There had been too many crashes, bubbles, swindles, and hyperinflations. Major financial disruptions had happened in every country at least once every generation, and most people had suffered personally and knew one or more people who had lost everything. The conventional wisdom was that stocks and bonds were risky, and that the stock market was safe only for rich people. The rich could do well in the stock market more often, because they knew the directors and other insiders, and their friends would tell them when to get out. Middle-class people were cannon fodder. They sometimes did well for a few months or years, but in the end they got burned. They were the ones left holding the bag when the smart money sold out. Older people who remembered the Depression felt gun-shy about every kind of paper asset, including savings accounts.

After 1934, savings accounts in the United States were guaranteed by the government. From then on, the middle classes came warily back, but they were cautious, as a dog that has been beaten is cautious as it moves gingerly toward its moody, violent owner. Insurance companies won back the trust of the middle classes, but it took until the 1980s for the stock market to win their acceptance. By the end of the 1970s, most middle-class people had money in bank accounts, and many of them had insurance policies, but most middle-class households did not own any stocks. And most middle-class people still had some of their wealth in safer things, like jewelry and gold.

There was a stock market boom in the United States from 1951 to 1966, and that boom presaged the big one that began in the fall of 1982. The 1950s and 1960s stock market boom drew in many middle-class people, and lasted long enough for some of them to make large amounts and keep the profits long enough to enjoy them. The flutter and excitement that people got who dabbled in the 1951 to 1966 boom presaged the sustained happiness that characterizes the modern era of stock ownership. Yet the 1950s and 1960s boom was different in feel and in reach. Much clearer memories of the Crash of 1929, the Depression, and World War II tempered its optimism. The 1950s and 1960s boom reached a smaller cohort of middle-class savers who got into the stock market. Most people stayed out. At the height of the 1960s bull market, in 1966, only about 15% of U.S. households owned common stocks. This figure includes the households that owned stock-oriented mutual funds.*

---

* Some sources cite a higher percentage because corporate pension funds in those days tended to be invested in shares of the corporation. The people who owned common stock in this way should not be included because they did not make a decision to buy. They owned shares in the companies they worked for, but only in the sense that their retirement funds were going to be paid for by the companies. They did not have any stock certificates as proof of their ownership, and they did not receive an annual statement of how much they had accumulated. The employees' pension fund was not a separate legal entity that was managed by an independent trustee. Instead, it was just a liability of the corporation, and once a year an actuary would compute how much the company was supposed to show in its accounts as earmarked for paying pensions to employees. A dollar amount called *pension liability* appeared in the corporation's annual report, and a footnote said that it was an estimate of how much the corporation would have to pay in the future to retirees. So owning stock that way was, for most employees, an accidental by-product of having a job.

Then, in the 1970s, and especially from 1973 to 1979, ordinary people went back to being wary of paper assets. Stock prices rose higher in 1972 than they had been in 1966, and the future looked bright. But 1973 saw crop failures, the first Organization of Petroleum Exporting Countries (OPEC) crisis, and a bear market in common stocks that cut their value in half over the course of a two-year decline. Money itself was knocked off its throne. The inflation of the Vietnam buildup from 1966 accelerated, and people questioned the ability of financial assets to deliver safety and positive returns. Many people returned to the old standbys of gold, silver, farmland, and other tangibles.

The Leap of Faith

Why has the period since 1980 been so different? Middle-class savers have put aside their caution and have poured money into paper assets. This is especially true in the United States, but is gradually becoming true elsewhere, most recently in Euroland. The acceptance of financial assets, including asset categories that had always been viewed with suspicion, has grown beyond any level that had ever been reached in the past. This growing acceptance has gone so far that many middle-class people under 40, and most who are under 30, do not know that financial assets in general and common stocks in particular were once viewed with skepticism.

The acceptance of financial assets has been accompanied by an equally strong acceptance of major financial houses like Merrill Lynch and Fidelity. Savers are completely relaxed about holding their securities indirectly—that is, leaving the stock certificates in the custody of a brokerage house or a mutual fund management company.

The sudden willingness to trust intermediaries is as new and striking as the sudden preference for paper assets. In 1969 and 1970, financial commentators were warning against leaving stock certificates in "street name"—that is, in the custody of a Wall Street firm. Stories were going around about year-end audits in which the brokerage firms' inventories did not match what their customer account statements said was supposed to be there. Ross Perot, whose Electronic Data Systems (EDS) shares made him a billionaire in 1968, tried to tame the paper tiger by taking control of the Du Pont brokerage firm, at that time the seventh largest on Wall Street. After a year-long struggle, he gave up.[1] At that point Wall Street firms were under a cloud of suspicion because the rumors were apparently true: The firms could not handle all the data and paper they were responsible for. Investors were advised to take delivery of the stock certificates every time they bought stock, and to keep the certificates in their own safe-deposit boxes. Then, when their brokerage firms failed under a mountain of unreconciled accounts statements, they would be safe with their certificates in their own possession.

Now these fears seem quaint, and most people have never heard that the paper tiger problem ever existed. Nevertheless, it is impressive that today's buyers take the leap of faith with such calm disregard for the risk that financial houses might fail. The risk is plain to see when one puts the typical transaction in mundane terms. Imagine buying gold coins and then leaving them in the vault of the coin dealer, or buying diamonds and leaving them in the care of the diamond merchant. Does this sound like a sensible thing to do? Isn't the point of owning gold and diamonds their safety? If there is a crisis, shouldn't the gold and diamonds be where the owners can get to them in a hurry? And what if there is no crisis, but the dealer fails because of embezzlement or mismanagement? Would any government agency then step forward and replace the investors' gold and diamonds? Today's middle-class savers apparently do not worry about such events. In fact, there are many layers of protection, so they really should not worry. But still it is remarkable what a feeling of comfort, safety, and familiarity middle-class savers have with financial houses.

The reality is that savers who have no expertise about the stock market are now willing to put most of their savings into financial intermediaries, which then put the money into common stocks. Savers' preferences no longer swing back and forth between paper assets and tangibles. The wariness of the 1970s now seems remote and quixotic. Proselytes of the New Economy look askance at people who talk too much about tangible book value, hard assets, and liquidity. The massive move to financial assets that began in the early 1980s, and has gathered steam since then, has been the dominant economic phenomenon of the past two decades. It presaged the fall of the Berlin Wall and was the principal underpinning and driving wheel of the 1990s wealth-creation dynamic.

Advantages of Paper Assets
There are good reasons for the middle class's growing preference for paper assets, and together these good reasons add up to an impressive advantage.

The advantage was slight at the beginning of the 1980s, and has grown larger over the past two decades. The advantage is still growing, and will probably continue to grow, but it is important to keep in mind that the advantage is always fragile and vulnerable no matter how large it becomes. Today's edifice of paper wealth can be likened to a very tall building that is narrow at the ground level. The building is made of girders that can bear weight but are brittle. The building keeps getting taller, and as it does it becomes more vulnerable to any strong wind that comes along. Its foundation is solid and strong, but the growing height of the building will put growing pressure on any flaw in its foundation. The fragility and the vulnerability of the edifice are constant companions of the world's growing wealth.

Each reason for preferring paper assets is a valuable social asset, which has to be created by consensus, then anchored firmly in the social contract. Well-functioning financial markets are one of the real advantages that people can acquire when they gather together to form cohesive societies. Each advantage of paper assets over tangibles is an asset that society holds in common, because it channels savings to financial markets. Tangibles are inert, and savings are more productive if they are put to work creating new productive assets. Keynes remonstrated against hoarding, and advocated putting money into circulation. He characterized interest as the reward for not hoarding. In the same vein, modern middle-class savers should not sink their money into gold or collectibles. Instead they should put their savings into the hands of people who will use the money to develop new production capacity. Each saver has to make the choice whether to do that or take the defensive posture of hoarding. One by one, the advantages of paper assets have induced savers to take the risk of not hoarding. As more savers have taken their first nibbles of riskier financial assets, they have been richly rewarded, and the rewards have induced other savers to take similar risks. The stock market has been in a virtuous circle, as its success pulls in more and more new participants. What follows are some of the advantages that paper assets can have over tangibles from the viewpoint of the saver.

First, paper assets can be superior to tangibles, even when financial institutions are functioning imperfectly. Financial assets yield a return, and are easy to buy and sell. They are easy to store, and now that most securities are registered, the legitimate owner does not have to worry that they might be stolen. Monthly statements and online access show the current market value. In comparison, tangibles are inconvenient and troublesome. They have to be protected against theft, and selling them sometimes requires costly assay and appraisal fees.

Second, paper assets can be tailored and structured to suit the needs of the buyer. They can be made to represent claims of any magnitude on any sort of underlying productive asset, ranging from office buildings to software development firms. They can easily be made to represent ownership of gold, diamonds, or rare stamps. So a saver who wants to own gold, farmland, or Impressionist paintings can buy a paper claim that will give the benefits without the inconvenience. Paper assets are divisible: It makes sense to speak of owning one share of a van Gogh, or one-millionth of a famous gemstone.

Third, paper assets can be combined to create efficient portfolios that satisfy investors' individual needs as they pass through the life cycle. Portfolios can easily be modified, taking into account the owners' changing attitudes toward risk, their changing financial commitments, their plans for retirement, and so on. Savers can change their portfolios daily or more often if they wish, when they consist of paper assets. Tangible assets can also be combined into portfolios, but fine-tuning a portfolio of tangibles is more difficult, because tangibles are not so divisible, and the costs of transacting them are higher.

Fourth, financial market institutions facilitate separating ownership from management, and also making ownership independent of geography. Professional portfolio managers can act as agents for the beneficial owners. A middle-class saver in Austria, for example, can own part of a food-processing plant in Argentina without ever going across the Atlantic and without learning Spanish. Auditors and financial journalists protect the investor. When these agents are properly motivated and vigilant, the beneficial owners do not need to worry about losing the fruits of their investments.

Fifth, paper assets can be protected against sharp declines in market value. Financial intermediaries can create investment vehicles that offer upside potential and downside protection. The protection against loss can be supported by a guarantee from an AAA-rated insurer. These vehicles can then attract savings from people who are too risk averse or unsophisticated to buy individual securities directly. The same type of insured structure could be applied to vehicles for investing in tangibles. But the design, packaging, and marketing of vehicles for investment in tangible assets have not been so highly refined.

Sixth, the cost of hedging a portfolio of paper assets against sudden price declines can be low. This means that aggressive investors can buy risky securities, then combine them with sophisticated risk management instruments, and create a high-yielding portfolio with downside protection. This fact means, in turn, that aggressive investors can use borrowed money in addition to their own savings. So the investors, with luck and skill, can earn returns well in excess of what they would be able to make if they owned the underlying productive assets directly.

This brief list of advantages does not do justice to the full advantages that paper assets have attained over tangibles. Many more pages would be required to add more and more points in favor of paper assets. However, although this list does show how extensive the advantages are, it does not show how fragile and vulnerable the advantages are, nor how easily they can be shattered. Two price trajectories will show how much difference these advantages can make, and how much wealth can be lost when they shatter and fall to pieces.

Gold was pegged at $35 an ounce from the end of World War II until 1971. In the London gold market, its price in dollars had begun to drift higher from 1968 onward. During the 1970s, primarily in response to the weakening of the dollar, gold skyrocketed, touching $800 an ounce in 1979. From 1968 to 1979, U.S. common stocks were clearly inferior to gold. They gyrated but did not show an uptrend.

The Dow Jones Industrial Average, which rose almost to the 1,000 level in 1966, fluctuated violently but ended 1979 at the dismal level of 750. During the 1970s, the Dow rose as high as 1,051 and fell as low as 574. Understandably enough, people stayed away from common stocks. Real economic growth in the United States stagnated, and sophisticated investors borrowed money to buy collectibles, including baseball cards.

Since 1980, the fates of gold and the Dow have been reversed. Gold has stagnated, falling to $285 an ounce in 1982, then bouncing along between $300 and $450 for most of the next 20 years. Lately it has had a struggle to stay above $300 an ounce. The Dow, meanwhile, has thundered mightily, rising from 750 to over 11,400.

Institutional Arrangements to Support Saving
via Paper Assets

All the advantages in favor of paper assets depend utterly and entirely on institutions of the modern social contract. Mixed-economy, pluralistic, capitalist societies evolve sets of rules, and the exact form of rules and the quality of their enforcement are absolutely pivotal. With any wavering, ambiguity, or breakdown of the rules, the advantages of paper assets are quickly lost. There can then be a disorderly liquidation of financial assets, and a switch back to tangibles. Images of people lining up to take their money out of banks are etched into the collective memory in many countries. If the breakdown is more extreme, productive tangible assets like farmland and cattle lose their value, and preferences switch to tangibles that are portable, like gold and diamonds. If a conquering army is marching into sight, a handful of gold coins is worth more than 1,000 acres of farmland or any amount of deposits at the local bank. Tangible assets and paper assets can be placed along a continuum that runs from complete safety to extreme risk. The safest assets do not require that any social institutions be operating. The riskiest assets require not only that all social institutions function, but also that they keep functioning without any changes in the rules, in order for their prospective claims on future value to be realized.

Paper assets are valuable if buyers are willing to give cash to buy them. For this condition to be met, the banking system does not have to be operating everywhere, but it does have to be operating *somewhere*. There has to be at least one currency that is not suffering hyperinflation or massive devaluation, and there has to be at least one place where savers can go to cash in their investments and enjoy the proceeds. There has to be at least one jurisdiction that will not tax the proceeds too heavily.

Right after deciding to save via the financial system, savers have to decide which currency to buy, and then which country to put their money into. The more credible currencies are the euro, the yen, and the dollar. Local currencies can be well managed, as the Chilean and Singapore currencies have been, or they can be traps to confiscate savings. The Mexican peso, for example, was devalued in 1976, 1982, and 1994. Each devaluation stripped Mexican savers of more than half of the purchasing power they had accumulated.

In consequence, many savers do not hold on to their home currency, nor save via their home financial system. Instead, they make the effort to acquire foreign currency and put it into financial assets issued elsewhere. This defensive behavior is distinctively pivotal because it deprives their home countries of local savings and raises asset prices in the favored countries where they send their savings. It raises the cost of capital and slows growth in their home countries, while lowering the cost of capital and spurring growth in the countries receiving the inflows.

Saving abroad used to be impractical or downright illegal for most savers. They had to overcome high transaction and communications costs, mail-drop fees, safe-deposit box rentals, and annual custodial fees that were higher than at home. If a saver needed only anonymity vis-à-vis the home government, there were many feasible arrangements, and costs could be affordable for a middle-class person. But as a practical matter, very few people went to the trouble or took the risks. Instead they opted for simpler defensive moves, such as acquiring foreign banknotes and putting them in the mattress.

So how should a financial system be designed proactively? The discussion until now has been about ways the advantages of financial institutions can be lost, whether through incompetence or malice, or subverted to dispossess savers. This is because financial institutions have not usually been set up ab initio with the objective of maximizing their attractiveness to savers, nor with the express purpose of maximizing the market value of financial assets. Instead, financial institutions have been set up under some chartering procedures intended to protect savers from abuses such as embezzlement, self-dealing, and insufficient diversification.

As an alternative, let us contemplate a financial system designed to attract depositors who are savvy and have alternatives within easy reach. This is a difficult thought experiment, because depositors have historically been taken for granted. They are usually caricatured as unsophisticated cannon fodder. They put their faith and their money into intermediaries because they have nothing else close at hand that looks better. However, in this thought experiment the intermediaries are enlightened, and deserve the faith that savers place in them.

These virtuous financial intermediaries charge low fees and give prompt, courteous service. The managers of these financial intermediaries do not stuff the money into their own pockets, lend it to themselves, or waste it on white-elephant monuments. Most important, they make, or facilitate, efficient allocations of capital. The money goes in the right proportions to the right borrowers, who do constructive, brilliant things with it. The depositors do well, economic growth accelerates, and asset prices rise.

The managers of these ideal financial intermediaries have to be paid well for being so good and wise. This is a requirement, because they will not be such paragons for the psychic rewards alone. They handle a lot of money, and the rewards for handling it well have to be greater than what they would get if they were short-sighted, self-serving, and rapacious. The reward structure that has evolved includes upside potential in the form of bonuses and stock options, combined with severe penalties for malfeasance. Salary plus bonuses for top executives at the largest financial houses in the United States and Euroland have grown. In addition, their stock options have appreciated massively, and now dwarf their annual pay including bonuses. For these managers, crime does not pay. The probability of getting caught is too high because auditors, regulators, journalists, and the public are vigilant, and the penalties for getting caught are severe. Creating value and giving good service are what pays, and pays so well that all their attention is directed toward doing those things to the limits of their ability.

Taxes, Inflation, and Risk—Stumbling Blocks to Buying

Buyers in the United States and Euroland have good reason to be satisfied with the financial services firms that vie for their savings. Service, transparency, and performance have all been improving, and so buyers have put more and more of their savings into financial assets. Other parameters, however, have to be in a favorable alignment before buyers will commit themselves wholeheartedly to buying. Those parameters are the tax regime, inflation, and risk.

Taxes on dividends, interest, and capital gains discourage buying because the buyers will have to hand over part of the profits to the tax collector. This is obviously true if the marginal tax rate is very high. Buyers would not keep very much of the profits, so they will not invest. When tax rates are lower, the evidence is mixed. Some studies find that buying is discouraged, and other studies find that it is not. The trend in the United States has been to reduce the effective tax rate on income from investments. Americans have been permitted to create tax-deferred accounts such as Individual Retirement Accounts (IRAs), 401(k) retirement accounts, 403(b) accounts, Roth IRAs, and the like. These have reduced the effective tax rate on income from investments, so the deterrent effect of taxation has been diminished.

Another problem, almost as severe, is that taxation leads to a loss of privacy. Bank accounts, stocks and bonds, and all financial assets have to be linked to an individual by a taxpayer identification number. Bearer shares and numbered accounts are discouraged. In countries where tax collection is most effective, all financial assets are registered. Every interest payment and dividend is linked to a taxpayer identification number, so that tax auditors can cross-check accounts and catch tax evaders. The result is that tax authorities can figure out quite precisely what each individual owns. From there it is a short step to a complete loss of privacy. Computer databases are too easy to decipher and download. Hackers, private investigators, and criminals can find out exactly what any person owns. Buyers who want to avoid paying taxes have to go to great inconvenience to move their official domiciles to tax-haven locales, set up numbered accounts, and refrain from leaving financial footprints that are easy to follow. Wealthy people who want to keep a low profile are finding it more and more difficult to do so. They have to hire lawyers, work through nominees, and convey assets to offshore trusts.

Not many people go to that much trouble. The relative sizes of domestic capital markets and the offshore capital market demonstrate that point. The growth rate of offshore capital markets has been less than one-third of the growth rate of domestic capital markets since 1990. The reason is that some governments, particularly those of the Organization for Economic Cooperation and Development (OECD) countries, have learned how to tax the middle classes without chasing their savings into offshore tax havens. The record of the 1990s indicates that there are ways of designing a tax regime that will collect enough revenue without penalizing savers.

The tax regime that will spur buying, or at least not discourage it, has to satisfy several criteria. If taxes are too high, or are arbitrarily enforced, savers will move their money to other jurisdictions, or cash in their financial assets and buy tangible assets that are easy to conceal, like gold and diamonds. Middle-class individuals can easily be frightened into a defensive posture of buying gemstones or foreign banknotes and keeping them in safe-deposit boxes or in their mattresses. Government succeeds when the people choose the more trusting stance and are not afraid of telling the local tax collectors how much they have. When this condition is met, the people turn their attention to making a high return, knowing they will have to pay the taxes that will be due.

Once people are sure that the government will spend tax monies wisely, and collect even-handedly from every citizen who owes taxes, then civic considerations come into play. Taxation is at the heart of the social contract. Citizens vote for taxes and pay them willingly if they can see the tax monies being spent on things the society really needs. Citizens stop paying willingly when they have no voice in how the monies are spent, and when they see evaders going scot-free. Evaders have to be caught, fined, and jailed.

The other criteria for a tax system are technical: Taxes distort incentives, and shift wealth from one group to another. For an extreme example of distortion and wealth shifting, suppose there is a town that has a river running down the middle of it, and there is only one bridge. The town council levies a toll to cross the bridge. The toll is a tax that is easy to collect, but the higher the toll is, the more it splits the town into two, and the advantages of agglomeration are lost. If the toll is set so high that nobody crosses the bridge, the bifurcation of the town becomes absolute, and the revenue collected falls to zero. It is as if the bridge had been torn down.

A subtler point is more important for the argument in this book. The toll affects the value of businesses on both sides of the river. If the toll is either raised or repealed, the market values of restaurants and other businesses in the town may be affected. The total demand for their services may not change, but traffic flow in the town will be different, and some of the restaurants will do better and some will suffer. In the extreme, there may be bankruptcies. So how high or low should the toll be? A test might be whether the aggregate value of the businesses in the town would be higher or lower with the toll at a new level. More generally, one way of optimizing a tax regime is to try to set the taxes so as to maximize the total market value of all the productive assets in the community.

Suppose that a country wishes to set its tax policy to maximize the market value of the income-producing assets located in that country.

Should tax rates all be set at zero? This tax policy works for a few very small countries that are trying to be tax havens. Larger countries, however, cannot set tax rates at zero. They need tax rates high enough to bring in enough revenue to provide needed public services, including police protection. A moderate level of taxation will not lower the market values of the income-producing assets in the country.

The next question is whether to tax income, profits, or assets. Taxing income seems to be the answer. Taxing profits or assets might seem more egalitarian, but OECD countries have steadily opted for lower taxes on profits and assets. For example, in the United States the percentage of total federal tax revenue that comes from corporate income taxes has declined from 13.4% in 1980 to 11.9% in 1999.[2]

There are two reasons for shifting taxes onto income and away from corporate profits. First, taxing income discourages consumption instead of discouraging investment. And second, the market value of corporations is hypersensitive to taxes on corporate profits. Shares are valued according to price/earnings ratio, among other benchmark indicators. Taking or leaving $1 of corporate profits makes a difference of $25 in the total market value of the company's shares, if the company price/earnings ratio is 25. For an illustration, consider a company that earned $1.4 million before taxes over the past 12 months. It pays $400,000 of corporate income tax, so its profits after tax are $1 million. It has 1 million shares outstanding, so its earnings per share are $1. Its stock is trading in the market at 25 times earnings, so the total market value of its shares is $25 million.

Now suppose the tax rate on corporate profits is lowered, so the company's tax liability is now only $399,999. The company's after-tax profits are now $1,000,001. The total market value of its shares is now $25,000,025. So by not collecting $1 of corporate taxes, the value of common shares has been increased by $25.

This sounds like an argument for collecting less tax from corporations. But suppose that total tax revenues have to remain the same. The $1 of tax revenue will then have to be collected from some other source. Who will pay the $1 that was not collected from the corporation? Some taxpayer has to pay $1 more, but it may not be obvious who really pays. To figure out who really pays more, it is not enough to look simply at who pays the tax to the government; you have to look at *tax incidence*—that is, on whose shoulders the tax ultimately falls.

A tax falls on the person whose real income declines as a result of its being levied. It does not fall on the person who pays it if that person can pass along the tax. A tax on salt, for example, does not fall on the owner of the salt mine if the mine is a monopoly, and the owner can raise the price of salt enough to recoup the tax payments. If those conditions are met, the tax falls on the consumers.

This discussion of tax incidence has a clear implication for designing a tax system that maximizes the total market value of all productive assets. Tax burdens should not fall on savers, and especially should not fall on buyers of risky financial assets. Risk taking should not be penalized. Economic growth requires investors that accept risk. For this reason governments debate what tax rate should apply to capital gains. They flirt with the policy of exempting capital gains from taxation. The practical restraint on this policy is that buyers of risky assets comprise most of the middle and upper economic strata. Too much of the total tax base would be exempted if taxes on capital gains were eliminated.

The United States has wrestled with this delicate trade-off and has come to an accommodation. Interest and capital gains are taxed, unless they are earned in a tax-deferred account, and there are many different tax-deferred accounts a saver can own. From the point of view of savers, and judging ex post facto how much financial wealth has been created, the U.S. accommodation has gone through a very successful evolution since 1980. Since the end of the 1970s, the tax on savers has diminished relative to the real after-tax gains they earn. For example, in 1979 a saver could earn almost 18% a year on government-guaranteed certificates of deposit (CDs). That may sound high, but inflation was running as high as 14%, and interest income was taxable. Worse, inflation had pushed many middle-class salary earners into the 50% marginal tax bracket. So the after-tax income was only half of 18%, or 9%; taking inflation into account, it was approximately −5% per year (9% − 14% = −5%). The modifications to the tax code since 1980, and the success in controlling inflation, have turned this dismal performance around completely. Twenty years later, in 1999, the same person who might have bought a bank CD in 1979 could have opened a tax-deferred retirement account and bought shares of a mutual fund that invested in U.S. common stocks. The annual rate of return could have been 30%, the tax zero for the time being, and inflation around 2%, for a real after-tax return of approximately 28% (30% − 2% = 28%).

Inflation is another deterrent to buyers. Since 1980 it has slowed almost to a standstill, so it has ceased to frighten buyers. It is always a threat, because governments constantly face the temptation to spend more than they collect. Prior to the 1990s, higher rates of fiscal deficit were the norm. Since then, however, Euroland and the United States have gone through high-profile self-imposed fiscal overhauls. They have tied themselves into tighter fiscal restraints, and have insisted that they cannot undo the knots. This rite of self-persuasion has been effective. Buyers of securities have believed that the restraints will hold.

Inflation trended toward zero in the OECD countries. It declined sharply in the 1980s, aided by the long slide in the prices of oil and other commodities. Inflation remained low through the 1990s, so now there is an entire generation of younger savers who have not experienced the disincentives it brings. They buy financial assets without giving much thought to the future purchasing power of the currency they will get later when they cash in. Buyers need to believe that inflation will remain low, or they will hesitate as they take out their wallets to buy financial assets.

Inflation makes a huge difference in the price that buyers will pay for financial assets. An example shows how dramatic the difference can be. Consider the price of a stock in a company that earned $1 per share after tax during the last 12 months and has real growth of 8% per year. When inflation is running at 10% per year, the price of the stock might be $8. When inflation is running at 2% per year, the price of the stock might be $35.*

Narrowing the Risk of Owning Common Stocks

To complete the panorama of attractions that will entice buyers, one more piece is needed: The risk premium has to be narrowed. The well-designed financial system that we have been contemplating gives buyers good reasons to buy paper assets, but the maximum power of financial intermediation is unleashed only if they buy risky paper, such as common stocks, instead of ultrasafe instruments, such as CDs. Capital markets can, by cleverly combining assets into portfolios, find owners for a larger amount of high-risk securities than savers want to own, but the amount of risky

---

* This calculation uses two formulas, and the result varies depending on assumptions, but the relative result is robust under a wide range of possible sets of inputs to the formulas.

placements cannot be in the aggregate very much larger than what buyers are willing to own.

The risk premium in the 1970s was too high. There is strong evidence that buyers will be willing to buy a risky security if its expected return is much higher than the return of a safe security. If Treasury securities are offering yields of 12%, as they were for parts of 1978 and 1979, buyers will take the risk of buying a corporate stock only if they think it will yield much more than 12%. During the 1978 to 1981 period, blue-chip common stocks were priced so low that a buyer could reasonably expect to make a total yield of 18%, including dividends and expected capital gains. Riskier common stocks had to offer yields that looked as if they were going to be even higher—for example, 20 or 22%.

The risk premium for U.S. common stocks was stuck at a high level from 1972 to September 1982. Anyone who bought U.S. common stocks during that period earned high returns on some stocks for brief time periods, but did very badly with other stocks. 1972 to 1982 was a difficult time for common stocks. Buyers had to be lucky or skillful to make more than the yield on Treasury bills or bank CDs. Some individual stocks did go up, but the broad stock market indexes did not. So hopeful buyers turned into rueful buyers time and again. This pattern kept the risk premium high. Sustained waves of buying would have narrowed it, but buyers continually were getting poor results and leaving the market, or giving up and buying Treasury bonds, bank CDs, or gold.

What lowered the risk premium was a long period when world economic conditions were stable. The 1970s were chaotic—two OPEC shocks and the world food crisis were just a few of the constant reminders that governments could not control events and corporate profits could fluctuate violently. By comparison, the 1980s and 1990s were stable. Corporations regained their old consistency: They got their costs and profit margins under control once again, they repaid debt, or refinanced high-interest debt, and their profits rose. Buyers got more return than they had expected, instead of less, so the adventuresome few who were buying stocks in the summer of 1982 were rewarded. The risk premium has been low most of the time since then, except when it has spiked upward at times of crisis such as the stock market crash of 1987 or the Russian default of 1998.

To see the damage a widening risk premium can do, consider a mutual fund that has just taken in $10 million from new shareholders. This fund invests in common stocks. The fund manager has, until now, bought stocks that are slightly riskier than the ones that are already in the fund's portfolio. This way, the fund positions itself more and more aggressively to profit from the rising prices of riskier stocks. In view of the widening risk premium, however, the fund manager cannot do that with the $10 million that has just arrived. The fund manager has to buy stocks that are safer than the ones that are already in the fund's portfolio. The fund manager has to start scaling back the fund's risk exposure, because if he or she takes more risk than other fund managers do, and the risk premium continues to widen, the risky stocks would go down, and the fund would underperform. So the fund manager stops buying riskier securities. Their prices fall as buyers back away, and the risk premium widens more. This sort of aversion to risk is contagious, so any widening in the risk premium can lead to further widening.

The effects of a widening risk premium would be seen first in securities markets. Prices of riskier securities would fall, and prices of safe securities, particularly Treasury securities, would rise. This would cause initial public offerings (IPOs) of common stock in new businesses to be delayed. Also, publicly listed high-technology companies would not be so easily able to issue new common shares to buy small high-tech companies that are not listed on any stock exchange. If that type of buying had to be scaled back, the growth rate of some high-tech sectors would slow down. Buyers who take risks need to be rewarded—not all the time, and not extravagantly, but if they go a long enough time without being rewarded, innovation and economic growth slow down.

In the 1990s, the risk premium narrowed and stayed small, with the exception of a few brief time periods. The risk premium between A-rated bonds and B-rated bonds also narrowed. For example, the yield spread between junk bonds and Treasury bonds was as wide as 8% in 1989, after hovering around 4% for most of the 1980s. In the 1990s, it narrowed to 2% before widening around the time of the Russian default.

This impressive narrowing of the risk premium is the triumph of economic stability and successful institutional arrangements. This happy conjuncture has created a preference for common stocks over bonds.

When institutions work really well, stocks are the choice, because the yield premiums they offer are larger than needed to compensate for the risk of owning them. Buyers ask why they should accept 6% on Treasury bonds when common stocks appear capable of yielding 14 or 20% on a sustained basis. Then subsequent events justify their optimism. The spectre of volatility that had been holding down the prices of the common stocks does not materialize; instead, the earnings of the companies rise steadily, and the prices of the stocks move up enough to deliver a higher yield than the 14% the buyers were expecting.

Making Sense of Buyers' Behavior and Sellers' Postponing Selling

So now we have laid out the complete rationale for buyers' actions since the 1980s. It is logical for them to buy—not only paper assets, but *risky* paper assets. Cash is trash, silver is obsolete, and gold is only slightly more interesting than dirt. In the buying stampede of the 1990s, moderates urging prudence fell out of favor. Survivalists and hermits living in the hills of thinly populated northern counties buy ammunition, canned goods, and gold coins. The middle class buys stocks, and people approaching retirement fret about choosing the opportune moment to shift some of their immense gains into bonds. Those who make the switch kick themselves later, because in the long stock market boom, every dip has been a buying opportunity.

Sellers are aware of the rationale for buying. They are influenced by the same arguments for holding on, so they sell less. They also look back on their earlier sales, and see that they should have hung on longer.

Sellers are also aware that buyers outnumber them. Net inflows into mutual funds and pension funds are as much as $50 billion per month in the United States. There are more people saving for retirement in the United States than there are retirees withdrawing savings from the financial system. As a result, money flowing into the financial markets exceeds the money flowing out of the markets. It is a question of intense concern how long U.S. demographics will support this happy pattern of net inflows into financial markets. There are many forecasters trying to predict when the Boomer generation will retire, and how much of their accumulated savings they will attempt to withdraw each year. All these models agree that after some number of years, the day will come when

U.S. retirees will try to take out more than the U.S. working-age population will be putting in. When that day comes, working-age people outside the United States will have to step in as substitute buyers, to add their buying power to that of the outnumbered Generation-X Americans. Otherwise, securities prices will fall sharply, and the Boomer generation will see its plans for comfortable retirement fall to pieces. A major challenge this book poses is how to make sure the working-age people outside the United States will be able and willing to buy securities when their buying power will be needed to bolster the meager buying power of the overburdened Generation-X Americans.

Sellers know all this. They do not know whether foreign buying will take up the slack when it will be needed, but they do know that for the next few years, the balance will be in their favor: more buyers than sellers.

An example will illustrate how the rising stock market can cause sellers to hold back and postpone selling. For simplicity, this example ignores taxes. Suppose that at the beginning of 1995 two U.S. 65-year-olds retired. Each had saved $200,000 and each was entitled to the maximum monthly Social Security check. Each was going to augment the Social Security check by taking $1,500 a month from savings. Each had $100,000 invested in short-term, high-quality bonds that earned 6% per year, and each had $100,000 invested in a mutual fund that made a total return of 30% per year. The only difference between the two retirees is that one takes $750 a month from each account and the other takes $1,500 a month from bonds and does not touch the initial $100,000 invested in the mutual fund.

The results of this example are illuminating. Both retirees are depleting savings at a rate of 9% per year ($18,000/$200,000 = 9%), well above the 4 or 5% rate that financial advisors recommend. Nevertheless, both retirees continue to be net accumulators of financial assets. The reason is that the value of their original $200,000 goes up by more than $1,500 a month. The more powerful point, however, is this: Their net purchases of common stocks rise at a rising rate. The first month they are retired, they buy $3,670 of common stock by reinvesting their gains [($100,000 × 0.0221 × 2) − 750 = $3,670]. The last month of the five-year period they buy $14,099 of new common stocks [($363,263 × 0.0221) + (274,689 × 0.0221) = $14,099]. It is equally telling that the one who sells the bonds and does not touch the stock mutual fund ends up 11% wealthier than the one who sells a little of each every month. The one who, in an attempt to be prudent, depletes the bond and stock accounts by equal amounts every month ends up with only 23% of the total holdings in bonds, and 77% in stocks. The total assets after five years of retirement are $361,801. The one who takes the entire $1,500 each month from the bond account ends up with $401,523 in total financial assets after five years of retirement, double the starting amount, but only $31,730 of it is in the bond account. The rest is in common stocks.*

---

* The calculations are from a spreadsheet called Two Savers.xls that is posted on the author's Web site, www.faculty.babson.edu/edmunds.

Chapter 3

Issuers Restrict Supply

In earlier eras, issuers were eager to print and sell new bonds and common shares. Governments and corporations kept issuing as long as there were buyers for the new paper. In the age of sail, financiers in Venice, Genoa, Amsterdam, and London would accept as much money as investors wanted to put at risk; they would launch joint-stock companies, raise funds, buy ships, and send the ships to Canton or the Spice Islands in hopes of bringing back riches. *Money* was the limit on how many ships could be sent. There was plenty of wood to build ships, plenty of sailors to crew them, and plenty of trade goods to bring back from Asia. What was scarce was money to pay for the ventures. Centuries later, during the canal-building and railroad booms, the situation was the same: Money was the limiting factor. There were plenty of promoters who would concoct schemes to build canals and railroads to the remotest hinterlands. The promoters would keep putting forth more schemes as long as investors would put up the money for construction costs.

Current Reluctance of Issuers

After 1980, however, and most markedly after 1992, issuance of new securities slowed to a trickle. For some categories of paper, repayments exceeded new issuance, so that the total amounts outstanding went down. This striking slowdown in issuance of new paper is one of the most important causes of the financial wealth phenomenon. The reasons for this sudden slowdown make sense when they are viewed one by one and when the motivations of each type of issuer are examined.

To see how much of a slowdown in issuance there has been, consider the well-publicized balancing of the U.S. fiscal budget. The U.S. fiscal deficit was $290 billion in 1992. By 1997 the deficit was only $23 billion, and in 1998 and 1999 the budget ended with surpluses of $70 billion and $123 billion, respectively. The surpluses are expected to continue into the future, so Uncle Sam will be paying off government bonds as they mature and issuing fewer new ones. The total face amount of U.S. Treasury debt held by the public is projected to drop from $3.47 trillion in the year 2000 to $0.865 trillion in the year 2009, and the remaining $0.865 trillion could be completely paid off by the year 2015.[1]

The outlook at this point is that there will not be as many U.S. Treasury bonds in the future as there are right now. For most people who grew up in the era of deficits, the idea of a coming shortage of Treasury bonds is hard to get used to. Surely Washington will go back to its old habits of spending more than it takes in? Crystal balls are murky on this point, but the indications are that fiscal deficits will not come back into fashion in the near future. Meanwhile, a less-publicized phenomenon has been taking place. Corporations have been buying back more stock than they have been issuing. In the United States, corporations bought back $207 billion of their own stock in 1998, up from $181 billion in 1997. The buybacks were almost double the amount of initial public offerings, which were $108 billion in 1998. Much more stock was taken out of the market by corporate mergers and takeovers: Acquiring companies bought $1.6 trillion of stock. They paid $672 billion in cash to the previous owners; the rest of the $1.6 trillion was paid for with securities. So the total amount of stock in the U.S. market went down by $1,027 billion (207 billion − 108 billion + 1,600 billion − 672 billion = $1,027 billion).[2] Let us be clear what this number means: It means that there was about $1 trillion less common stock for investors to buy at the end of 1998 than there had been at the beginning of that year. So if all U.S. common stock were worth $10 trillion at the beginning of 1998, and prices of U.S. common stocks had not risen during that year, it would have been worth about $9 trillion at the end of the year.

These figures help explain why securities prices have gone up so much. Buyers have been putting money into the market, buying paper every day, but the amounts of paper available for purchase have been going down. The reduction in the total supply is the major driver of the price increases. The amount of purchases that savers have made is small relative to the total amounts of paper that exist. For example, U.S. investors made $176 billion of net purchases of mutual funds in 1998.[3] That is less than $15 billion a month. U.S. stocks and bonds were worth more than a thousand times $15 billion—that is, more than $15 trillion. So the steady buying would not have moved prices very much. What moved prices was the much more massive repurchases and repayments. These were at least 5 times as great in 1998 as the new purchases of mutual funds.

Governments and corporations each have good reasons to be issuing less paper and paying off the paper they issued in the past. Their reasons are different, but they happen to be synchronized. Their combined effect is to create a scarcity of high-quality paper in the capital markets. The reasons why each type of issuer is putting out less paper need to be examined in detail. You need to understand why issuers are so reluctant to offer more securities in order to be able to see what will happen to prices of high-quality securities in the future and to see where capital will flow in the future.

Government Bonds

Government bonds are the best known and most widely held category of paper asset. Government bonds are issued when a taxing authority plans to spend more than it will collect during some time interval. Bond buyers supply the extra cash. The modern form of government bonds has evolved from bonds' origins in earlier eras. It is convenient to trace the evolution of bonds in the West from the forms they took under feudalism.

In the Middle Ages, European princes frequently borrowed from bankers and gave promissory notes or bills of exchange to secure the loans. These notes or bills matured some number of days or months after they were issued, and the bankers would wait the requisite amounts of time and then present them for payment. A prince developed a credit history with the bankers by paying on time or by defaulting. Some monarchs and princes became very adept at using loans from bankers. Philip II of Spain, who ruled from 1545 to 1598, was an overachiever in this regard.

He owned the silver mines of the Americas, and a fleet laden with treasure arrived every year in Seville. If Philip had been a man of little ambition, he might have been content to spend the annual bonanza of silver on himself and his friends, and give a bit to the populace from time to time. But he had ambitions, and he knew bankers in Genoa. The bankers of Genoa saw how much treasure he was receiving from the Americas every year, so they loaned him enough for his many projects and wars. He built the cathedral in Quito and *El Escorial* castle outside Madrid and paid for most of the Christian fleet in the battle of Lepanto. He also bankrolled the Spanish Armada.

Philip II managed the Spanish Crown's affairs personally, with the help of a staff of secretaries. He was conscientious and hard-working and paid great attention to detail. During his lifetime he maintained the Crown's credit rating and always contrived to have the cash to pay off each note when it fell due. Because of his expertise in borrowing money, for most of his reign he was able to spend much more each year than the Crown's annual revenues. In that sense he took the art of deficit spending to the highest level it reached prior to the modern era. Unfortunately, many of his projects were unproductive, so the Crown's revenues did not go up enough to repay all the loans easily. There was no enormous inflow to compensate for all his ambitious outlays. Several times during his reign, Philip's spending was so far ahead of his income that he overextended the Crown's credit. He put the Crown so deep in debt that he sometimes had to pay high interest rates to get money to pay off notes that were falling due.

Philip II knew the most important rule: When a note falls due, the issuing government is supposed to have collected enough taxes to pay it off; alternatively, the government is supposed to have borrowed the cash from some other source. This day-to-day job of cash management is easy if a government's total expenditures do not exceed its revenues over some time period, such as a year. In that happy circumstance, the government can issue notes during periods of the year when revenues fall short of collections, and pay the notes off at other times of the year, when revenues exceed expenditures.

For some governments, however, the demands on the purse exceed the amounts collected for much longer periods of time. In that case, longer-term loans are called for. In the Middle Ages, commercial banks did not like to make long-term loans and charged high interest rates for the few long-term loans they did make, so governments began to borrow in a different way. They would borrow a large sum from a syndicate of bankers. The bankers would then sell loan-participation certificates to individual investors. Each certificate would represent, for example, one-thousandth of the total loan. If the certificates had a face value of 1,000 florins, then the entire loan would have been for 1 million florins. Individual investors liked these loan-participation certificates because they were safe. The bankers would try to set the terms of these loans so that they could sell the participation certificates at a profit. If the bankers could successfully sell all the certificates, they would recover the cash they had loaned and would then be able to arrange another loan. Braudel writes, "This was how the . . . bank of Henry Hope & Co. . . . managed between 1787 and 1793 to make nineteen Russian loans of three million francs each, a total of . . . 57 million. It was with Dutch money then, . . . that Russia was able to conquer a vast territory stretching to the Black Sea. . . ."[4]

Transactions like these showed that there was a demand for government bonds. Amsterdam at the time was a thriving metropolis, wealthy from long-distance trade, so there were people in the city with cash who were ready to buy safe investments that paid a return. Bonds paid interest and gold did not, so bonds were better than gold as long as they were safe enough. There were bonds of different maturities, and some were payable in gold. From that time on, governments in Europe routinely issued bonds to pay for projects that would take a long time to come to fruition. There were many projects, and many buyers for government bonds, so the amount of government bonds in circulation grew steadily, except during times of war, revolution, or financial collapse.

Through the 1800s, government bond issues were linked to specific projects. Sometimes the links were tenuous or fictitious, but governments were careful to maintain the image that each bond issue was for some capital investment project that could not be financed from ordinary revenues. The projects were supposed to generate enough government revenue to pay off the bonds that were being sold to fund them. That way there would be no permanent drain on the state's revenues. The idea of issuing government bonds to pay current fiscal outlays took its modern form during the 1930s and 1940s. During the Great Depression, tax collections in the United States and Europe fell, while the needs of the poor and unemployed increased. Many experts were uneasy about governments borrowing money to spend it supporting a minimum standard of living for the poor and unemployed. The question of how the bonds would be repaid came up frequently. Then World War II broke out, and the question had to be put aside. The need to win the war pushed the question of repayment into the background. The U.S. Treasury issued unprecedented amounts of bonds, and ordinary Americans bought them.

The question of repayment came up again many times from 1946 onward. Government bonds are safer than corporate bonds but still are vulnerable to inflation, devaluation, or outright repudiation. Buyers give up purchasing power and need to believe that they will later get back more purchasing power than they have given up. If the bond issue is to fund a project that will pay for itself, bond buyers do not worry. But if the bond issue is to pay for soup kitchens or wars, bond buyers have to look to other sources of revenue for their repayment. They believe they will be repaid with more purchasing power than they have given up if either or both of two conditions hold: First, the issuing government has to have a tax base that is large enough, or growing fast enough; second, the amount of bonds that is outstanding cannot be too large relative to the tax base.

For the U.S. Treasury, repayment was in doubt from the late 1970s until the summer of 1982. Inflation was high, federal tax collections were stagnating in real terms, and the nation's technological preeminence appeared to be fading. Comparisons with the United Kingdom, which had lagged other industrial countries from 1914 onward, were appearing in the financial news media. The total amount of Treasury debt was not large compared to the country's gross national product (GNP), but the market's assessment was ominous. In late 1980, the market prices of long-term U.S. Treasury bonds were so low that buyers who were willing to take the risk of buying one were being offered yields of 15.5%.

Fears about repayment faded in the second half of 1982, and a strong economic recovery became visible early in 1983. The future prospects for U.S. prosperity and fiscal health began to look better, and buyers were rewarded when they bought U.S. Treasury bonds. Market prices of existing bonds went up, and the Treasury was able to place new issues without having to offer such high rates.

Euroland and Japan, meanwhile, were having similar experiences in the late 1970s. Then in the 1980s their paths diverged. Japan's savers bought every security that was offered, and their buying pushed prices up higher and higher for the rest of the decade. Euroland's savers were hesitant. They continued to demand high rates, and did not buy enthusiastically enough to push up prices.

The United States and Euroland had large fiscal deficits during the 1980s and narrowed those sharply in the 1990s. These were large enough that the total amount of government bonds rose as a percentage of GNP for both. The turnaround was widespread and almost synchronous. The U.S. turnaround from 1993 onward was striking against the backdrop of persistent deficits throughout the 1980s (Figure 3.1).

There are many explanations for this synchronous and clearly demarcated turn to fiscal austerity. A plausible one begins with the demographics of the United States and Euroland. The people who are now over 40 had always questioned whether their Social Security checks would have much purchasing power. Before they turned 40, however, they were more interested in seeing current government expenditures rise. Outlays seemed necessary and made more difference to them than the integrity of the Social Security payments they would receive at some date in the distant future. But after they turned 40, their perspective began to lengthen,

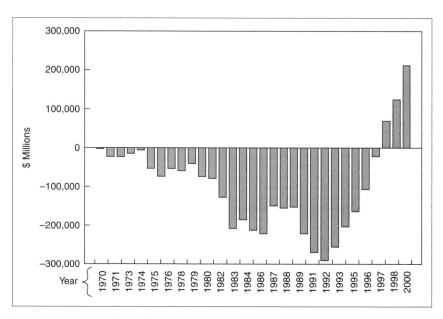

Figure 3.1 **U.S. federal budget deficit/surplus, 1970 to 2000.**

and their scheduled retirement seemed to grow nearer. They began to think more seriously about their future retirement.

Voter participation rises with age, so older people have more electoral weight than their numbers would indicate. Compounding this fact is the demographic bulge of the Baby Boomer generation, which outnumbers the one following it both in the United States and in Euroland. So voting patterns quickly favored the longer view: As the Boomers moved into the higher age brackets, they outvoted people in the younger age brackets, and fiscal policy quickly became more austere.

In Euroland, the move to fiscal austerity was orchestrated. All the countries joined together to tighten fiscal policy at the same time, with checkpoints and certification dates. The group discipline and the mechanisms for imposing it were formalized at Maastricht in 1991. This meeting, and the treaty that was signed there, set the criteria that countries had to meet to qualify for being included in the single currency. The Maastricht treaty called for all countries to meet criteria of low inflation and fiscal deficits of less than 2% of GDP. Countries that flagrantly failed to meet these criteria would not be allowed to merge their national currencies into the euro. At the time the treaty was signed, inflation rates and fiscal deficits were quite divergent among the countries that joined to form Euroland. Countries with later baby booms and younger populations, like Spain, had higher inflation rates and larger fiscal deficits than countries with older populations, like Germany and Denmark. The Maastricht treaty forced these divergences to be narrowed so that all members of the bloc could obtain the benefits of currency unification.

The benefits of currency unification can be illustrated with a simplified example. Suppose that in 1993 Spain's national debt was 70% of its GDP. Suppose that this debt was represented entirely by fixed-rate, noncallable bonds yielding 14%, with a maturity of 7 years. Before currency unification, the market price of the bonds would be the same as their face value, so their market value was 70% of GDP. Spain's fiscal deficit before it cut spending to conform to the Maastricht criteria was 4% of GDP. The spending cuts brought the deficit down to only 2% of GDP, so expenditures decreased by 2% of GDP per year. Because of the cuts in spending, Spain qualified for the currency unification. Market participants then changed their view of Spanish government bonds. There used to be a risk of devaluation but now there was not, since the Spanish currency disappeared, to be merged into the euro. So Spanish inflation as such now no longer existed. In its place there was only Euroland inflation, and Euroland's monetary policy was set in the European Central Bank in Frankfurt. Immediately, Spanish government bonds were repriced in the market. They were now 14% bonds denominated in euros. Buyers bid up the price of the bonds until they were yielding only 6%, the same as German government bonds. When the repricing had finished, the bonds were worth 1.45 times as much as they had been before. The holders of the bonds would have a gain worth $0.70 \times (1.45 - 1) = 31.5\%$ of GDP.

This enormous gain in the market value of Spanish government securities has to be compared to the cutback in Spanish government spending. The relative magnitude of the gain can then be seen: It is 15 times greater. In fact, the gain that investors experienced may have been even greater, because the rally in securities denominated in Spanish currency was not limited to Spanish government bonds. There was a similar increase in the market value of mortgages, corporate bonds, and common stocks. The total gain may have been 60% of GDP. The cut in government expenditures of 2% of GDP was a relatively small price to pay, but it was a hardship for the people who ceased to receive government payments.

The Euroland currency unification was controversial at first. Voters were suspicious of it, and its fate was in the balance because each country had to hold a plebiscite to ratify the treaty. Voters in Denmark rejected it by a narrow margin, and French voters barely passed it. But it passed, and as it progressed toward passage, asset prices began to rise. The increases in asset prices began a virtuous circle that is one of the serendipitous benefits of the Maastricht approval and convergence process. As the unification date approached, the convergence process delivered financial windfalls that were higher in the countries that had to make greater spending cuts. To see why, consider two Euroland countries that had fiscal deficits of 2.5 and 3.5% of GDP, respectively. The Maastricht approval process required both deficits to be cut to 2%. The country that was at 2.5% was already close to meeting the criterion, so its currency was not as vulnerable to devaluation as was that of the country that was at 3.5%. Government securities of both countries rose as the national legislatures cut fiscal deficits to 2%. The country that had to cut its deficit by only 0.5% of GDP did not see such a large gain in prices of its government bonds as did the country that had to cut its deficit by 1.5% of GDP.

The reasons given here for the trend to fiscal austerity in the United States and Euroland are only a few of the many that may have caused it. The outcome, however, has been very clear. There has been less inflation and less new issuance of government bonds, especially during the years from 1995 to 2000. Forecasts of fiscal deficits and surpluses for the period from 2000 to 2030 are numerous and cover a wide range. The demands on national social security systems are looming. In view of the current composition of the electorate, and the slow rate of change in voting patterns, two points seem obvious.

First, inflation and fiscal deficits make it harder for governments to provide for the coming bulge of Boomer retirements. A deficit today uses up the government's borrowing power too soon, before many Boomers have retired. Inflation today means that in the future government bonds will have to offer higher yields in order to attract buyers. So inflation today raises the cost of financing a fiscal deficit later on. As more and more Boomers retire, the cost of supporting them will be easier to bear if the government can easily sell bonds. It follows that today's government bond buyers have to be rewarded for their investments. If today's bondholders suffer, later on there will be fewer buyers for government bonds. So today's aging voters have a very strong reason to oppose fiscal deficits and inflation. Voters will be protecting their own standard of living when they oppose fiscal deficits and inflation.

Second, the voting power of the elderly will get stronger, and will remain strong at least until 2030 and perhaps beyond. To see why, consider a simplified example. Suppose there is a country with 74 million people of voting age. At the beginning of the example their ages and participation rates are as follows:

Age	Total Voters	Average Participation Rate	Total Votes
20–29	10 million	20%	2 million
30–39	10 million	30%	3 million
40–49	15 million	40%	6 million
50–59	15 million	50%	7.5 million
60–69	10 million	60%	6 million
70–79	8 million	70%	5.6 million
80–89	6 million	80%	4.8 million

Total votes: 2 + 3 + 6 + 7.5 + 6 + 5.6 + 4.8 = 34.9 million
Total votes cast by people over 40:   29.9 million, or 29.9/34.9 = 86%
Total votes cast by people over 50:   23.9 million, or 23.9/34.9 = 68%

Now consider what happens as this population ages 10 years. The people who were in their forties and fifties dominate more than they did at the beginning. The 40- to 49-year-olds are now 50 to 59, and their participation rate rises from 40 to 50%. The 50- to 59-year-olds are now 60 to 69, and their participation rate rises from 50 to 60%. For simplicity, assume that 1 million people each year turn 20, so that the number in each of the younger brackets remains steady at 10 million. Also assume that these younger voters do not become politicized, so their participation rates remain at 20, 30, and 40%. Also assume for simplicity that the number of voters in the 70 to 79 and 80 to 89 age categories remains the same, and their participation rates do not change.

After 10 years, the number of people is still 74 million, but the number of votes cast goes up from 34.9 million to 37.9 million. The tilt toward older voters has increased. Total votes cast by people over 40 is 30.9 million, or 30.9/37.9 = 82%. This is lower than the 86% it was 10 years earlier. Total votes cast by people over 50 is 26.9/37.9 = 71%. This is higher than it was 10 years earlier.

This simple example shows that the concerns of voters over 50 already weigh heavily in the outcome of elections, and will weigh more heavily in the future. People over 50 comprise 53% of the population and 68% of the votes at the beginning of the example. Ten years later, they comprise 61% of the population and 71% of the votes.

The implications of this discussion of government bond issuance are as follows:

- Fiscal austerity is consistent with the demographics of voters in Euroland and the United States. The shift from larger deficits to smaller deficits to fiscal surpluses is reasonable in view of the needs of the voters.
- Fiscal austerity has delivered windfall gains to owners of government securities. To the extent that fiscal austerity has been the

cause of lower inflation, it has delivered windfall gains to owners of other financial assets.

- The demographics of voting-age populations in the United States and Euroland will continue to favor fiscal austerity and low inflation.
- The supply of government bonds will grow more slowly than it did in the 1950s through the 1980s, and might shrink.
- The prices of government bonds will remain high and their yields will remain low. Government bonds will continue to be safe to hold and easy to sell.

Common Stocks

In the days of Horatio Alger, the American Dream was to start a company and work hard to make it prosper. Since World War II, the American Dream has been speeded up: Now it is to start a company and then sell shares to the public. The American entrepreneur's career arrives at the benchmark of success when his or her company makes its initial public offering and the company's shares trade at a premium to the IPO price. Creating a corporation is one of the first steps, and nobody tries to hang onto 100% ownership anymore. And the initial sale of stock is only the beginning of a long, carefully planned campaign to create a stock market clientele for the company. Later, after the company has grown some more, it sells more stock. If the stock performs well it splits 2 for 1 or 4 for 1. Secondary offerings, automatic dividend reinvestment plans, and stock splits are subsequent milestones in the company's campaign to make the shares widely distributed, well known, and highly regarded.

In Europe and parts of Asia, selling stock does not have this same eminence in children's career plans. The dream there, in its business variant, is to start a business, make it prosper, and then pass 100% ownership on to the next generation. Selling stock is not part of the plan. Selling stock is a sign of weakness. The conventional view is that selling stock is like taking in partners on disadvantageous terms. Business owners are reluctant to sell stock because public opinion will judge them negatively for having done so. Many owners state that their first responsibility is to their families, and they put their businesses in the same category as their houses, farms, and personal effects. For this reason they consider selling equity a defeat or a disgrace, almost as shameful and blameworthy as mortgaging the family homestead. Selling stock leads to losing control, and that is clearly undesirable. The business is to be kept in the family; outsiders complicate decision making and meddle in the affairs of the business.

The act of issuing shares sends loud, attention-grabbing signals. In the United States, the signals proclaim power, optimism, and the potential for super wealth. The issuer announces a business worth scrutinizing and opens the books for all to see. Investors are invited in and are given access to a business with extraordinary upside potential. The managers, directors, and other insiders willingly put themselves in the spotlight. They put their rank and standing in the community on the line, and they run the risk of being thrown out if the company does not perform as well as market participants expect.

Outside the United States, the signals are more dissonant, and in some countries they are muted. Managers and directors do not put their necks in a noose. Their job security does not depend so heavily on the performance of the company's stock. The shares the public buys are not instruments of power. The shares may have a vote, but the buyers do not have voting in mind. Control of the company resides in the board of directors, or with nominees, or with a committee of bankers. Shareholders get dividends and annual reports that do not say much, except that the company is in good hands and is performing satisfactorily in the judgment of experts who are privy to the details of the company's affairs.

To illustrate how different the conventions surrounding common stock are outside the United States, consider that in Europe and much of Asia there are shares that are not entitled to a vote. These are called *savings shares*. The name carries no stigma. Savings shares exist alongside ordinary shares and "golden" or super-voting shares. Many companies, including many that are large, conservative, and well capitalized, have issued savings shares and sold them successfully. These nonvoting shares are credible and respected outside the United States, and European financial advisers often recommend them for client portfolios. Widows and orphans are often advised to buy them. These nonvoting common shares are entitled to the same dividends as the voting common shares and have equal rights in liquidation. They are slightly cheaper than the voting shares because the right to vote is worth something, even though control is rarely disputed.

The signals and symbolism of common stock are so different because they manifest deep differences in business cultures. The United States is skeptical of traditional elites and is continually spewing up new elites, exalting them, and then casting them down. Europe and Asia are more hesitant to declare new heroes, and more willing to turn to traditional authorities for continuity and decisions. The United States has many pyramids of power, some rising and some falling, and new ones cropping up frequently, but does not have an overarching hierarchy that can consistently exert decisive authority in business situations. In Europe and Asia, the top decision makers in business are still concentrated on the boards of directors of the biggest banks. The banks are losing power rapidly, but the path to the top for a young man from a good family is still to go to a top-ranked traditional school and then get a job at a large bank. This career path leads to the pinnacle of power in countries where financial decision making is centralized, and where the main engines of value added in the country's economy do not change.

The differences in business cultures around the world are more profound than this characterization has described so far. To understand what common stock signifies it is necessary to dig deeper, to a visceral question of identity: The business either is or is not a separate entity, distinct from the person who owns it. In the United States, the business is clearly separate. The stockholders own it, and they own it in proportion to the percentage of the total shares they have. Outside the United States, the separation is not always so complete. The distinction between the business and its owners may be formalized by making the business a limited-liability corporation. But in casual conversation, people will blur the business and its owner together. And when there is a dispute over control, or over distribution of benefits, people outside the United States may casually assume that the dispute will be resolved in favor of the owner of the business.

There is also a difference over whether the business belongs to the entire nation or only to its shareholders. Outside the United States, the conventional views are in juxtaposition with views regarding the rights of the "owner" vis-à-vis the other shareholders. A business begins as an extension of the individual or family most closely identified with running it. Alternatively, it may be linked from the beginning to a group of companies controlled by a family or by a bank, or it may be linked to a regional power group or an ethnic or religious minority. After the business has become large, it passes into a new relationship to society. When many ordinary citizens depend on the business for their livelihood, it becomes part of the national patrimony. The business is then a collective asset of the entire nation, and the dominant shareholder no longer has the right to make big decisions about the business without consulting representatives of other elements of society. In the United States, the business is distinct from its founders, from their families, from other businesses, from regional power groups, and from religious and ethnic identities. It is in a capsule and it belongs exclusively to its shareholders. The managers make decisions without consulting other elements of society, and they do not conceive of themselves as stewards of the nation's destiny; nor are they charged with upholding the nation's standing in the worldwide rankings. They routinely make decisions to close factories, fire people, and change suppliers, all with the goal of raising the share price. They may be conscious that their actions have social impacts, but their responsibility is to the shareholders, and they do not define it more broadly than that.

Stock Options

The economic fate of employees is always linked to the success of the company they work for. On the downside, if it fails, they lose their jobs. If their pension fund is invested in the company's stock, they lose their retirement savings at the same time. So they have a clear and tight link with the company in the downward direction. But if the company does well, employees do not necessarily benefit proportionately. They keep their jobs, and probably get raises and perks. But they do not benefit completely from the company's success unless they are stockholders.

The trend around the world is to give stock options to employees and to decouple their pension funds from the affairs of the company. Stock options give employees better participation in the company's upside potential. Separating the employees' pension fund from the company's books and putting it in the hands of an independent trustee gives the employees better protection on the downside. The trustee invests the pension fund in a diversified mix of assets not linked to the company's fate. If the fund is large enough, the trustee divides it into tranches and chooses different portfolio managers to manage each tranche. Every year an outside auditor checks the pension fund's accounts, and every year the trustee reviews the performance of the portfolio managers and fires any of them that are performing poorly. These actions improve the employees' position and make the employees' incentives more congruent with the shareholders'.

When employees get more of their total compensation in the form of stock options, they become more committed to making the company successful and more focused on its future value in the stock market than on its previous performance. The company may have attracted them with the good pay it offered, or with its stability and safety, but after they get stock options they become more interested in its upside potential. They get more options every year, and if the company's stock rises steadily, they become millionaires on paper long before they are able to cash in and become millionaires for real. The longer they work for the company, the more their financial success is tied to its future stock market performance. If their options vest, they may wait before cashing them in, so as to defer the taxes that will be due. They may exercise a few options, get the shares, and then pledge them at a bank to get cash. This way they get some tangible benefits from their paper wealth without having to pay the tax collector. But most of their wealth remains on paper, with a constant risk of disappearing, until they cash in and pay the taxes, retire, or get fired.

A steady rise in a company's stock produces a paradoxical spectacle: millionaires on a treadmill. The employees are wealthy on paper, yet they work long hours. It appears they are striving to get more millions, but in reality they may only be striving to hang onto the paper millions they already have, until the day comes when they will be able to convert those millions into cash. The stock market, however, is a relentless taskmaster. Stocks do not stay at the same price for long. Most of them keep rising or begin falling. The rule of thumb in the stock market is that the stock price keeps rising as long as the company's growth rate stays high. If the company's growth rate slows, the stock price falls, and very suddenly the paper millionaires are millionaires no longer. An option to buy 75,000 shares at $20 a share is worth $2.25 million when the stock is at $50. If the stock falls to $19, the option is worth very much less. Sharp drops in price happen often. High-flying stocks often crumble where there is a minor disappointment in the company's performance. A new product is launched and fails to meet expectations, or its launch is delayed, and down comes the stock. Setbacks like this happen often enough to keep the paper millionaires on tenterhooks, and when a stock slides far enough the golden options turn sour, and then yesterday's paper millionaires have to start over again at the bottom of the ladder.

Shareholders' Clout

When so many middle-management, technical, and support employees have stock options, the price of the company's shares takes on paramount importance. Employees with stock options check the price daily and talk about it with their coworkers and friends. Some of them calculate how much the stock has to go up before they will have $100,000 on paper, or $500,000, or $1 million; or enough to buy a house, a new car, or a vacation. Some of them try to forecast when they will be able to cash in, and how much they will be able to get in cash.

The top managers are responsive to the employees' aspirations, and they have their own stock options to motivate them. So they devote a lot of effort to communicating with shareholders, portfolio managers, and institutional investors. Top managers do road shows, where they present the company to the investing community and try to show why investors should buy the company's stock. They listen attentively to questions from shareholders and answer questions candidly and completely, with the caveat that they cannot divulge inside information.

Shareholders in the United States know how much influence they can exert. They can publicize their dissatisfaction in investor chat rooms or on bulletin boards. They can telephone the company and give their opinions. A shareholder-relations person will talk with them and communicate their arguments to top management. Often, top managers will call a shareholder back, listen to suggestions, and explain why they are not following those suggestions.

Top managers give shareholders such courteous and respectful treatment because a few small purchases or sales of the company's stock can make a big difference in the stock price. The daily trading volume in the shares of most companies is tiny compared to the total amount of shares that exist. Less than 1% of the stock, and sometimes less than one-tenth of 1%, trades most days. When there is news, or a massive shift in investor sentiment, more than 5% of the shares may trade in a day, but this is unusual. So the marginal buyers, the ones that are sitting on the fence with a few thousand dollars to invest in one stock or another, have a tremendous influence on the day-to-day fluctuations of a stock's price. They have to be treated as valuable potential allies, or else they turn into damaging enemies.

Outside the United States, top managers do not usually pay such attention to communicating with shareholders. Outside the United States, perks do not include stock options, and when they do the options are so newfangled that they have not yet influenced top managers' behavior very much. Daily trading volume is low, and top management has no reason to be concerned about who is selling or why. Most shareholders have owned their stock for a long time and are not thinking of selling it. Shareholders know what the annual dividend is, and will sit up and take notice if the dividend is cut, but do not have a compelling reason to know what the stock price is from day to day. If control of the company has not changed for many years, and if there is no likelihood of control passing in the immediate future, the stock price may be chronically depressed, compared to what it would be if a buyer suddenly tried to acquire control.

This panorama of inertia and indifference to day-to-day price fluctuations is changing, but it still describes the situation for many companies. When a stockholder or someone who is considering buying stock telephones the company, the call may be shunted aside, or it may be routed to a junior person who handles shareholder relations along with other low-priority assignments. The shareholder-relations person, if there is one, takes the call and listens politely, then reads the caller the company's latest press release, sometimes because that is all the person knows about the questions the shareholder asks, or because that is all the shareholder-relations person is authorized to do. The person then notes the shareholder's opinions but takes no further action, because the shareholder-relations person does not have access to top management. The person also does not personally own any stock or have any stock options.

Raising the Stock Price

Stock prices do not rise all by themselves. Some investors, with charming naivete, believe that stock prices go up because diligent stock market analysts investigate the companies and then buy the shares they think will go up the most. This is folklore for schoolchildren. The stories children hear about capitalism are a caricature of what the stock market is really like. American children mostly hear positive stories, some so positive they are fanciful or utopian: Every individual pursues his or her rational, enlightened self-interest. The listeners picture hard-working managers who come to work early with clear-eyed idealism and good-naturedly plug away all through the long day, sticking to their knitting, steadily and prudently creating value for shareholders. Observing the managers are busy analysts who visit companies, kick the tires, and then go back to their offices, where they plough tirelessly and diligently through corporate reports in hopes of uncovering some little-known fact that will lead to fame and fortune.

This caricature never was accurate, even in bygone days. Stock prices go up because managers *make* them go up. That is how stock prices have always gone up, and today it is the *only* way they go up. It is not true, and never has been, that a company can raise its stock price merely by doing what it does especially well. Good performance helps, but it is not enough all by itself to raise a company's stock price. There are too many good companies clamoring for investors' attention. Any stock can be overlooked for years. Somebody has to call attention to it, and keep calling.

Wooing the analysts is essential. Top managers go on a road show when the stock is being sold to the public for the first time. Then, after it is listed and analysts are following it, top management has to keep going on road shows. Two or more per year are required. Otherwise, the stock falls off the analysts' and portfolio managers' radar screens. Their attention spans are short, and new publicity campaigns are constantly being directed at them. Turnover is high among analysts and portfolio managers. The newcomers may not know the company exists unless somebody tells them. Or they may know, but the company's name may slip their minds because some other company's publicity has gotten their attention. They are bombarded so constantly with information that they rarely have time to ferret out any overlooked, undervalued, underowned stocks.

Marketing the stock to individual investors is also important, and for some companies makes all the difference, because individual investors can buy enough shares to create an uptrend. Direct communication aimed at individual investors makes them aware of the company. But they will not buy on the recommendation of the company itself. The company is too obviously biased. Before individual investors will take the leap and buy shares, they need to find out about the company from sources that appear to be objective or savvy. Consequently, the company can address individual investors in its own guise, but it will then need to work to impress "objective" third parties. For this part of the marketing effort, the company has to work through intermediaries, or work in disguise, cloaking itself in other identities, if it is going to induce individual investors to buy.

Raising the Stock Price through Financial Engineering

In addition to publicizing its stock to analysts and investors, a company can adopt financial policies that will maximize its stock price. A company's stock price depends in part on how the company is financed and on how much risk it asks its shareholders to bear. These ideas are novel to many observers. Most uninitiated people think that a company's assets are what matters. Those are what produce the cash flows that ultimately reward investors. But it is true that the company's liabilities also matter; the company may be using too much debt financing or too much equity financing. And the company's hedging policy also matters; the company may be asking shareholders to take more risk than is necessary.

The idea of optimizing the mix of financing sources is easy to understand for a middle-class household. Suppose that there is a family that owns a house worth $400,000 and has household income of $100,000 a year. Suppose also that the family owes $50,000 on credit cards and only $25,000 on its mortgage. Obviously, the household can lower its annual interest expense by refinancing the mortgage and using the proceeds of the refinancing to pay off the credit card debt.

A company that is borrowing from different sources can often do the same. It can replace high-cost debt with low-cost debt. After it does that, the interest it saves increases earnings, so the stock price should go up, as surely as if the company had found a way to increase the profit margin on the products it sells.

Some companies may also gain from rebalancing the mix of debt and equity financing. Debt is cheaper because it is senior to equity. Interest expense is also deductible, while dividends are paid from after-tax income. An example will illustrate this. Suppose that a company is earning $100 million before interest and taxes. It has no debt, so its financing is 100% equity. Suppose that its assets have a market value of $500 million. Its common stock therefore should have a market value of $500 million. It has 20 million shares of stock outstanding, so the shares are trading at $25 each in the market. Suppose its earnings would be taxed at 30%. In this case, the company's after-tax income would be $70 million, and its return on common equity would be 14%. This is its cost of capital.

The company's capital structure, 100% equity and 0% debt financing, is not optimal. Its cost of capital is higher than it needs to be. The company can lower its cost of capital below 14% by issuing bonds and then using the proceeds of the bond issue to retire shares of common stock. Suppose the company sells $200 million of bonds. The interest rate on these bonds is 8%. It then uses the $200 million to repurchase common stock. At the $25 price, the $200 million will pay for the repurchase of 8 million shares of stock. The company will then destroy the 8 million shares of stock that it has just repurchased. There will then be only 12 million shares outstanding.

What will be the effects of these transactions? First, the company's earnings after interest will be reduced. It was earning $100 million a year before, but afterward it will be paying $16 million a year of interest on the bond issue, so its pretax earnings will decline to $84 million. Its taxes, which were $30 million a year, will also be lower; taxes will be $84 × 0.30 = $25.2 million. So its earnings after tax, which were $70 million, will fall to $84 − $25.2 = $58.8 million. Its earnings per share will increase, from $70 million/20 million = $3.50 a share, to $58.8 million/12 million = $4.90 a share.

The company's earnings per share rise from $3.50 to $4.90 because it uses a cheaper mix of debt and equity financing. Also, it pays less tax, so more of the $100 million it earns each year go to holders of its securities and less of it goes to the government. At a first approximation, its cost of capital declines from 14% to [$200 × (1 − 0.3) × 0.08 + $300 × 0.14]/ 500 = 10.6%.

The cost of capital falls because the company uses cheaper, tax-advantaged debt financing instead of using only equity financing, which is more expensive. Debt financing is cheaper because bonds are safer than common stocks. Bondholders have the senior claim on assets. If anything happens to the company, they have priority in liquidation. For this reason, bond investors do not expect or require such high rates of return as do buyers of common stocks.

The company's stock price also rises as a result of these financial maneuvers. It does not rise by the full amount of the increase in earnings per share, which would be ($4.90/$3.50) × $25 = $35. Instead it rises less than that, because after the recapitalization the stock is riskier. The $200 million of bonds are a senior claim on the company's assets and cash flow, so stockholders are in a riskier position. They do not bid the stock all the way up to $35 a share. There is a formula that calculates the new stock price, taking into account the proportion of debt the company uses in its capitalization. This formula says the stock price would rise to $27.72. This increase is greater than 10%. That is enough to earn an annual bonus for the managers. They did not raise earnings before interest and taxes, but they made the stock go up. Borrowing money and using it to buy back stock adds value as surely as inventing new products or finding new markets.

Since the maneuver of borrowing money and using it to repurchase common stock works, people often wonder how far down that path a company should go. Will it keep working to borrow more and use the cash to repurchase common stock, until the company has repurchased all the common stock and is entirely financed by debt? The answer is no; to go that far is to err in the opposite direction. The correct policy is to keep adding debt to the company's capital structure until the proportion of debt reaches an optimum. At that point the company is using as much of the cheaper debt financing as it should. If it borrows more than the optimal amount and uses the borrowed money to repurchase more common stock, the maneuver backfires. Buyers of common stock shy away, because the company's few remaining shares of stock are then too risky. Its earnings per share are higher, but the vulnerability of the shareholders' returns to any fluctuations in the company's operations is too high.

Besides optimizing its capital structure, the company can benefit its shareholders by reexamining its dividend policy. Historically, companies paid dividends according to rules of thumb, or in accord with legal requirements. Paying dividends regularly signaled market participants that the company was solid and stable. There were shareholders who depended on the dividend. They were long-term holders of the stock, not short-term traders.

Now the clientele are different. Stockholders are not holding on for decades. Instead their horizons are shorter, and they want to collect their rewards in the most tax-efficient way. Capital gains are taxed more favorably than dividends, so companies now try to deliver capital gains to shareholders instead of dividends. If shareholders want cash, they can borrow it using the stock as collateral, and then sell the shares later to repay the loan. By doing this they can defer their tax liabilities.[5] It is also true that delivering $1 of capital gains can cost a company less than delivering $1 of dividends.

An example illustrates some of the computations a company might use to decide what is the most efficient way to deliver returns to its shareholders. Consider the company described before, after its recapitalization. Its stock price is $27.72 per share. Now suppose the company has $27.72 million it wants to dedicate to rewarding shareholders. Suppose this money is from profits that the company just earned, and the profits have already been taxed. The company can reinvest the $27.72 in the business, it can use it to pay a dividend, or it can use the money to repurchase 1 million shares in the market. Let us consider the effect of each in turn.

Reinvesting the cash in the business will increase future earnings. The company was earning 20% on assets before interest and taxes, or $100 million on assets worth $500 million. After the reinvestment it would have $527.72 million of assets. It would continue to earn 20% on assets, so its earnings before interest and taxes would go up to $105.54 million. Applying the 30% tax rate to the $5.54 of new earnings, after-tax earnings would increase by $3.88 million. This works out to $0.32 per share. Applying the price/earnings ratio from the earlier part of the example, we get the new stock price of $29.59. So each of the company's 12 million shares would be worth $29.59 − $27.72 = $1.87 more. The total pretax gain to shareholders would be $1.87 × 12 million = $22.44 million.

Paying the cash as a dividend to the shareholders will give them $27.72 million pretax, but the amount they keep will be substantially less because they will have to pay taxes on the dividend soon after receiving it. Considering that some of the shareholders are wealthy, their marginal tax rate might be 40%, so they would keep only $16.63 million after taxes.

Using the cash to repurchase 1 million shares can be the most effective way of rewarding shareholders. After the repurchase there will be 11 million shares remaining. The company's earnings in the year after the repurchase will be $100 million before interest and taxes as before, and its interest expense will be $16 million as before. After the repurchase there will be only 11 million shares, so the market price of each one can be expected to increase to $27.72 × 12/11 = $30.24.

There is no magic in the repurchase. The repurchase delivers $27.72 million to the shareholders but it does it in a way that gives shareholders the choice of a return of capital, which is not taxed, or capital gains, which can be deferred until the shareholder chooses to pay. The $27.72 million appears twice, once as the value of the shares that are retired from the market ($27.72 × 1 million = $27.72 million), and again as the increase in value of the remaining 11 million shares [($30.24 − $27.72) × 11 million = $27.72 million]. So the earnings are paid out not as dividends but to pay for stock that is being retired, and the company's market capitalization is the same as it was before ($27.72 × 12 = $30.24 × 11).

In this example, which captures the essential dimensions of the choice, the company rewards its shareholders most by repurchasing common shares and destroying them. Reinvesting the $27.72 million in the business at a 20% pretax rate of return rewards them less. And paying the money out as a cash dividend also comes out badly, because shareholders are not given the flexibility of choosing when to take the gain.

This example could go into more detail, but the point has already been made that companies reward their shareholders by repurchasing common stock and then tearing up the certificates. Shrinking the supply of stock makes sense at the level of individual companies. It also stokes the wealth-creation machine by aggravating the shortage of securities.

There is another kind of financial maneuver that companies can use to raise the price of their stock. This is to buy specialized financial products that shift risk. These are called *derivatives*. Some of them are very complicated, and when they are used improperly they can backfire, but when they are used correctly they can raise the value of the company's stock.

One example will suffice to illustrate how this can work. Consider the company in the previous example after its recapitalization. It has $200 million of debt and 12 million common shares worth $27.72 each. It earns $100 million before interest and taxes and pays $16 million of interest, leaving $84 million. Its share price is held down by the risk that earnings may not be sufficient to pay the interest. In that event, the bondholders would be able to take the company and manage it for their own benefit.

Now suppose that the company's earnings before interest and taxes can fluctuate between $10 million and $190 million. They average $100 million but can be much lower or much higher; in particular, they can be

less than the $16 million that has to be paid each year to the bondhold-
ers. Also suppose that the fluctuations are entirely due to the price of oil.
The company uses oil and cannot pass on any increases in the cost of oil
to its customers, so its earnings swing up and down.

The company's stockholders are informed, intelligent, and risk averse.
They know that they run a risk when they buy the company's shares, so
they refuse to pay more than $27.72 for the shares.

The risk of owning the shares disappears when the company buys protection against oil price fluctuations. It pays $10 million a year to hedge
itself completely against fluctuations in the price of oil. Its earnings before
interest, hedging costs, and taxes are now certain to be $100 million each
year. Interest expense remains at $16 million a year. Hedging expense is
$10 million a year. The company's pretax earnings are now $74 million
a year instead of $84 million per year as before, but now there is no risk
of earnings falling or rising. After-tax earnings will be $74 million $\times$
$(1-0.3) = $51.8 million. This works out to $4.32 per share. In view of the
hedging, stock market investors will now pay more than $27.72 for the
shares. Formulas indicate that investors would pay between $30.84 and
$72.00 per share. The latter price is an upper limit; in reality they would
probably pay $30 or $31 per share. This is an improvement of 8 to 11%.

Using derivatives, as in this case to protect against fluctuations in the
price of oil, opens up a further possibility for raising the company's stock
price. If hedging reduces the volatility of the company's earnings before
interest and taxes, the company can use more borrowed money in its capital structure. It can borrow more than $200 million to repurchase com-
mon shares. For example, it can borrow another $100 million and agree to
pay 10% annual interest. It can then use this cash to buy 3.22 million
shares at $31 each. After buying these shares, the company destroys them.
There would then be only 12 million − 3.22 million = 8.78 million shares
remaining. The market price of the remaining shares would be higher
than $31 each. To see how much higher the stock price would be, it would
be necessary to know how effective the hedging really was. The company's
earnings per share would be $5.10. If the hedging were effective, the stock
price might go up to $36.14.

The effect of these maneuvers, in these simple examples, is to raise
the company's stock price from $25 to $36. The exact amount of the increase, and the exact financial maneuvers that would be done to make it

happen, are debatable, but the main point is clear. Companies are finding intelligent ways of rewarding their shareholders. Many of these ways involve buying back their stock and then destroying the shares bought back. The supply of stock is shrinking.

New Issuance and the Supply of Common Stock

During calendar year 1999, a total of $4.2 trillion of new securities were issued.[6] This seems like a large amount, considering that world output was approximately $39 trillion. Is this large amount of new issuance the beginning of a change in the supply of securities? No, it is not. The increase is more apparent than real.

In 1999 there were mergers and share buybacks, just as there were in 1998, and these reduced the net amount of new securities that investors could buy. There were also shares held off the market under *lockup agreements*. Because of these buybacks and lockup agreements, the amount of new securities that was really available was much less than $4.2 trillion.

When a company sells stock to the public, 100% of its shares are included in the total new supply of stock, but much less than 100% is really available. Usually only 20% of the shares are offered to the public. The investment-banking syndicate that distributes the shares to the public usually asks for a *green shoe option*, allowing it to sell slightly more than 20% of the shares if there is enough demand. The remaining 80% is not released to the public. It stays in the hands of the founders and venture capitalists. The 80% includes the control block, which may be a large portion of the 80%. There are also shares held by employees, officers, directors, friends, and family members. These shares are restricted. The investment bankers require that these shares not be sold during the months immediately following the IPO. The Securities and Exchange Commission (SEC) investigates any sale by an officer or director during the lockup period because the seller may have acted on inside information.

The shares are locked up under several kinds of restrictive agreements for long periods following the IPO. Many of the holders would come under suspicion of improperly enriching themselves if they sold. Their freedom to sell increases with time but is always restricted by some rules of fair play or team spirit. For example, if a founder sells a large amount of stock one year after an IPO, some employees and shareholders may feel undercut. The founder's sale depresses the price by adding to the visible supply of stock (the free float), and SEC regulations require that the sale be disclosed no longer than two weeks after the event. So the sale depresses the stock twice, once on the days of sale, and again when market participants learn that the sale was by an insider, presumably well informed.

In practice, several conventions have evolved that effectively prolong the lockup for many years. First, the insiders and the holders of large blocks schedule their sales for four dates a year. This convention gives four windows when insiders can cash in without sending any alarm signals to the market. Selling shareholders are encouraged to say well in advance how many shares they are selling in total, and over how many quarterly window dates they are going to spread their sales. Second, if an insider or a large block holder has an emergency that requires selling outside of this quarterly window scheme, the holder has to say that the selling is motivated by a personal situation, not by any loss of faith in the company's future prospects. The effect of these lockup conventions is to hold stock off the market.

An IPO in October 1999 provides an extreme example of how restricted the supply of stock can be. Akamai Technologies sold stock to the public but did not sell anywhere near as much as the public wanted to buy. Instead of offering the usual 20% of the total amount of shares, Akamai offered only 9 million shares of 91.4 million, or just under 10% of the total. The remaining 90.2% was retained; part of that was the control block, and part was restricted or covered under lockup agreements. Besides those restrictions, there were other de facto restrictions in effect. In each IPO, members of the underwriting syndicate give selected retail investors the privilege of signing up for shares at the IPO price. This is a privilege because very often the shares trade to a premium on the first day, so anybody who is allowed to buy at the offering price gets an enormous windfall gain. In exchange for the privilege of buying shares at the offering price, investors are often required to agree not to flip the shares on the first day, or during the first 60 days. These *no-flip agreements* are different from the lockup agreements that officers, directors, and employees sign. The no-flip agreements are not legally binding. The underwriter enforces the no-flip agreement by threatening to cut off the investor's access to subsequent offerings.

The price of Akamai Technologies shares went from $26 to $299 on the first day of trading. It is clear what happened. First, the company was a hot prospect because it had a track record and its product was in great demand. Its IPO was widely announced weeks and days before the event. The underwriting syndicate had a successful *book-building period,* which means its order book for the issue was oversubscribed. Consequently, the shares were allocated, and buyers did not get all they had requested during the book-building period. Second, very little stock was offered. Third, the retail investors who were lucky enough to get a few hundred or thousand shares had to promise not to sell the shares for 60 days. So a retail investor who did not get any stock, and who was determined to buy some, had to put out an offer and hope that somebody who had agreed not to sell would relent and let a few shares go. Day traders usually bid for shares of any hot IPO, to see if they can pry a few shares loose. They then flip the shares for higher prices during the first day. So suppose there were 10 retail investors, each determined to get 1,000 shares, and there was only one person who got shares at the offering price who was willing to break the no-flip promise and sell. The stock would officially begin trading at 9:30 A.M. The shares would be electronically posted to the accounts of the people who were lucky enough to get them at $26 each. Immediately there would be offers to buy at $27 or $28. The offers would rise quickly until some transactions took place.

Trading an IPO stock on its first day is tricky. Traders need to know how much unsatisfied demand there really is. Underwriters usually manage to get orders for more stock than is being offered, but it is hard to tell how many of those orders were from buyers who ordered twice as much as they really wanted. The first few minutes of trading sometimes tells the story. The stock price rises above its offering level and then keeps on going up, or begins to fall back down. In the case of Akamai Technologies there really was unsatisfied demand, and there were traders who were determined to have some of the stock. Traders can use *limit orders,* saying in effect that they will not pay more than a stated price for the stock, or they can use *market orders,* saying that they will pay what they have to in order to get the stock. In the case of Akamai there were traders offering to buy at the market price. Those orders gave a blank check to sellers, who succumbed to the temptation to let go of a few shares, even at the cost of losing their access to future IPO issues from the underwriting syndicate.

About midday, when the stock price was going up faster than an express elevator, there was an opportunity to push it even higher. The people who are under lockup agreements are allowed to buy the stock in the market during its first 60 days of trading. What they cannot do is sell. Some stockholder could have chosen that moment to add to his or her position, offering to buy 100 shares of stock *at the market*. This hypothetical buy order would have intensified the frenzy. Traders can find out how many shares are demanded at the bid price and how many are offered at the ask price at any moment during the trading day. This is called the *size* of the bid and ask. At a moment when the price of the last trade was, say, $186, the bid may have been $185 and the ask may have been $187. This would be a typical spread during a day of active and volatile trading, and the $2 difference between bid and ask price would not convey much information. The more important information is the size: There may have been only 100 shares offered at $187, and 22,800 bid at $185. The size information would tell traders that there was much more demand than supply at the $186 price level; very soon one of the buyers would break ranks and buy the 100 shares that were offered at $187. So the next trade would be at $187, up from $186. Somebody who already had a lot of stock could buy several times during the day, and push the price higher. In the case of Akamai Technologies, there was no reason for anybody to do that. The company's prospects created the buying frenzy, and the stock went to the stratosphere on its own steam.

How much money was really involved in creating Akamai's eye-popping market capitalization of $27.3 billion at the end of the first day's trading? That valuation is the number of shares, 91.4 million, times the $299 price. Nowhere near as much as $27.3 billion really moved. Only 9 million shares were sold that day. The IPO was supposed to raise $26 × 9 million = $234 million for the company, for the selling shareholders, and for the underwriting syndicate. It did raise that much. What happened after that was that the owners of some small fraction of the 9 million shares let them go after trading began at 9:30 A.M. More than 5 million shares traded that day, but some shares traded more than once. The buying frenzy was evident from the opening moment, because the lowest price during the day was $143. To see the maximum amount of money that changed hands, suppose that 5.5 million shares traded that day, at an average price of $200 a share. That is $1.1 billion—still a lot of money, but less than 5% of the $27.3 billion figure.

So the total supply of securities issued in calendar year 1999 was, in effect, much smaller than $4.2 trillion. Suppose that $1 trillion was held off the market, and another $1 trillion of previously existing securities were bought up and destroyed by mergers and takeovers. That leaves only $2.2 trillion net new issuance that buyers could have bought. That is only about 5.6% of world output. Considering that gross world savings were more than twice that, and considering that fewer and fewer savers are buying tangibles, one can see that 1999 was another year of demand for securities exceeding supply. Consequently, securities prices had to go up, and they did.

Chapter 4

How Much Can a Stock Be Worth?

As the stock market continues its near-vertical rise, investors continually wonder whether stock prices have risen above what they can possibly be worth. News analysts question whether prices of common stocks have soared far above the reasonable range. Investors seek to understand how high a stock can rise and still be in proportion to the company's future prospects. So they search for rules of thumb and benchmarks that they can apply to common stocks.

Are Traditional Yardsticks Still Applicable?

There are traditional yardsticks, and experts have come forth with many new ones, but now the search is much more urgent because stock price increases have outpaced so many of the old parameters of value. Investors who look at a stock carefully and balk at paying the market price for it often find themselves buying the same stock a short time later for 2 or 3 times as much. Then they feel totally unsure of themselves because they have paid so much. So they watch the stock in trepidation, holding their breath and crossing their fingers. If it doubles or triples again, they are giddy and euphoric; if it falls, they agonize in self-recrimination because they paid so much more for it than it should have cost. If they had bought a "good" stock at a "reasonable" price and then lost money, they would not have suffered such agonies.

Today's high stock prices look too high but are not. The price rises of many stocks make good sense and correspond well to the parameters of valuation models that have been in use for many decades. This chapter looks at two typical companies and shows how much their common stocks can reasonably be worth. It shows that traditional benchmarks are rooted in the environment of the past and are valid in that environment. The current environment is more favorable to common stocks and consequently allows stock prices to be much higher. The high prices can persist, and can go still higher, as long as the new favored environment for common stocks continues.

The central thesis of this book, that financial wealth can continue to grow very rapidly, depends on stock prices continuing to rise. If financial wealth is to reach the astronomical levels that this book projects, the most likely way is for common stock prices to rise higher. Common stocks would have to be a greater part of the mix of financial wealth. When the stock market rally began in 1982, common stocks accounted for only about one-third of financial wealth. By 2000, common stocks were around 40% of financial wealth. By 2014, if financial wealth has grown by 5 to 10 times the amount it reached in 2000, common stocks will probably account for 70 or 80% of financial wealth.

Stocks will be a larger and larger portion of total financial wealth because the amount of bonds usually does not grow very fast. The reason is that bonds tend to be closely tied to assets and cash flows that already exist. Bond buyers have to be skeptics because they can lose their entire investment if things go wrong, but if things go especially well they do not usually enjoy much upside potential. Bond buyers usually demand that productive assets collateralize the bonds they buy. Another reason why the value of bonds in existence cannot grow very much is that issuers usually sell the entire amount of a bond issue instead of holding most of it back. If a company needs $400 million to build a new power plant, it sells $400 million of bonds, and investors usually buy all $400 million in a short period of time. Buyers actually have to pay for the bonds before getting a claim on them. Another fact holding down the market value of bonds is that bond prices do not usually rise very far above their initial face amounts. So the amount of bonds in existence bears a close relationship to the amounts that people saved during previous periods, and it does not usually grow much faster than total savings.

Common stocks, in contrast, are claims on future potential. Stocks are forward looking and not so closely tied to the here and now. Their market value can grow much faster than output. Stocks depend for their value on how much companies will earn in the future, and how much of those earnings will go to shareholders. Investors often change their views on these questions quickly and capriciously. Since 1995 investors have become much more optimistic about future earnings, and about the portion of future earnings that will go to shareholders. Their optimism has so far been justified (Table 4.1).

The conventional factors that investors have historically taken into account to determine a common stock price are as follows:

- The company's future earning potential
- The riskiness of the company's lines of business
- The company's debt burden
- The company's policies and priorities for rewarding shareholders
- The outlook for inflation

Table 4.1   **U.S. Corporate Profits, 1990–1999**

Year	Corporate Profits, $ Billions	Percentage of U.S. GNP
1990	408.6	7.01
1991	431.2	7.31
1992	453.1	7.14
1993	510.5	7.66
1994	473.2	8.11
1995	668.8	9.01
1996	754.0	9.63
1997	838.5	10.10
1998	848.4	9.70
1999	892.7	9.67

Source: DRI Global Economics.

This list may sound utterly obvious and reasonable, but it has its limitations. These become obvious when one looks at how to value the shares of two companies. These two are representative of two broad categories of stocks in the market, blue chips and New Economy stocks.

The Stable Manufacturing Company (SMC)

The first stock is easier to value because the procedure for valuing it stays close to the traditional approach. This company, Stable Manufacturing Company (SMC), is representative of prominent Old Economy companies like General Foods, Caterpillar, Ford, and International Paper. SMC has a solid position in the market and an excellent reputation, and its annual sales are growing a bit faster than the economy. Its products are in everyday use, and production technology for those items is well known but expensive to copy. The barriers that keep other companies out of SMC's market are high but not insurmountable. Replicas of SMC's product are in the market, but they are not as good, not as well marketed, and not a serious threat to SMC's growth and profitability. Securities analysts rate SMC stock a blue chip and recommend it for long-term value-oriented investors. In this example, its sales have grown 7% per year for the past five years, and its profits have grown 11% per year for the past five years. During those five years, SMC's best year and its worst year were quite similar. SMC's fastest sales growth was 8% for one year, and its slowest was 6%. Its worst year for profit growth was 10%, and its best was 12%. SMC is often compared to Gillette, Johnson & Johnson, and Procter & Gamble.

SMC's annual sales are $5 billion. Its direct manufacturing costs are $2.5 billion, and its marketing expenses, administrative staff, and headquarters overhead cost $1.35 billion, so its earnings before interest, taxes, depreciation, and amortization are $1.15 billion ($5 billion − $2.5 billion − $1.35 billion = $1.15 billion). SMC pays interest on its debt and lease payments on its equipment and facilities amounting to $300 million a year. SMC also owns some equipment and buildings, and the depreciation expenses on those are $250 million a year. There are also some intangible assets, and the amortization expenses for those are $50 million a year. Interest, depreciation, and amortization together add up to $600 million a year. SMC's earnings before tax are therefore $1.15 billion − $600 million = $550 million. The company pays taxes equal to 40% of pretax earnings, so its net income is $330 million. SMC has 100 million shares, so its earnings per share is $3.30.

The historical price range for SMC's stock is from $23 to $63. This is between 7 and 19 times earnings per share. The stock fluctuated in this range from 1960 to 1993. There are a lot of reasons why this was the normal range, and why any price above this range had to be unsustainably high. The reasons include assumptions that are not usually stated. Let us state what those are, and see how much difference the assumptions make. The conventional view is that if SMC's stock price is higher than 19 times earnings, it is clearly overvalued. Here are the assumptions:

- SMC's profits will cease growing faster than its sales; indeed, its profit growth may slow down more than its sales growth.
- SMC's sales will soon cease growing faster than the economy; they will have to slow down to match the growth of the economy.
- The corporate tax rate will remain at its present level.
- SMC's employees have a claim on the company for their retirement and future health care costs in excess of the claim that is specifically shown on the company's books.
- SMC will be unable to acquire or merge with other companies in its industry sector because combinations within a sector are anticompetitive and will be blocked.

The conventional method for valuing a stock requires a growth rate for earnings per share going forward into the future. This requirement is hard to deal with if the conventional assumptions are no longer valid. Corporate profits have historically been cyclical, so periods when they have risen have always been followed by periods of decline. It used to be customary to assume that the average company's earnings per share could not grow faster than the economy for long periods of time. Growth companies could exceed the average by 2% per year, and stagnating companies would grow more slowly than the economy. In the aggregate, company earnings could not grow faster than the economy, and their performance would track the business cycle. Lately, however, earnings have been well above their usual performance, and there is some doubt about how they will fluctuate in the future. They may keep rising longer than they did during previous cycles, and then oscillate around some higher average level.

There are two reasons why SMC's earnings may keep growing for longer than they have done in the past. One is simply that business cycles seem to be getting longer, so the upswing may last longer, and the upswing after that may be longer still, so the lengthening of upswings will raise the trendline of earnings growth. The other reason is even harder to put into the conventional framework for valuing common stock. Corporate profits may now have a greater role in society than before, and for this reason the social contract may allow corporate profits to claim a higher portion of total output than before. If this is correct, then SMC's profits can grow faster than its sales, and much faster than the economy, for a very long time.

The conventional valuation method also requires a discount rate, to compute the present value of SMC's future earnings per share. The discount rate has to be high if the stock is volatile and if there is much inflation. But because inflation has been low and because SMC's stock price has risen steadily, the discount rate that investors will use to value SMC's future earnings is not very high, perhaps only 14%. This discount rate may appear too low because profits have historically fluctuated widely. The stability of recent years might look like an aberration, as if nature has been particularly benign. But the stability does not come only from a favorable alignment of the planets. Instead, it is the result of more systematic hedging. Companies like STC now place much higher priority on managing risk and on damping the volatility of the underlying fluctuations of the businesses they are in. They use derivatives to offset the unpredictable ups and downs of commodity prices, interest rates, and exchange rates. They are no longer willing to tolerate levels of volatility that were acceptable in the past.

If SMC's earnings can grow at 11% a year, and investors use a discount rate as low as 14% to value SMC's earnings, then SMC's price/earnings (P/E) multiple can be as high as 33.3. Many analysts use the following simple formula:

$$P/E = \frac{1}{\text{discount rate} - \text{earnings growth rate}}$$

This formula takes into account the riskiness of the company's future earnings growth and the rate of inflation. These each influence the discount rate. This formula awards a high P/E ratio to a company if the discount rate investors apply to its earnings is low. The discount rate can be as low as 10% if the company's earnings are stable and if the company's future looks safe. The formula also awards a high P/E ratio to a company whose earnings growth is high. The earnings growth rate in the formula is supposed to go on for many years into the future, so it is usually less than 15%. If the company's earnings growth rate is zero, the formula is particularly simple. For example, if a company's discount rate is very low, say 10%, and its earnings growth rate is zero, the formula says its P/E ratio should be 10 [1/(0.1 − 0.0) = 10]. At the opposite end of the normal range, if a company's discount rate is fairly low, say 14%, and its earnings growth rate is high, say 12%, the formula says its P/E ratio should be 50 [1/(0.14 − 0.12) = 50].

Using the numbers in this illustration for SMC, its P/E should be 33.3 [P/E = 1/(0.14 − 0.11) = 33.3]. In this case, the ceiling P/E ratio is no longer 19; instead, it has risen to 33.3. So SMC's stock price is no longer capped at $63. In the circumstances described, it is reasonable to pay much more than $63 for the stock.

Already this has raised the ceiling price of SMC stock to $110. This figure is its earnings per share of $3.30 times the new, higher price/earnings ratio of 33.3 ($3.30 × 33.3 = $110). It arrived at this new level by overturning only one of the conventional assumptions, namely that earnings growth will have to slow down and revert to its former cyclic pattern.

Now let us overturn another assumption and see the effect it will have on SMC's stock price. The corporate tax rate will not remain the same; instead, it will decline from 40% down to 20%, at the rate of 1% per year for the next 20 years. This decline will add to SMC's earnings growth because more and more of SMC's pretax income will go to shareholders and less will go to the government. So for the next 20 years SMC's earnings growth will be even higher, as high as 12.4% per year. Using the same formula as before, the new price of SMC's stock could be as high as $206 [$3.30/(1.14 − 0.124) = $206].

Now let us overturn the last three remaining assumptions and see how much more SMC's stock could go up. Most companies that were founded before 1980 face some uncertainty about future retirement costs, and SMC is one of those. But now let us set that assumption aside. For the rest of this numerical illustration, assume that SMC's future liabilities toward its employees now are entirely known. SMC's only liability to its employees for their retirement or for their health care expenses after retirement is to pay a defined contribution to their 401(k) accounts and to pay a portion of their health maintenance organization monthly fees. SMC makes these monthly payments and shows its employees and its auditors that it is doing so. These contributions go to a trustee who issues a receipt to SMC; after that, SMC has no further long-run residual liability toward its employees.

With the assumption that SMC's obligations toward its employees are fully accounted for and expensed during the current accounting period, the uncertainty that shareholders face is reduced. Prior to 1980, the shareholders did not know how much of the company's future earnings would be spent on retired employees. Retirees were entitled to defined retirement benefits and health care. Now their future claims on the company are nil, because their claims have already been paid. Shareholders can count on getting a more predictable portion of earnings. This reduction in uncertainty can be incorporated into the formula for P/E. The usual method is to lower the discount rate—for example, from 14 to 13.9%. That small reduction in the discount rate might not seem important, but it raises the price investors can justify for the stock from $206 to $220.

The last assumptions to be removed are about sales growth and mergers and acquisitions. SMC's sales can grow much faster than the economy even though its products are not high-growth items. SMC can keep buying companies and merging them into SMC. This will allow SMC's sales to maintain their growth even after SMC's individual products achieve market saturation. Mergers and acquisitions, especially the ones that create monopoly power, used to be blocked if they would give a company too much pricing power. Now let us relax that assumption. Suppose that SMC would be allowed to merge with the other companies in its sector, and after merging, SMC would be able to raise prices 1%. Suppose further that SMC's costs would not change, so the price increase would flow to pretax earnings. Pretax earnings would then go up by $50 million, and the increase would be sustained in subsequent years. The effect on earnings and earnings growth could be impressive. One could assess the impact of relaxing the assumptions one by one, but it is more illustrative to set them all aside at the same time.

For the effect of relaxing all the assumptions at once, use 40% as the beginning corporate tax rate and 20% as the ending tax rate. The freedom to merge raises SMC's revenues by $50 million, and its pretax earnings by the same amount. SMC's tax payments to the government rise $20 million in the first year, and SMC's earnings after taxes rise $30 million in that same year. The new earnings after taxes are 9% higher than before.

Investors would not immediately assign a 9% higher growth rate to SMC's earnings. They would fear that if SMC acts too much like a monopolist it might cause a backlash or attract new competitors. So they would raise their estimate of SMC's growth rate only a small amount, perhaps to 12.6% from 12.4%. Again, this small increase makes a big difference in the ceiling price of SMC stock.

To complete the calculation, suppose that earnings per share rise 9% from $3.30 to $3.60, and the price/earnings ratio rises to 77 [1/(0.139 − 0.126) = 77]. The stock price could then be as high as $277 without exceeding the parameters of the earnings-based valuation approach that traditionally is used for blue-chip stocks. For comparison, the historical valuation range for SMC was $23 to $63 per share.

This illustration shows one of the conventional methods of valuing stocks of stable blue-chip companies. It also shows that the valuation formula builds in assumptions about the relationship between the corporation and the society. These assumptions have been valid until recently, but now are being relaxed or set aside. Each of these assumptions has an impressive effect on the ceiling price that a reasonable buyer might pay for SMC stock. In the illustration, relaxing them all at the same time causes SMC stock to more than quadruple in price.

Note that shareholders are not the only players in the economy who benefit when these assumptions are relaxed. Consider just one assumption, the prohibition against monopolies. If SMC merges with its large competitors and gains enough market power to raise the prices of its products 1%, there are two clear winners. The winners are the government and SMC stockholders. The government collects more tax revenue, and the stockholders gain an amount of paper wealth equal to 100 times the dollar amount of the price increase. To compute the amount of paper wealth the stockholders would gain, suppose that the stock is at $220 per share before the merger. Since there are 100 million shares of SMC outstanding, the market capitalization before the merger is $22 billion ($220 × 100 million). After the consolidation, the stock price rises by $57, to $277. The new figure for total stock market value is $27.7 billion, an increase of more than $5 billion. This is 100 times the amount of the price increase. SMC's revenues before the increase were $5 billion, and they have increased by 1%, which is $50 million.

Consumers pay $50 million a year more, and stockholders then have paper wealth of $5 billion more. Government also collects $20 million more taxes in the first year. Considering that many consumers are also stockholders or government employees, it is reasonable to expect that mergers and consolidations will be allowed.

The assumptions being set aside in this illustration, however, are bedrock postulates of the social contract in the United States. They have been in place at least since 1932, the year of the Roosevelt landslide, if not since 1890, the year of the Sherman Antitrust Act. Monopolies are against the law in the United States, and corporations are subservient to the interests of the people. Would investors really believe that those inalienable principles of the republic have all been permanently set aside? One can gauge their degree of belief by looking at the market price of stocks like SMC's. Investors put their beliefs on public display when they pay prices approaching the $277 level for SMC stock. SMC, after all, is not a glamour company. It does not make products with exceptional growth potential. The growth potential that drives SMC stock to that high level comes from a new source: SMC's rising status in society. SMC gains its new higher status because it has become a generator of wealth. The sky-high price of SMC stock speaks loudly, affirming that new clauses have been put into the social contract. Buyers must believe that these new clauses are already in effect, because the high price they pay for SMC stock is reasonable only if all the assumptions have really been set aside.

Can companies really achieve the preferential status that setting aside these assumptions implies? The answer is that they have already done it. Gillette stock climbed by a factor of 10 in less than 20 years. Procter & Gamble stock did almost as well. So did many other blue-chip stocks. Every increase in these companies' status raised the justifiable price of their stock, and the process became self-reinforcing.

The process can continue into the future. SMC stock can rise higher. If SMC raises its prices a further 1%, and if the corporate tax rate drops to 10%, SMC's earnings per share would rise more, from $3.30 before the assumptions were relaxed to as much as $5.85 afterward. That would raise SMC's justifiable stock price to $450 a share.

Now this exercise seems to be going too far! Are investors really going to be crazy enough to believe that a company with products as ordinary as SMC's can reasonably sell for 77 times earnings? They do not have to be crazy to believe that, because if the social contract really has been rewritten, then SMC stock really is worth that much. That price/earnings level is justified if inflation is low, if interest rates are low, and if SMC can keep its growth rate high enough. Both the formula and common sense say so. If there are no other assets for investors to buy that are more attractive, and if it appears that SMC can keep acquiring more companies, its stock price can indeed trade at that high level, and remain at that high level for a long time.

The High-Growth High-Technology Company (HHC)

The second stock is harder to value because the traditional approach to valuation does not work directly. New Economy companies are valuable for their potential, not for their accomplishments. Trying to infer what a New Economy company will be worth in the future is difficult but can be extremely rewarding to any investor who can do it successfully. There are many possible approaches, and this discussion first looks at the current practice of valuing a high-growth company as a multiple of its annual sales. Then comes a valuation of High-Growth High-Technology Company (HHC), an exemplar high-growth company, using a straightforward extension of the methodology for valuing companies growing at a normal rate. This methodology divides the valuation problem into two parts. The first part is to select a date in the future when the company's growth will slow down to a normal rate. At that point it can be valued as a blue-chip company like SMC. The second part is to assess how big and how valuable the company will be at that time. Then, with those two results in hand, it is a simple matter to compute what the high-growth company's stock price should be today. Finally, after going through those calculations, comes a valuation of HHC using the *real options* approach that has lately become popular with analysts.

Real companies that are like HHC include Amazon.com, e-Trade, Yahoo!, Lycos, and Palm. Since each of these is controversial, and since each one's financials are complicated, this discussion values HHC, the archetypical simple New Economy stock. This valuation exercise is much less precise than the one used to value SMC stock. There are more uncertainties and fewer data that might be applicable. Here are some of the uncertainties:

- Will HHC's high growth rate slow down sooner than predicted, or later?
- Will HHC be dominant in its sector when its growth slows down?
- How large and profitable will HHC be when its growth slows down?
- Will HHC's technology be leapfrogged?

Answering these questions is a guessing game. The investor's optimism may have more to do with the answers he or she gives than the data that are at hand. Nevertheless, let us proceed with an illustration.

Suppose that HHC is an online retailer. For convenience you may think of Amazon.com, but the numerical illustrations are for HHC, the simpler, uncontroversial exemplar. Choosing an online retailer removes from the analysis the risk that its technology will be leapfrogged, because its technology is no longer risky. But there is no loss of generality because the remaining uncertainties are adequate substitutes for technological uncertainty. There are many ways a company can fail to live up to its early promise, and for the purposes of this analysis all the ways are interchangeable. The uncertainties of surviving and dominating the sector are enough to illustrate the method and show how wide the range of plausible valuations is.

Investors can protect themselves against some of the risks of HHC's stock quite easily. For example, they can buy shares of other online retailers that sell the same product line. Then if only one survives, the investor will own shares of it and will do well. In online retailing of books, for example, an investor would buy shares of Amazon.com, Barnesandnoble.com, Varsitybooks.com, and a few others.

The remaining risks are still large and hard to assess. Nevertheless, the investor has to have a view of how those risks are going to be resolved. Many investors deny this and say that they are only trying to assess the psychology of other investors. Still, there is some segment of investors who are trying to gauge the company's current price vis-à-vis future scenarios of the economy and judge how big the company will be at that time. Let us follow the thought process of one of those investors. Consider HHC in 2000, early in its life.

Suppose that HHC's sales for 2000 are $1 billion and that it is showing losses instead of profits. HHC has been in business only five years and has not shown any profits yet. When HHC was in its infancy, its sales grew at 100% per quarter, then later at 100% per year. HHC's business plan is not to make a profit until it is already a large company and dominant in its sector. In these first years of its life HHC is more concerned about killing its competitors, so it launches price war after price war, and will keep doing that until it finally kills or absorbs all of them. HHC sold stock to the public and has enough cash to last until it has a monopoly in its sector. Only then will it raise prices and finally begin to earn profits.

There are many other reasons why HHC will not earn profits until it is already dominant in its sector. HHC has to hire people very rapidly to support the growing level of business. Its revenues trail behind its costs, so HHC loses money for this reason, too. Finally, HHC has to invest in research and development, new hardware, and advertising. And every time HHC buys one of its competitors, it has to pay a premium, and the excess over book value has to be amortized. This amortization of acquisition premiums is another expense, so HHC chronically shows accounting losses.

During these early years, investors value HHC shares by assigning a multiple to the company's annual sales. For example, in 2000, when HHC's sales are $1 billion for the year, investors assign a multiple of 16 to its sales, and value HHC at $16 billion. Because the company has no debt and there are 100 million shares outstanding, the share price that emerges from this computation is $160 [($16 billion − $0)/100 million = $160].

Valuing a company at a multiple of its sales might seem absurd, because sales are not profits, but the convention makes sense. In a crude way, it takes into account the front-end expenses the company has to pay and the company's future size and profitability. To see how it takes into account the company's growth, consider how a company that is not growing could be worth $16 billion if its sales are only $1 billion. If its net profit after taxes were 100% of its sales, the company's stock would still be overpriced, because its earnings yield would be only 6.25% ($1 billion/$16 billion = 6.25%). So investors who pay that much for the stock must think that the company is going to grow much larger. And the company must be growing rapidly, because if the company were growing at a normal rate, its stock would still be overvalued even if its after-tax profits were 50% of its sales. To see this, consider that if the company's after-tax profits were $500 million, its earnings per share would be $5. For the stock price to be $160, the company's price/earnings ratio would have to be 33. Normal growth is 7 or 8% per year, so the formula

$$P/E = \frac{1}{\text{discount rate} - \text{growth rate of earnings}}$$

shows that the discount rate would have to be only 10%, and that is too low for a risky company [1/(0.10 − 0.07) = 33].

Consequently, the valuation of $16 billion makes sense only if the company would grow much bigger—for example, to an annual rate of sales of $10 billion. Then its after-tax profits could be high enough to justify the valuation of $16 billion. Its after-tax profits could be, for example, $750 million, and its P/E ratio would be 21.6, and then the company's $16 billion market capitalization would be consistent with normal valuation standards.

There is another important point, however. The $16 billion valuation would make sense when the company's annual sales reach $10 billion and its annual profits reach $750 million. Investors who are valuing the company at that level in 2000, when its sales are only $1 billion, must think that it is going to be even bigger than $10 billion in annual sales. The evidence is that they are paying $16 billion for the company in 2000, several years before the company's sales will reach the $10 billion level. So they must believe that the company's sales will keep growing beyond the $10 billion level.

The Two-Part Valuation Approach

One can see that HHC has great potential and has annual sales of $1 billion in 2000. Now let us make some assumptions about when HHC's growth rate will slow down, and about how big it will be at that time. Then one can figure out what HHC should be worth at that future date, and then figure out what its shares should be worth in the year 2000.

Suppose that by 2015 HHC's sales have reached $50 billion and its after-tax profits have reached $5 billion. Also suppose that by 2015 HHC's earnings growth rate has slowed down and is 12% per year. Investors in 2015 consider HHC a blue chip, secure in its segment, which it dominates. They therefore apply a 14% discount rate to HHC's future earnings. At that date HHC's price/earnings ratio would be 50 [1/(0.14 − 0.12) = 50]. This implies that HHC's market capitalization would be $250 billion ($5 billion earnings × 50 P/E = $250 billion). Because there are 100 million shares of HHC, this implies that as of 2015 HHC's stock price would be $2,500.

Is this scenario for HHC's sales, profits, and stock market value in 2015 more optimistic than what investors believed in 2000? Let us try to reconcile HHC's valuation in 2000 to the scenario for its value in 2015 and see if the two are consistent.

An investor buying a risky stock in 2000 must think it is going to pay an annual return of around 20% per year. This is higher than the long-run average rate of return on risky stocks, but lower than their rate of return from 1994 to 1999. HHC stock costs $160 a share in 2000. It pays no dividend, and it is assumed that it will not pay any dividends until sometime after 2015. With this assumption it is simple to compute how high the annual return would have to be for $160 to grow to $2,500 in 15 years. Solve the following equation:

$$\$160 \times (1 + x)^{15} = \$2,500$$

The answer is 20.1% per year. This completes the two-part valuation calculation. This example creates a scenario of how big the company might be in the future and what it might be worth at that future date. As of that date in the future, the company's growth is supposed to have slowed down, and it is supposed to have killed or absorbed its competitors. So its pricing policy as of that date allows it to make "normal" profits. Then as of that date in the future, the example uses the traditional formula to value HHC's stock. Then it takes the stock price in the year 2000 and computes what a buyer's annual rate of return would be if the scenario turned out to be realistic.

The computation indicates that a company with a stock market value of $16 billion in 2000, that is risky and does not yet dominate its sector, would need to be worth $250 billion by 2015 in order to give a 20.1% annual rate of return to an investor. Because investors in 2000 expected to make about 20% a year, it follows that investors believed that HHC would have a stock market value of $250 billion in 2015.

The Real Options Approach

The analysis of HHC's value is simplistic and needs to be examined more closely. All investors do not really believe anything so optimistic or so precise about HHC's prospective value in 2015. Instead, they believe something much more plausible and much more susceptible to precise valuation. HHC's value of $16 billion in 2000 includes a component that has not been discussed until now. HHC has several options. One of these is to diversify into retailing other merchandise online. For example, HHC can add clothing, airline tickets, toys, and computer software to its product line. It can try to turn itself into a one-stop shopping portal, where consumers could get everything they need, not just a few types of merchandise.

This option might not seem to be worth very much as of mid-2000. But online retailing has already suffered one shakeout, and there may be waves of consolidation in the future. HHC has an advantage in entering these new lines of business vis-à-vis competitors who are not already major players in online retailing. This advantage is a *growth option* and it can be valued. The method involves computing the value of the new lines of business and the probability of being able to enter into those lines and establish a profitable foothold. The value of the option has to be set against the cost of obtaining it. HHC bought the option by building up market share in its initial line of business. HHC launched price war after price war to buy market share, and has made itself one of the biggest players in online retailing. Those price wars have been expensive. Part of the justification for the expense is the option that it purchased to go into other types of online retailing.

HHC's common stock has many other growth options incorporated in it, and each one is valuable. Two more are worth mentioning. One is the option to abandon a new line of business. HHC's heavy investments in buying market share bought more than the option to get into new lines of online retailing; they bought an inside view of the online retailing industry. So HHC not only has a lower cost of launching a new product line, it also has a lower cost of abandoning a new product line if the launch does not go well. A competitor that does not have such a strong position in online retailing has to spend more to launch a new product line, and will not so easily be able to abandon the new line. This *option to abandon* is valuable to HHC.

The last option to mention is obviously valuable. That is the option to sell out. This option explains a big part of why New Economy stocks are valuable even if the companies have no immediate prospect of making a profit. Suppose that HHC has 10% of the market in its industry sector, and suppose that three other competitors each have 10% of the market. All other competitors are much smaller. None has made a profit, and none is running out of cash. The competitive situation is in equilibrium, and no competitor will take any precipitous action.

Now suddenly something upsets the competitive equilibrium. One of HHC's competitors suddenly gains market share. Its 10% jumps to 15%, and another competitor's 10% falls to 8%. Then the one with 15% buys the one with 8%. HHC now faces a completely changed competitive situation. The competitor now has 23% of the market and may be able to acquire the other companies in the industry. That would give the competitor a 90% market share to HHC's 10%.

HHC would have to choose when to sell out. The competitor would pay the most for HHC when HHC's market share would give the competitor the whip hand over the industry. That would be long before the competitor reaches a 90% market share. HHC's heavy investment in buying market share would pay off handsomely because of selling out at an opportune moment. So HHC could pay rich returns to its shareholders without ever making a profit and without becoming the dominant player in its industry.

These growth options are all valuable, and their combined value can account for more than half the market value of a company's stock. For some New Economy companies, the prospect of breaking even and the prospect of becoming a dominant player are both remote. But the prospect of selling out to a competitor who needs market share is very real and, consequently, very valuable.

Are Investors Rational to Pay So Much for Shares of HHC?

After reviewing these valuation approaches, one can see how many twists of fate may be bad for HHC without being fatal for HHC's shareholders. The value of its future potential may in reality be zero, in the sense that HHC may never make a profit, but a competitor may buy HHC before that becomes certain. A valid motivation for buying HHC can be to close it down.

Now it is clear that investors do not have to believe that HHC stock will be worth $2,500 a share in 2015 in order to buy it in 2000 for $160 a share. Some investors who pay that price in 2000 do believe that HHC will be worth that much by 2015, and some believe that HHC will be worth even more. But other considerations intervene, lowering what HHC would have to be worth in 2015 to a more modest figure. Skeptics can sell HHC stock short and hope for disappointing news, but they run a tremendous risk when they do so. A favorable news announcement will make the stock jump, so skeptics mostly stay on the sidelines.

What if HHC's performance is good, but not as good as the scenario assumes? Suppose the people who buy HHC stock for $160 in 2000 make an annual return of only 10% for the 15-year period from 2000 to 2015. In that case HHC stock would rise only to $415, and HHC's stock market value would rise only from $16 billion to $41.5 billion. HHC could have annual sales of only $20 billion and profits of only a bit more than $1 billion and be worth that much in the stock market. A more modest scenario like this does not seem so spectacular, and HHC might achieve it easily. For investors who paid $160 a share in 2000, this outcome would be disappointing but not disastrous.

Even that modest performance would deter short sellers. If HHC stock trends from $160 to $415 in 15 years, selling it short does not seem suicidal. During those years the stock might backtrack several times, and at those times short sellers would have a chance to make a profit. But they would still be putting their heads on the chopping block, because HHC stock would probably also make several vertiginous runs upward during those years. A short seller who is caught in an updraft often does not survive, so an uptrend, even a weak one, warns off short sellers. There are too many ways HHC stock can jump up, and bad earnings do not necessarily mean the end for HHC. This fact makes the bulls more fearless. They can buy knowing that most short sellers will be intimidated by HHC's potential to jump upward on any flimsy pretext. So the bulls have yet another reason to pay up for HHC stock.

Valuing HHC is obviously a much less precise exercise than valuing SMC. The calculations about HHC's stock show that it very easily could be worth the high price investors paid for it at a very early point in the company's life. The rate of return they would earn on their investment, even after paying a very high price at the beginning, could easily be high enough to justify the risk they take.

Conclusion

Stock prices in the last days of 1999 and in 2000 certainly were high by historical standards. The high-growth, high-technology stocks seemed particularly high, but their valuations could be reconciled with conventional standards of value quite easily. The calculations reveal that investors who buy stocks like HHC must be very optimistic about how large and profitable those companies will become in the future, or about how valuable HHC may be to a competitor. If companies like HHC continue to perform well, their stocks can keep rising.

For most observers, the mighty rise of the technology stocks is the hardest part of the U.S. stock market rally to accept. Commentators balk at the prices of premiere technology companies like Sun, Cisco, Lucent, and Qualcomm. This chapter shows that these prices can easily be reconciled with the traditional approach to valuing companies. Growth options that these companies have created make up part of their value. Prices of these companies have risen because investors believe their prospects are excellent.

The most notable result of the calculations in this chapter is that the prices of stable, blue-chip companies like SMC are harder to reconcile with historical standards of value. The massive stock market rally lifted prices of shares like SMC well above their historical ceiling. The old ceiling price for SMC stock was $63 according to the traditional rule of thumb. The example in this chapter raises the ceiling to $277 and shows how the maximum justifiable price could rise even more, to $450! The way this is done, however, is to set aside some very fundamental assumptions about the role of the corporation and the role of common stock in the U.S. social contract. In effect, the example puts the interests of consumers, employees, and tax collectors behind the claims of shareholders. Once this is done, a standard formula for the value of a common stock puts forth the higher valuations. The indicated stock price for SMC tracks upward, obeying the new realities, and its increases track the performance that many blue-chip stocks have achieved during the market rally the U.S. has experienced from 1982 onward.

The main fact that this chapter reveals is that stock prices of many companies have risen more than they would have done during any previous rally. Prices have risen well above what companies like SMC could have been worth if they had remained in their traditional place in the hierarchy of American society. This stock price rally, therefore, is not a cycle, and it is not a bubble. It is instead a major upward move in the status of some corporations, particularly the ones with highly valued stocks listed on the NASDAQ or the New York Stock Exchange. The major upward move does not apply to all corporations or to all business. The rise in status is not simply a swing of the pendulum in favor of business. It is more selective and powerful than that. It is a swing in favor of companies that have identified themselves and distinguished themselves as generators of financial wealth.

The answer can now be given to the question of how much a common stock can be worth. The answer for a high-growth, high-technology stock is simple: If the company's prospects look brilliant enough, its stock can rise even higher than it did in 1999 and 2000. The stock can double or quadruple without exceeding the parameters of conventional valuation. A dramatic rise only has to mean that investors have reassessed the company's future potential. The answer for blue chips is more problematic. Can Coca-Cola stock sell at more than 35 times earnings? Can Gillette stock resume its meteoric rise? Can General Electric continue its sparkling record of high returns to shareholders? Yes, they all can do that. So can all the other blue chips, not-quite-blue chips, laggards, and wallflowers on the New York Stock

Exchange. They can repeat the performance they have given in the past, and they can surpass it. But they cannot do it if they are limited to the old role they held in U.S. society. They will have to keep breaking out of the restraints that held them. They will have to keep asserting the priority of rewarding shareholders. They will need to keep pushing their new role as wealth generators if their stocks are to keep performing as they have recently done.

Chapter 5

How Did the United States Become So Wealthy?

The United States is noted for its low savings rate and for its underinvestment in social infrastructure. Yet its economic performance, particularly since 1992, has put it near the top among Organization for Economic Cooperation and Development (OECD) countries in economic growth, job creation, and stock market returns. These facts appear contradictory: A country cannot disregard frugality, and underinvest in its human resources, and at the same time move up in the performance rankings. But that is what the United States has done, and no sobering day of reckoning has arrived. Instead, the U.S. economy is marking new peaks of prosperity with each passing month. This chapter discusses how the United States has been able to do that, and how the country's set of policies will enable it to continue prospering into the future, and also assesses whether other countries can apply the same policies successfully. U.S. prosperity has a solid, if unorthodox, foundation. America is not living beyond its means. Private net saving as a percent of gross national product (GNP)

Mark Potter coauthored this chapter. An earlier version entitled "Yankee Doodle Soufflé: Can Blighty Copy the Recipe for U.S. Economic Success?" was published in *New Economy*, vol. 6, no. 1 (Institute for Public Policy, Blackwell Publishers, London, 1999). Reprinted by permission.

has been negative, meaning that people are spending more than they are earning; and that usually augurs ill for the future. But in this case, that fact only shows that national income statistics are now tracking an incomplete set of aggregates. The net worth of American households is rising steeply. U.S. asset prices have risen so much that the average household is much wealthier than before, despite having increased expenditures faster than income.

Accolades or Condemnation?

America has always been willing to borrow and to live on its future prospects, but this daredevil streak in the national psyche has always been stigmatized as brash and imprudent. This self-indulgent, spendthrift characteristic has never been held up as a national virtue and a wellspring of economic advantage. Instead, America's intemperate streak has been maligned, as if it were a perverse national predilection to take unnecessary risks. This disparaging characterization of America's risk-taking is a huge mistake. America's debt-fueled lifestyle is one of the main locomotives of the country's impressive record of economic accomplishment.

The explanation of Yankee Doodle's startling wealth that is advanced here treats America's borrowing, spending, and unrestrained importing as one of the cornerstones and prime movers of the country's de facto national economic strategy. This chapter argues that the current de facto strategy can continue to deliver strong performance into the future. Americans are not borrowing future consumption and dissipating it today. The country has not been staving off an unpleasant day of reckoning when it will have to pay for its profligacy. America is living well within its means, and is on a prudent and viable growth path. No comeuppance, whether minor or bone-rattling, is presently on the horizon.

The Strategy with No Name

The strategy the United States is following stands mercantilism on its head. Classic mercantilism advocated running a trade surplus in order to accumulate foreign exchange and gold. Wealth was equated with gold, so it followed that the successful mercantilist country would be wealthy. The United States, in contrast, runs a trade deficit, so foreigners accumulate dollars, U.S. securities, and U.S. properties. In the Yankee Doodle version of mercantilism, dubbed here *mercantile soufflé*, wealth is equated with current consumption, growth of consumption, and rising asset prices. In Yankee Doodle's upside-down mercantilism, the successful country enjoys high current consumption and growth, while foreigners accumulate its currency and the securities it issues. Moreover, in this new, upside-down mercantilism, the United States can continue importing more goods than it exports for an indefinitely long period, because foreigners use their accumulated dollars to buy land, buildings, and businesses in the United States. The United States reacquires its currency from abroad, and then can spend it once again to pay for more imports.

But the U.S. strategy of upside-down mercantilism goes beyond the trade account. The United States grows not only by importing goods and services. It imports savings from abroad, and has successfully become the world's largest debtor country: It exports capital, but imports more capital from abroad, and so increases its dominance as a debtor. The United States has become rich in installed capacity and infrastructure, built in part with money borrowed from abroad. The United States is also rich in highly educated people and has successfully become the largest importing country of highly educated people. The United States trains people and sends some of them abroad, but it imports more, and so increases its dominance as a knowledge-intensive country.

This preliminary caricature of the United States's de facto economic policy makes it seem foolhardy, shortsighted, and libertine. The policy appears to condone profligacy and disdain the hardscrabble virtues of work, frugality, and sacrifice. Yet in spite of all its apparent flaws, the de facto policy is working, and can work for many other countries as well.

Foreign Demand for U.S. Assets: Climbing the Staircase to the Penthouse

Many foreigners see the United States as glamorous, trend-setting, and technologically advanced. It has the image of the land of opportunity, and as a country that launches new ventures. Many people who grow up outside the United States want to visit, and the United States promotes tourism. At the same time, the United States keeps itself exclusive. Not everybody can come. Only the elite, the lucky, and the wealthy will be able to get past the hurdles.

This combination of appeal and selectivity works. Many foreigners desire to see the United States, and to establish a foothold there (Figure 5.1).

They need to be able to get a visa. In some countries, having a multiple-entry visa to the United States is a mark of membership in the elite. Owning some U.S. assets helps foreigners get a U.S. visa.

The United States is promoted as the place to get a university or graduate education (Figure 5.2). This transmits U.S. values around the world and creates intellectual seigniorage.

Selling Pieces of the United States

Both Americans and foreigners make constant efforts to sell pieces of and claims on the United States. The United States has a strong image as a place to invest: more exciting than Switzerland, and just as safe. Even the most humble foreigner can own something American. The first U.S. financial asset that most foreigners acquire is some U.S. currency. This is the first step up the ladder of U.S. financial assets, and the first step is easy to reach: The amount of U.S. currency outside the United States is estimated at $150 billion. Foreigners view it as a safe investment because it maintains its purchasing power fairly well in the United States. For the

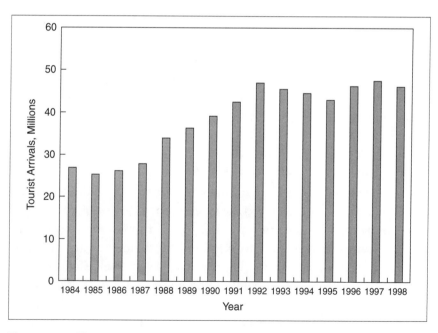

Figure 5.1   **Foreign tourist arrivals in the United States, 1984 to 1998.**

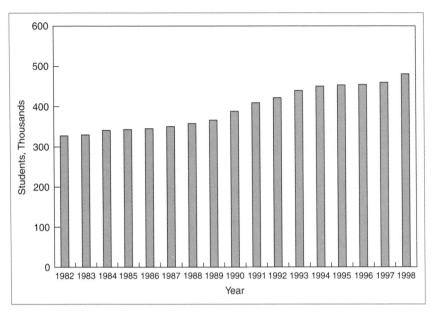

Figure 5.2   Foreign students enrolled in U.S. colleges and universities, 1982 to 1998.

U.S. Treasury, and indirectly for the U.S. population, it is a windfall gain that people overseas are willing to hold greenbacks. The currency they hold can be viewed as part of the U.S. national debt, cheaper than the rest because dollar bills do not pay interest.

The next assets that many foreigners acquire are Treasury securities or U.S. bank accounts. Foreigners, including foreign central banks, own $2 trillion of the $5.5 trillion of U.S. Treasury securities outstanding. Of the $4.4 trillion of total bank deposits, they own as much as $0.5 trillion. They are willing to own these financial assets because the United States protects the ownership rights of both Americans and foreigners. The International Monetary Fund (IMF) estimates that in total at year-end 1996, foreigners owned investments in the United States with a gross worth of $5.12 trillion, a figure 79% as large as the U.S. gross domestic product (GDP) for that same year (Figure 5.3). Evidently, foreigners feel confident that they will be able to collect the income from their investments and the proceeds when they sell them. The Federal Deposit Insurance Corporation (FDIC) guarantee of bank deposits up to $100,000 is an important drawing card. Foreigners also know they have equal protection under the law in business disputes with Americans.

The next assets foreigners buy are U.S. houses and condominiums, land, buildings, and businesses. Or they buy stocks, bonds, mutual funds, and insurance products. U.S. policy is to protect them from losing their investments to fraud. They buy because they do not fear expropriation, confiscation, or nationalization. They also buy because if they buy enough they can enter the United States and reside there to monitor their investments. They can also make the case that members of their families should be allowed there to monitor their investments.

Selling the United States to Foreigners as Part of a Growth Policy

Paradoxically, by selling pieces of the country, the United States increases its financial clout around the world. The policy of encouraging foreigners to buy bits and pieces of the United States makes the country richer because it raises the value of all U.S. assets by increasing the number of po-

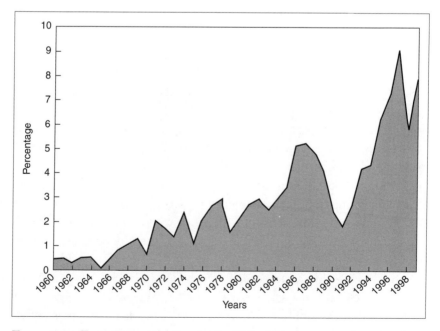

Figure 5.3   Foreign-owned assets in the United States as a percentage of GDP, 1960 to 1998.

tential buyers. It also builds repeat business, because foreign investors who make profits will consider additional investments. This policy increases the economic clout of the United States in the following ways:

- It brings capital into the country. U.S. citizens receive cash for the assets they are selling to foreigners. They can use the cash to buy imports, or to make investments inside or outside the United States. In 1995, a total of $467 billion came in from abroad (portfolio investment only). In 1996, the figure was $488 billion.[1]
- It makes the dollar go up versus other currencies, or keeps it from falling.
- It allows Americans to have a low savings rate, without causing stagnation or slow erosion of living standards. Foreign portfolio investment in the United States is large in relation to total capital formation. For example, in 1995 and 1996 it was equal to 46 and 45% of private gross fixed capital formation.[2]
- It supports larger issuance of Treasury securities. The U.S. government can run a fiscal deficit without pushing up the interest rate, and without causing inflation, as long as foreigners keep buying more Treasury bonds.
- It allows the United States to have a balance of trade deficit without having to finance it by foreign borrowing. The balance of trade deficit has to be financed by foreign borrowing only if it is larger than the net spontaneous inflow of capital into the country. In 1996, the current-account deficit was $148 billion. During that year the Federal Reserve Dollar Index, a trade-weighted composite of the dollar's value in terms of other currencies, went from 86 to 89.
- It discourages other countries from making war against the United States. Key decision makers in other countries own assets in the United States, or have their children in school there. They would be destroying their own holdings, or bombarding their own family members, if they ordered an attack. They would also deny themselves the chance to visit the United States.

Reflex Reactions: A Policy Counter to Common Sense

The conventional objection to selling pieces of the country is that the new foreign owners have to be paid a return on their investments. The return, however, does not have to be in gold or foreign currency. Foreign owners willingly accept U.S. dollars or more assets in the United States as payment. The strategy of selling pieces of America fails only if a time comes when there are no new foreign investors who want to buy U.S. assets. If that happened, the United States would face a currency crisis. No currency crisis need ever occur, as long as the United States is careful not to expand the effective supply of dollars too rapidly, and as long as the United States continues to defend the rights of foreign investors to enjoy the income from their investments.

A more visceral objection to selling pieces of the country is that somehow Americans might sell it all, and end up as vassals in their own land. This could happen in some countries, but not in the United States, because the definition of U.S. citizenship includes everybody who becomes naturalized. A tenth-generation American has no more rights than someone who was naturalized a week ago. If somehow a few billionaires in Switzerland, Tokyo, and Singapore bought the entire United States, they would not be able to exercise complete control, because they could not vote in U.S. elections without becoming naturalized.

Selling the entire country, though possible, is harder than it sounds. The United States has been a net importer of capital for most of the years since the Mayflower arrived. The country draws in money from abroad, and also attracts people who come to look after the money. In a generation or two the new arrivals, and hence the money, have become American. Merchants in London loaned money to Virginia tobacco farmers, then sent their sons and nephews to find out how their investments in the colonies were doing. The children remained in the colonies, and two or three generations later turned against their British forebears and signed the Declaration of Independence. The same pattern has been repeated many times since, because when foreigners buy assets in the United States, they are only steps away from becoming Americans.

A Policy without a Spokesperson

No group of experts is urging the United States to import more than it exports, to invite highly trained people and naturalize them, to disregard saving, nor to sell pieces of the country to foreigners. The official U.S. position is usually to deplore the trade deficit and to urge trading partners like Japan and China to import more goods and services from the United States. On the other points the official U.S. position is harder to characterize and sometimes is muted. The current U.S. immigration policy is a curious mélange. Part of it makes family ties paramount, so that relatives can be brought in, and part of it is quintessentially pragmatic. Skill categories that are in short supply, such as engineering, get quotas allowing foreign experts to be brought in. The shadowboxing in mid-1999 over the increase in H-1 visas (for computer programmers and other highly trained experts) was a rare public display of the positions of important power groups. The high-tech lobby wanted an increase, and organized labor opposed the increase. President Clinton leaned one way, then another, and finally came down in favor of the increase. The increase was, of course, temporary.

Despite whether any advocate will step forward, there does not need to be any group of experts or leaders stage-managing the policy of de facto upside-down mercantilism. There are no manifestos, no sacred texts, and no keepers of the eternal flame. Instead, the policy is a series of steps along the path of least resistance. Habit, convenience, inertia, and indifference all favor it. Financial markets are pricing common stocks as if the strategy were going to continue, and continue to work successfully. So it continues onward, and spreads to other countries with the speed of telecommunications and by the power of compound interest.

Can Other Countries Copy the Successful Recipe?
The United States may be the only country that is pursuing the full set of policies described here. There may be others, but they would not admit it; and the United States itself would deny that it is doing these things in any systematic or intentional way. But the policy has its appeal, and adopting pieces of it can work. Countries do not have to adopt all of it or none of it; many other countries have successfully adopted parts of the recipe. Growth through importing other countries' savings and highly trained people cannot work for all countries at the same time, but it can work for many at once, and it can work for many that have not tried it.

Skeptics might argue that the United States is singularly able to raise its living standard with goods, savings, and education produced abroad because of the following reasons:

- The United States is, in effect, extracting payment for the umbrella of military security it provides.
- The United States is singularly able to attract highly trained immigrants, whereas other countries cannot draw in so many.
- U.S. currency is used as a reserve currency, as a store of value, and as a vehicle for transactions between parties outside the United States, and those uses create a demand for U.S. dollars abroad, which allows the United States to run a trade deficit to satisfy that demand. Other countries, according to the skeptical view, do not enjoy these advantages, so the de facto U.S. policy would not work as well for them.

These skeptical objections overlook or discount several dynamic advantages the policy has in its favor. These are advantages that accrue to any country that adopts the policy, not just to the United States:

- Yankee Doodle's upside-down mercantilism can make the value of the country's capital stock go up. Any country that intends to run a trade deficit for a long time will have to import capital. Countries can import capital by borrowing it or by attracting equity investment. Attracting equity investment from abroad is better than borrowing because equity investment does not have to be repaid. Equity investors want quarterly returns and do not demand repayment of principal as long as they get them.

  To keep the equity investments coming in from abroad, the country will have to treat foreign investors fairly and keep the investment climate favorable. From time to time foreign investors will buy enough of the equity in a local business to acquire control of it. The change of ownership has to be welcomed, and the rights of the new owners have to be protected.

  When these conditions are met, portfolio investment, including equity investment, will come into the country. Enough will come to pay the trade deficit. Enough will also come to make up for deficient local savings. Enough will come to pay for experts from abroad. And finally, enough will come to drive up the market value of the capital stock. So local owners of land, buildings, and businesses will be enriched. They will be able to sell their holdings at higher prices or borrow increasing amounts of money against their assets.

- Upside-down mercantilism pushes the country to become more competitive in attracting capital. Any country can attract a small amount of capital from abroad. But if it is to keep attracting larger amounts of capital, it will have to keep improving its image and positioning in the minds of investors. There are now a growing number of countries that are trying to attract capital from abroad, and some of them are becoming more adept at doing so. Many countries are wary of financing their growth and supporting their standard of living with capital from abroad, but a growing number are more sanguine and are willing to live that way, at least for a time. Most intend to stop someday, after they have been able to raise domestic savings rates and develop their export industries; but for the time being, there is competition to attract capital from abroad.

- Upside-down mercantilism requires transparent financial disclosure and openness to information. Opaque regulatory regimes and restrictions on telecommunications inhibit attracting capital.

- Upside-down mercantilism requires the country to move toward sustainable economic policies and toward a social contract with its citizens that gives them health and education, equitable taxation, pluralistic representative government, property rights, and rule of law. Portfolio investors abroad know they will earn high returns if they invest in a country that is out of compliance with benchmarks of sustainability, but which then moves quickly toward compliance. Prices of common stocks reflect, at any given moment, the consensus scenario for the country's economic growth. If the scenario improves, the prices rise.

Selling a Positive Image to Local Electorates

Once a country embarks on the path of import-driven growth, its policy-makers begin to feel pressure to outperform the prevailing economic forecasts. More and more foreign capital will come in, permitting the country to import more and more, provided that the country's economic performance continues to produce surprises on the upside. At first it is easy to outperform expected growth, because the earliest investors expect little. As time passes, however, the country needs to do better and better to keep rates of return high.

One way a country can improve its growth outlook is if news and entertainment media transmit positive images of quality of life and if people accept the images and work to attain that quality of life. For example, movies and television shows can show a middle-class lifestyle in a favorable light. They can show poverty, large families, low educational attainment, soil erosion, and deforestation unfavorably. They can also show corruption, tyranny, and brutality in a negative light. When consumers accept the images, and buy products associated with them, they pay for the cost of the messages they are receiving. Their purchases maintain the profitability of the entertainment and telecommunications companies. The intent of television shows is innocent; television moguls do not set out to devalue, disparage, or displace local indigenous culture. The objective of telecommunications and media companies is to exceed forecasted growth targets so that the rate of return to shareholders will remain high. At the macro level economic policymakers have the same objective, because if the rate of return stays high, new capital will keep coming in from abroad, and the policy of import-driven growth will keep working.

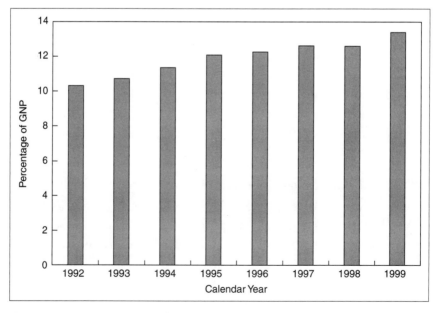

Figure 5.4   U.S. Imports of goods and services as a percentage of GNP, 1992 to 1999.

Mainstreaming the Recipe for Mercantile Soufflé

Economic innovations usually happen before they gain acceptance and mainstream legitimacy. The policy of growing by importing seems incongruous at first, but as import surpluses continue year after year, they lose their novelty and finally are considered ordinary. By now the U.S. import surplus (or trade deficit) is part of the economic landscape, tolerated and accepted without being loved (Figure 5.4). The rest of the United States's de facto policy is perhaps farther from acceptance. Though most of it has been going on for longer, its good features have not been pointed out as often. The full recipe has not been portrayed as a formula for success that fits together logically. If it has been mentioned at all, it has been portrayed as an odd set of anomalies. The inescapable reality, however, is that the de facto policy is a coherent set of ingredients for growth that go together, work better than the other alternatives that are advocated, have been implemented, have become accepted without the formalities of legitimization, and appear to have a long and triumphant future ahead.

Chapter 6

The Direct Route
to Prosperity

The idea of winning the lottery appeals to people everywhere. The winning ticket breaks the shackles that chain people to poverty and humdrum toil. Lotteries give hope because even the poorest person can become a multimillionaire overnight. The new-found wealth suddenly rains down from heaven. The winner had no prior warning that the big win was coming, and did not have to work hard for years to earn it.

Sudden Wealth

The conventional view is that that there is no analog to winning the lottery for entire countries. The teachings of our elders and our hard-won experience tell us that countries cannot scamper up the ladder of prosperity a dozen rungs at a time. It is true that some countries have achieved growth rates higher than anyone thought possible, but even those few that have done it needed decades to reach adequate standards of living. And they had to put themselves through rigorous reorganizations and bootstrap drives to industrialize. At the level of entire countries, there are no lotteries big enough to pull millions of people up from poverty. The consensus of

John Marthinsen coauthored this chapter.

mainstream opinion is that there are no magical forces or short-cuts to prosperity.

There is reason for hope, however. Standard economic theory has focused its policy recommendations on flow variables, like production, government spending, and exports. If a country is poor, the explanation is that its production is inadequate: Because it does not produce much, it cannot consume. Recently, however, world markets have been awash with overproduction of commodities and manufactures. The abundance of goods casts doubt on the continued validity of the explanation. This book argues that a short-cut to prosperity does exist. However, to implement the needed policy changes, governments must redirect their attention from traditional flow variables, such as gross domestic product (GDP), investment, consumption, and balance of payments, to stock variables, such as the value of productive assets, stock and bond market capitalization, and human resources.

Attempts to increase the output of goods and services through monetary and fiscal policies have proven to be of marginal, if any, value, especially since the Asian crisis of 1997. This chapter proposes that economic authorities direct a campaign toward increasing shareholder value and the value of productive assets. This new objective is such a departure from the previously accepted objective, and is so contrary to established precepts, that to a skeptic it might seem chimerical or imprudent. Nevertheless, the long-run effects that will result from government policies targeting shareholder value are more likely to raise the level of real GDP in stagnating industrial nations and in emerging nations than the more traditional demand management remedies tried in the past.

There is a tautological identity between production and consumption in the national income and product accounts. This chapter contends, however, that the identity applies only for the world economy as a whole and for countries with closed commercial and financial systems. The identity does not hold for individual countries with open economies. Countries wishing to sustain high standards of living over long periods of time must be able to produce a substantial portion of their own needs. Nothing in this argument disputes that, but the focus here is on bridging the gap between the short-run reality of stagnation and poverty and the long-run goal of sustained growth. Happily, such a bridge can be created, and this fact gives hope to millions of people who are enduring daily hardships, unemployment, and economic frustration.

Problems with Conventional Views on Growth, Development, and International Resource Flows

The conventional view is that poor countries do not produce enough because they do not invest enough. They do not invest enough because they do not save enough, and they do not save enough because they are poor. Summarized, this states that poor nations are poor because they are poor.

International capital and labor flows could lift such countries out of poverty, but many of the nations that would benefit the most from these flows are reluctant to allow either capital or immigrants to come in. Their misgivings are different for each type of inflow. Short-term capital inflows have the drawback that they might leave suddenly. When short-term capital flows out, it puts pressure on local banks, capital markets, asset prices, and foreign exchange markets. Foreign direct investment has a more constructive image, but it does awaken the fear that the government will lose economic control to powerful multinational companies, then uncaring investors pressing to repatriate earnings will drain away the country's resources. Finally, immigration brings workers with new skills and youthful vigor, but it stirs deep-seated fears about the new arrivals usurping jobs that rightfully should belong to local workers.

These apprehensions are real, but the economic basis for them has to be set alongside the economic dynamism that capital movements and immigration can bring. The closed-economy bootstrapping model of economic growth still has its appeal, but in a world of open economies there is no hiding from external effects. Still, there is a desire to insulate against volatility coming from the world market. Volatility is what causes violent outflows of investment, and it used to be outside the control of national economic policymakers. But nations can and should explicitly manage volatility, just as corporations manage the risks than can hurt their shareholders. Modern risk management products exist, and they work when they are applied correctly. This fact undercuts the rationale for prohibiting both the inflow and outflow of foreign capital and labor. To do so is to turn away from all the advantages that come from exploiting comparative international differences in relative resource endowments, technologies, and investments in human capital. Similarly, the advances in modern capital markets weaken the economic logic for preventing the inflows and outflows of foreign resources, but permitting them for domestic citizens. It used to be feasible to have a double standard for foreigners and local nationals. Some countries reserve a portion of each stock issue for local citizens, and keep that separate from the portion that foreigners can own. This policy gives local investors more clout and partly neutralizes foreign investors' advantage of greater buying power. These schemes have the virtue of holding local savings in the country, and they give small investors an entry into owning shares. Unfortunately, these schemes to give preference to local investors are difficult to administer, and there are "arrangers" who make a business of circumventing them, and "straws" who lend their names to foreigners for a fee. The schemes also convey a discouraging message, namely that local investors would send their money abroad if the preferential treatment did not keep it at home. This last point, that local savers would send their money abroad, is revealing. Policymakers know in their guts that local savings will leave, so they devise preferences to give local investors some extra juice that ordinarily would go to the foreigners. A preference of this sort can serve its immediate purpose but does not constitute a really satisfactory solution. The local investment climate needs to be favorable enough to hold local savings in the country. Instead of devising preference schemes, countries can more constructively put their efforts into improving the local investment climate and monitoring the treatment of skilled workers.

A New Focus

Shifting the economic focus from flow variables to stock variables broadens the policy alternatives for nations seeking growth. One of the simplest and quickest ways to grow is by enacting policies that promote capital market development and using the windfall gains from capital revaluation to purchase and encourage the inflow of foreign savings, technology, and skilled people.

The potential gain from such a revaluation can be illustrated numerically by considering pairs of countries that are alike in annual corporate profits but different in price/earnings ratios. One country's stock market is valued at 20 times earnings on average, while the other's is valued at 12 times earnings. Corporate profits in each country are $10 billion, but in one country the market value of common stocks is $200 billion, while in the other the value is only $120 billion. In a world of mobile international capital, how can such differences persist?

Part of the difference may be attributed to lower interest rates in the country with the higher valuation. That difference is not the cause of the higher valuation but rather is a manifestation of the underlying reason. Investors should not be rewarded for holding risky securities if these risks can be eliminated by diversification.[1] If the two countries' capital markets were of equal perceived risk, capital should move toward the country where the interest rate is higher until the interest differential is reduced to zero. Because interest differentials persist, there must be risks in those markets that cannot be avoided by diversification.

For the shareholders in the country with the lower valuations, it is easy to calculate the gain they would obtain if the multiple of price to earnings went up to 20 (Table 6.1). A major objection to emphasizing *shareholder value* as a route to prosperity is that its success depends on confidence and trust, two assets that may take years to earn, but which can vanish in a moment. The inputs that are needed for growth can go anywhere in the world, but they tend to migrate toward regions with relatively desirable combinations of risk and return. Given the relative abundance of capital in the industrialized nations, the return to capital should favor developing nations, but this is not where the capital and educated labor are flowing. Increasingly, resources are shifting toward high-tech start-ups in already-rich countries.

At year-end 1999, the 10 most highly valued New Economy companies in the United States (led by Microsoft, Cisco, Intel, Sun, and Oracle) had a stock market capitalization that exceeded all the emerging stock markets combined.[2] The total market value of all claims on the emerging markets, including bonds, international bank loans, and loans from mul-

Table 6.1 Wealth Effects from a Higher Price/Earnings Ratio

Parameter	Country A	Country B
P/E ratio	12	20
Corporate profits	$10 billion	$10 billion
Common stock market value	$120	$200
Gain to A from higher P/E ratio	$200 – $120 = $80 billion	

tilateral agencies, does not exceed $5 trillion.* By comparison, the value of U.S. common stocks alone is $14 trillion.[3]

In the aggregate, the gross national product (GNP) of the emerging countries exceeds the U.S. GNP, so their aggregate stock market capitalization should be able to reach $20 trillion, or more than 10 times its current level. That would be equal to an increase of approximately $3,600 per person in the emerging nations. Such an increase can be achieved only if the emerging countries successfully attract foreign portfolio investments, direct investments, and an educated labor force.

The Wealth Effect

Raising the market prices of capital assets is easier than raising the output of goods and services, and it may have a much larger economic impact. For most countries, the stock of capital assets (i.e., factories, buildings, houses, infrastructure, agricultural resources, and intellectual capital) is worth 2 to 5 times annual GDP. For resource-rich countries, or nations with very depressed annual output, the capital stock might potentially be worth 10 times annual GDP. If the market prices of capital assets rose, for example, from 2 times GDP to 3 times GDP, the wealth effect would be equal to 100% of annual GDP. The increase in wealth would be a windfall, because it would not require the building of new productive capacity, loss of consumption, or invention of new technologies.

But will this increase in wealth spark any increase in spending, jobs, and payrolls? When a nation's wealth goes up, the conventional view is that the rise has an anemic effect on household consumption expenditures. To the extent that wealth is owned by pension funds or is part of the estate holdings of "old money," the prices of capital assets can fluctuate without having much effect on flow variables such as economic growth, employment, or real living standards.

In the rather distant past, wealth was not widely distributed, and those who owned it spent more or less the same amounts regardless of whether

---

* Total market value of emerging markets stocks was $3.06 billion at the end of 1999. This figure would make it seem that total claims on emerging countries must exceed $5 trillion. The $3.06 trillion figure for common stocks, however, includes stocks that foreigners are not allowed to buy, and it also includes stocks that do not trade very often, or are not followed by analysts. The emerging market stocks that are suitable for international investors have a value of only about $2 trillion.

the prices of capital assets rose or fell. Capital assets were largely immobile, often staying within families from generation to generation. As a result, the annual value of transactions was 1% or less of the total value. Asset-rich owners were not constantly reminded of what their holdings were worth, so changes in wealth did not make much day-to-day difference. Nowadays, in contrast, 48% of U.S. households have some direct or indirect ownership of common stocks, and 70% own their own homes.[4] In the United States, ownership of wealth is much more dispersed than it was in the days of the classical economists. People buy and sell capital assets much more frequently than they used to, and owners of assets know more precisely what their holdings are worth, so an increase in the value of the capital stock can have a dramatic effect on the level of real economic activity in a country.

Estimates of the *wealth effect* (i.e., the percentage change in consumption due to a percentage change in wealth) in the United States range from 1 to 5%.* Both numbers look low, but because consumption is the largest component of U.S. (and most nations') GDP, a significant change in wealth can still translate into meaningful increases in consumption expenditures. There is great potential for this to happen in nations where capital markets are especially undervalued. Furthermore, there could be knock-on effects that accompany revaluation, which would stimulate increases in capacity building, employment, and consumption.

Capital Asset Prices Not Merely a Reflection of Annual Output and Profit

The market prices of capital assets do not move in lockstep with changes in the flows of real output. In classical and preclassical economics, prices of capital assets are little more than faithful companions of flow variables such as output. The standard elementary treatment of capital valuation discounts the annual product of land and equipment by "the" cost of capital. Using this paradigm, an asset with a perpetual stream of annual earnings equal to E and a cost of capital equal to R should have a current value equal to E/R (Figure 6.1).

---

* There have been reports in the financial press of a "wealth effect" in this range. The authors have not seen an econometric study estimating the size of the wealth effect for Americans whose stock market holdings have recently soared.

$$\text{Value} = \frac{E}{R}$$

- E is the portion of total annual output attributable to land and equipment.
- R is the opportunity cost of capital.

Figure 6.1   **Asset value for perpetual stream of earnings.**

More advanced valuation models put R in the spotlight. The value of R is determined by (1) the real risk-free rate of interest, which equates an economy's ability to trade off present and future goods and services with the public's preferences to trade off present and future consumption; (2) the expected inflation premium; and (3) a risk premium, which can be further decomposed into credit, inflation, currency, and country risk. Any risk that can be eliminated by diversification should not penalize an asset's market value. The technical distinction is that as long as the risk is nonsystematic and can be diversified away or cheaply transferred, investors will not be compensated for bearing it. What penalizes an asset's market value, and causes buyers to shun it, is risk that cannot be diversified or shifted.

A nation's risk premium has a close connection to the legal, financial, and political safeguards provided to investors. When funds are lent, a social contract is transacted alongside the legal contract. Part of that social contract is the implicit assumption that there will be legal protections for savers and investors, and sufficient penalties for dereliction of fiduciary responsibility. The more even-handed the auditors, corporate executives, and judges are, the lower the risk premium demanded by investors will be. The more savers feel their rights are protected and that agents act on behalf of the beneficiaries they serve, the more elastic international capital inflows will be to small changes in real interest rates.

Therein is the essence of the poor countries' image problem. Sophisticated investors believe, with good reason, that poor countries do not protect them. They realize that diversification can protect them against nonsystematic risk, but nothing protects against embezzlement, self-dealing, securities fraud, and market manipulation. If an entire category of investments is vulnerable to these abuses, it gets a low weighting in most portfolios and is penalized with a high risk premium. This risk premium is one of the primary reasons for the undervaluation of many nations' capital markets.

Capital Sales and the Road to Prosperity

Promoting policies that increase shareholder value may seem beguilingly simple, but how long can a nation sustain its consumption and growth by this means alone? At what point will the revalued capital stock be entirely sold off and the means for further wealth-fed growth all used up? A numerical example with three variants might be illuminating.

Consider a country whose capital stock is worth $2,000, twice its GDP of $1,000. The market for its capital assets is not very organized, and foreigners do not own any of the capital assets. Suppose that this country abolished all international capital restraints and successfully developed the market for its capital assets, causing foreign money to come in and the domestic cost of capital to drop. The same stock of capital might then be worth $3,000.

This increase would be an immediate windfall gain of $1,000, or 100% of GDP. Consider three scenarios of what the country could do with this windfall. In the first, called *Pure Profligacy*, the owners of the revalued assets would sell part of their holdings every year to foreign portfolio investors and spend the proceeds on luxuries. In the second, called *Prudence and Profligacy*, the owners would sell more of their holdings each year and spend half the proceeds on imported capital goods and half on luxuries. In the third, called *Pure Prudence*, the owners would spend the proceeds on imported capital goods.

In the Pure Profligacy scenario, this nation uses its new wealth to increase consumption by 5% percent each year and finances it with the proceeds from capital asset sales to foreigners. It takes more than 13 years for the wasteful habits of the local owners to deplete their holdings to the preliberalization market value of $2,000. It takes 22 years before the local owners run into an obstacle. They sell 5% of their remaining holdings but have to use all the proceeds to pay dividends on the shares they sold earlier. At that point they can keep up their profligate lifestyle for more years because they still own 32% of the local capital stock.

In the Prudence and Profligacy scenario, the nation sells enough of its capital stock to support both an increase in consumption and an increase in investment. In this variant the local owners can continue their higher consumption for 34 years. After that they would have to sell more than 5% of their holdings to pay the dividends on the shares that foreigners bought earlier. The local owners can go on a surprisingly long time dissipating their patrimony. The local economy grows because some of the money goes to pay for imports of capital goods, and the capital goods support higher output. The local owners spend lavishly, but the value of their holdings rises, so it takes many years before their spending outstrips the value of their holdings.

In the Pure Prudence scenario, the nation sells enough of its domestic capital to finance a 5% increase in domestic investment and uses the proceeds to import foreign capital goods. By swapping one type of capital (e.g., portfolio investments in the form of shares) for another (e.g., direct investments), the absolute level of domestic-owned capital never changes, but the absolute level of foreign ownership increases each year. This variant is dramatically better than the two preceding ones. Local wealthy people own less and less of the capital assets they held at the beginning, but they own the new capital goods they import with the money they get from foreigners. The total amount of capital employed in the country goes up, and the value of capital assets rises. The local wealthy people sell some of their holdings every year, but it takes more than 30 years until foreigners own as much as one-quarter of the nation's capital stock. Output grows each year because of the imports of capital equipment, and the market prices of capital assets rise. The foreigners buy and buy, but their purchases do not overtake the holdings belonging to local wealthy people.

So, selling 5 or 10% of the capital stock to foreign portfolio investors each year does not get rid of it as fast as common sense or back-of-the-envelope calculations would indicate. What happens is that the capital stock becomes more valuable after the foreigners begin buying. Also, in two of the scenarios some of the proceeds are reinvested instead of simply being consumed, so once again the value of the capital stock rises after the local owners begin selling.

It would have been more accurate to have the market value of existing assets keep rising as foreign portfolio investors buy more of the capital stock. The increase would be due to continuing declines in country risk. This was not done here, because the power of the revaluation growth path is convincing enough in the elementary scenarios, including Pure Profligacy. If the market value of the capital stock keeps rising, it is easy to create a scenario where the local owners sell and sell, but the value of what they still own remains higher than it was when they started. And if the country can attract skilled immigrants, the local owners can sell at even higher rates, and end with wealth higher than their original holdings.

It all seems so easy. Surely, there are problems with the suggestion that a nation sell off its wealth to finance its development. Common sense would dictate that prosperity built on selling the capital stock to pay for imports cannot be a viable long-run strategy. If for no other reason, why would foreigners want to buy bits of the country's capital stock if it exported nothing? How would they ever get paid? The answers to these questions are startling, and are points in favor of the growth strategy based on selling parts of the capital stock.

The Role of Exports

There is no one-to-one relationship between a nation's imports and exports. A country's exports can lag far behind its imports, provided that during each time period the proceeds from selling bits of its capital stock are large enough to cover both the trade gap and the net payments on invested capital. Moreover, the cash to pay foreign investors can come from local nationals, who consume the output of the businesses in which the foreigners have invested. In this case, repatriation of earnings would have its major impact on the nation's short-term capital account and the net investment income portion of the current account. Payments could also come from other foreigners, who buy the holdings of the foreigners who are cashing out. In such a case, only the financial (i.e., capital) account of the balance of payments would be affected.

The doctrine that exports pay for foreign investment is old, and presupposes an outdated mode of foreign investment. When there is a large pool of portfolio investment capital in the world, seeking to earn a return, the demand for shares of a country's capital stock depends on the local investment climate more than it does on export success. Portfolio investors will buy a share of a business if they think they will later be able to sell the share at a profit. In this case, a sustained rally in the market prices of local capital goods can substitute for export success, and the sustained rally can be a valid substitute for an indefinitely long period.

Competitiveness and Technology

The perception exists that countries can achieve wealth only if their industries are competitive, in the sense that quality and cost have to meet world standards. Yet the laws of comparative advantage indicate that, regardless of how unproductive a nation is relative to the rest of the world, free markets should always endow it with a comparative advantage in the production of something. Typically, exchange rates and resource prices adjust so that the nation commands an advantage in a range of low-technology products.

In most nations, internationally traded goods and services do not account for a majority of GDP. The majority of products is domestically produced and consumed and does not necessarily conform to the laws of comparative advantage. Services and bulky products (e.g., beer and processed food) for which transportation costs are prohibitive are in this nontraded category.

Why, then, is competitiveness deemed so important? The reason relates to exports. The conventional view is that if the country cannot export, or if it can export only by offering its goods at low prices, the country will be poor. Without exports, the country will be unable to pay for imports, and its standard of living will inevitably decline. Therefore, the conventional wisdom equates competitiveness and technology with living standards. However, as previously seen, the connection is not so direct if the country successfully attracts buyers for bits and pieces of its capital stock. And the connection breaks completely if the country successfully attracts skilled immigrants.

Externalities from Selling Domestic Capital Assets to Foreigners

Selling pieces of the domestic capital stock has advantages beyond the obvious one of paying to support temporarily higher living standards. It could raise the value of the remainder by lending credibility to the value of the remaining assets and to the country's legal system. By making the nation's assets more internationally visible, it would improve the perception that they are safe to buy.

The sale of domestic fixed assets to foreigners would raise the average level of value of human capital in the country. Progress toward prosperity can be greatly facilitated by educated people poached from other countries. If they can be assimilated, naturalized, and retained, a nation can quickly raise the average quality of the work force using a top-down approach and afford itself the luxury of time to work from the bottom up. The key to success is in aligning the long-run interests of these skilled workers with those of their adopted country, and vice versa.

Some Conclusions

A direct route to prosperity exists, and it is a route that is open to many countries that are poor today. The route does not require massive amounts of investment or years of self-sacrifice. It has only two requirements: First, the country must make the appropriate legal changes to improve the investment climate for foreign portfolio investors; second, the country must attract and retain skilled immigrants. These steps will work because there are large amounts of foreign portfolio investment that will flow into a nation where the conditions are right, and there are skilled people who will immigrate and stay if they can make a better life for themselves.

Taking this route will require countries to make fundamental changes in the way they treat the world—and this is the rub. The proposed policy goes beyond attracting skilled immigrants and portfolio investment. It calls for countries to renounce economic nationalism. Countries that seek to attract foreign investments and skilled immigrants will have to be completely neutral to the citizenship of owners and managers. They will have to give foreign investors the same legal treatment as local investors, because a them-versus-us attitude will result in higher costs of capital and lower capital valuations. They will have to encourage the use of expatriate and immigrant managers whenever their skills are needed. They will have to promote widespread and globally diverse business ownership. This means changing corporate law, and it means national companies' selling shares (millions, dished out at a rate the market can absorb) on listed stock exchanges. In short, these countries will need to uncouple nationality from ownership, from management, and from control as well.

To support this shift in philosophy, countries will have to make investments, but instead of focusing on roads, military armaments, and utilities, countries will have to commit resources to modernizing their local financial markets.

There is an urgent need for poor nations to leapfrog the decades usually needed to grow. After stagnating for most of the period from 1994 to 1998, the emerging stock markets are in danger of being written off as too small, too volatile, and too low yielding. The IFC Investable Index yielded −6% per year from January 1994 through December 1998.[5] During the same time period, the Standard & Poor's index of 500 U.S. common stocks yielded 22.1% a year.[6] A real and pressing threat exists that securities analysts, financial advisors, and multinational companies will continue to shun the emerging markets. If that trend continues and capital continues to stay out, these countries will be stuck in a pattern of anemic and erratic investment flows. Growth will continue to be based (as it has been since 1994) on limited domestic savings, a weak technology base, and a large pool of unskilled labor.

Wealth-Increasing Scenarios in Detail

The following numerical examples show how a poor country can dramatically increase its wealth and consumption by selling small portions of its capital stock each year to foreign portfolio investors. In this example, the owners of the country's businesses start out owning 100%. They sell a small percentage of their holdings each year. Skilled immigrants come into the country and increase production by a constant amount each year. The local population goes on producing exactly as much as it was producing in the beginning. It saves and invests only enough to maintain that level of production capacity. All the increase in production comes from immigrants, and the increase in consumption comes mostly from the sale of shares of the country's capital stock.

Three variants are discussed. All three can be found in the spreadsheet Profligacy.xls, posted at www.faculty.babson.edu/edmunds. The first is the extreme case of Pure Profligacy. In this variant, the owners of the country's businesses sell their ownership bit by bit and consume the proceeds. The government steadfastly pursues probusiness policies and never does anything to frighten foreign portfolio investors. The sellers always dedicate part of the proceeds of each year's sale to paying cash dividends to foreign portfolio investors. These annual dividends are 4% of the price the foreign portfolio investor paid. The example is expressed in dollars;

expressing the example in local currency complicates the illustration without altering the main points.

The example begins with the emerging country's output being worth $1,000 a year, with annual exports of $200 and imports of $200. The country has growth potential, in the form of underutilized resources and underemployed workers. Its existing capital stock at local prices is worth $2,000, or 2 times annual output, and at the beginning is entirely owned by local nationals.

The initial event is an announcement that the country welcomes foreign portfolio investment. The local owners of the capital stock then sell 5% of their holdings to foreign portfolio investors. These assets account for output of $50 per year, and have a local market value of $100, but the foreign investors pay $150 because their opportunity cost of capital is lower. Local owners now have $150, and they use $144 of it to import goods. These imports are entirely luxuries, which add nothing to the country's productive capacity. The beginning population produces the same output as it did previously—that is, output worth $1,000 during the 12 months following the sale. Exports remain at $200. Imports rise to $344, and the country has to pay dividends of $6 ($150 × 4%) to the foreign portfolio investors.

What is the new situation after the $6 of dividends is paid? The country's income level immediately goes up 14.4%, from $1,000 to $1,144. The announcement welcoming portfolio investment draws attention, and the country attracts skilled immigrants. These immigrants come into the country right after the first sale, and they create new economic activity in the amount of $30 per year. Consequently, income for the first 12 months following the sale is $1,174. The remaining 95% of the capital stock is now worth $3,346 [$150 × (95/5) × (1,174/1,000) = $3,346]. This completes the first year of the example.

Now, after one year, the country has gained credibility and investors now pay slightly more for shares of its companies. Initially, before foreign portfolio investment, its capital stock was worth 2 times annual income. Then, when foreigners made their first purchases, they drove prices up to 3 times annual income. Now, after one year of favorable news, they drive prices up to 3.1 times annual income. The remaining 95% of the capital stock that belongs to local nationals is now worth $3,458, not $3,346.

Local owners now sell 5% of their remaining holdings of the capital stock. This sale brings in $173 ($3,458 × 0.05 = $173). As before, the local population produces output worth $1,000. The first year's immigrants produce output worth $30, and the second year's immigrants produce output worth another $30. The country also takes in $173 from sale of assets. Total income is therefore $1,233. Dividends to foreign portfolio investors of $13 must be paid [4% × (150 + 173) = $13]. The new figure for national income is $1,000 + $173 + $30 + $30 − $13 = $1,220.

After the second annual dividend of $13 is paid, the first year's portfolio investors now have a paper profit. Their 5% of the capital stock is now worth $150 × (1,220/1,000) = $183. In addition they have received two annual dividends of $6 each. So the portfolio investors who put in $150 have an annual rate of return of 14%, including their paper profit. The second wave of portfolio investors have a similar rate of return, because their $173 investment has received a $7 dividend, and has a market value of $173 × (1,220/1,174) = $180.

Surprisingly, despite the profligacy of the local owners of the capital stock, this growth process can go on for many years. Each year the local owners sell 5% of their remaining holdings to foreign portfolio investors. These local owners then spend all the proceeds on luxury consumption, except for what is needed to pay dividends. Each year a new wave of skilled immigrants comes in and produces enough to add $30 to annual output. The original population continues to produce $1,000 worth of output each year. Exports remain at $200 each year. The country's policies continue to be favorable toward foreign portfolio investors, so the value of the capital stock goes up each year, from 3.1 times output to 3.2 times output, and finally reaches 5 times annual output after 20 annual increases of 0.1 each.

The Profligacy spreadsheet shows how well this growth strategy can work. It takes the local owners a surprisingly long time to sell, because every year they sell 5% of their remaining holdings. After 10 years, for example, local owners would still own 60% of the capital stock [100 × (1 − 0.05)^{10} = 59.9%]. Furthermore, the 60% would be worth considerably more than the 100% they owned at the beginning. Ten years of immigration would have raised output to $1,300 ($1,000 + 10 × $30 = $1,300). The favorable treatment of foreign portfolio investment would have raised the value of the capital stock to $5,453, so the sale of the eleventh tranche would bring in $165, and dividends of $67 would have to be paid from that. So the local owners of the capital stock would be able to spend $98 and still retain holdings that would be worth approximately as much as they were before.

This engine of profligacy comes to a halt after 22 years. At that point the proceeds from selling 5% of the remaining assets held are $139, and dividends payable on previous sales amount to $139 also. Although by that time the local owners only own 32% of the country's capital stock, their holdings are still worth $2,739, or 37% more than the $2,000 they were worth in the beginning, before the first sale to foreign portfolio investors.

This variant of the direct route to prosperity works because there is a huge pool of money seeking portfolio investment opportunities. Portfolio investors are on the lookout for countries that will give them favorable treatment. When they find a favorable investment climate, they bid up the market prices of capital assets located there. There is also a huge pool of skilled people who will move to a new country where they can apply their skills and make a good life for themselves. What can sustain the growth process for longer than 22 years? If portfolio investors bid up prices of the country's capital stock faster, so that it rises from 3 times annual income to 5 times annual income in less than 20 years; or if more immigrants come in.

Revaluation of the capital stock and skilled immigration are enough to lift up the original local population to new levels of prosperity. By assumption, the local population does not increase its output, invests only enough to maintain its original productive capacity, and does not achieve any increase in exports. In this first variant of the direct route, labeled Pure Profligacy, the local population is enriched by two windfalls: the upvaluation of its capital stock and the contributions of skilled immigrants to the local economy.

The second variant of the direct route, Prudence and Profligacy, is more reasonable. In this variant, the local owners of the capital stock do not consume all of the proceeds from selling bits to foreign portfolio investors. Instead, they invest one-third of the proceeds at a capital/output ratio of 3. The initial sale of $150 for 5% of the capital stock happens just as in the first variant, and $6 of the $150 proceeds is paid as dividends one year later to the portfolio investors, but the entire $144 net proceeds is not spent on luxury consumption—only two-thirds of it, or $96, is spent.

One-third, or $48, is invested in new productive capacity. The local population uses this new investment, so the output of goods and services rises by one-third of $48, from $1,000 to $1,016. Immigrants come in as they do in the first variant, and they add $30 of new output each year, so annual output goes up faster.

This variant works for 34 years. At that point the dividends to foreign portfolio investors are equal to the proceeds from the sale of 5% of the remaining assets held. After the thirty-fourth sale, local owners still own 17% of the capital stock, and that 17% is worth almost as much as their original holdings of 100%.

If cash dividends paid to foreign portfolio investors are only 3% of the amount they invested, this variant works for 45 years. The crucial assumption is that the lower cash dividends do not discourage the foreign investors, and they keep paying high prices for the shares of the country's capital stock.

The third variant is Pure Prudence. Local owners sell part of their holdings each year to foreign portfolio investors, hold back some of the proceeds to pay dividends, and use all the rest of the proceeds to import capital goods. In the first year they spend $144 on capital goods, and these add $48 to GDP. As always, immigrants come in and add $30 to GDP, so GDP rises from $1,000 to $1,078 in the first year. This scenario produces the fastest rise in the total value of the capital stock. You may want to modify the parameters in the spreadsheet so that the market value of existing assets keeps rising as foreign portfolio investors buy more of the capital stock. The increase would be due to continuing declines in country risk. This realistic modification is one of several that will produce explosive growth. It is easy to create a scenario where the local owners sell and sell, but the value of what they still own remains higher than it was when they started.

Chapter 7

The Propagation Mechanism

Financial wealth propagates differently from income. The two seem tightly linked together, and casual observers often think they are two names for the same thing. But they are different and they do not spread in the same ways.

The Distinction

Income grows and spreads in its own set of ways. Wealth increases and spreads in ways that are different, and it travels through different channels as it spreads from country to country. The difference is pivotal to the argument in this book, so this chapter examines how each one propagates. It begins with a review of how rising income in one place can lead to income growth elsewhere. The income-propagation section is brief and the arguments proceed along familiar lines. The chapter then shows how financial wealth spreads from one country to another via stock market wealth propagation. The wealth-propagation section is longer because the phenomenon is newer and less familiar, and because it is the main topic of this book.

Income Propagation

Higher income spreads from one place to another in ways that seem mundane because they are so well known. Its capability of spreading is one of its most important attributes, but not one that most people would mention first. Higher income can stem from innovation or from cooperation. It does not necessarily require very much cooperation, however. Some rudimentary set of relationships has to be in order, but the conditions are not very demanding. Higher income can occur even when social and military conditions in the surrounding country are hostile. Cooperation between two people can be enough. A person who knows a better method can teach that method to somebody else. At the level of an entire country, only a few conditions have to be met for higher incomes to propagate from small groups to larger groups. Internal trade does not require a very highly ordered society to be feasible and advantageous. Higher income can propagate from one part of a country to another via internal trade.

Higher income can also propagate via international trade. Trade from one country to another can propagate higher income and can raise incomes more powerfully than internal trade. International trade requires that more conditions be met, but it does not require as many conditions as stock market wealth propagation. International trade has a remarkable capability: It can raise incomes in places that are geographically distant from one another. International trade is a controversial propagation mechanism. Its virtues and failings have been studied and debated vigorously for centuries, and many thoughtful people today are wary of it or opposed to it. But the debate over international trade has now been intensified and supercharged. Its power and controversy have been supercharged and overshadowed by the new mechanism, stock market wealth propagation.

Stock Market Wealth Propagation

Stock market wealth propagation is newer, less familiar, and obviously more dynamic. It might have enough power to accomplish what international trade has been unable to do—namely, raise the entire world to an adequate standard of living. It might also hasten the ultimate ecological doom that awaits humankind. Wealth propagation has appeared only recently, and it has been capricious and erratic when it has appeared at all. It has also generated storms of controversy. It has been like a newly discovered kind of engine that has coiled within itself the power to create an order of magnitude more wealth than the world has seen before. This wealth would be large enough to free all of humankind from drudgery. This new engine, unfortunately, has not worked consistently. Most of the time it sputters and misfires, or sits idle waiting for a part or a repair. But when it does roar into life, it propagates more prosperity than any mechanism that has come before. The propagation mechanism operates in plain view, and you can see what it does, and where it works its magic. You can also see the mechanism suddenly come to a halt, and leave its job half done; or turn its attentions toward a new place, and deliver wealth somewhere else. Regrettably, it most often delivers wealth to people who are already wealthy.

The stock market wealth propagation mechanism is like a hothouse plant that is not hardy enough to thrive in all conditions. It grows only when many preconditions are all satisfied. It needs a larger polity and a high degree of consensus about the legal framework, the tax regime, and other institutions of society. For stock market wealth creation to occur, older people need to put their savings into the hands of financial intermediaries who lend to younger people. The financial intermediaries have to assess risks and allocate the available funds to the borrowers who are most likely to repay the loans. There has to be a market where financial claims are traded; if there is not, older people would be foolish to buy financial assets. They might have to sell them before the maturity date, and if they might be unable to do that, they should not buy.

Financial assets have to become the trapping of wealth that the local community uses as its yardstick. They have to supersede land, gold, cattle, cash, and other heirloom markers of wealth. This requires that the financial system attain all-pervading precedence throughout every atom and molecule of the economy. To do this, financial markets have to be large relative to the economy where they are operating, and financial intermediaries have to be competent, efficient, transparent, and guaranteed. If financial intermediaries are incompetent, they give the money to the wrong borrowers, then cannot collect it when it is due. If they are inefficient, they give the money to the right borrowers, but charge too much for their services. If they operate in secrecy, people do not trust them, and too many people feel that the intermediaries are serving the interests of some small group rather than the larger interests of society.

And if they are not guaranteed, depositors will hold back because they do not have enough protection against fraud, disaster, incompetence, or inefficiency.

Stock market wealth, and the process of creating it, are very different from income and the process of creating it. The statement is both obvious and contentious, because for centuries economists viewed financial wealth as an incidental concomitant of production. Financial wealth had no independent existence, any more than the shadow of a factory exists independent of the factory. Economists at opposite poles on every other issue—for example, Marx and Marshall—agreed on this point. They saw an isomorphic identity between financial claims and productive capacity, and in their minds the financial system had no power to cause wealth to increase. Money was neutral, meaning that if there was more of it or less of it in circulation, the only difference would be higher or lower prices and wages. As a consequence, there has been a very tight linkage between financial wealth and production in most people's minds. Wealth was the passive companion.

To the classical economists, financial wealth was the current reading on a gauge that told how much income people had saved during prior periods. They did not consider the reading very reliable, because it would fluctuate with inflation. They would have normalized financial wealth by dividing it by the value of current production. But such a calculation was, in their minds, hardly worth doing. For economists like Henry George, who were fixated on land and production, financial wealth was a chimera and a distraction, but most of them just thought it didn't matter. Financial wealth was nice to look at, like a banner flying atop the mast of a sailing ship. The banner was brightly colored, and everybody could see it as the ship sailed by. They could admire how jaunty and bold it was. Everybody realized, however, that the banner was just along for the ride; the sails, the masts, the hull, and the crew did all the work. The banner was just there to look good, and could not even reach its position at the top of the mast if the crew did not put it up there. It told viewers who the ship belonged to, and what its capacity was. So in past days it was correct to ignore the banner and focus on designing the hull and the sails to make the ship go faster, or maneuver better, or stay afloat better in a storm. The insignia on the banner and the signals it sent were secondary.

The message of this book is that the banner is now more significant and highly valued than the ship. The ship used to be important, but now the most valuable thing it does is to hold up the banner. The ship itself and its voyages are no longer essential, because there are more ships than anybody needs, transport is cheap, and new ships are easy to buy. There is nothing secret about their design or construction, and the shipyards are often idle and need new orders.

Documents conferring ownership are the new markers of success. The physical assets themselves are important only if there is something special about them. Ships, factories that make ordinary goods, and warehouses full of ordinary goods are too abundant. Those mundane assets are useful as collateral for securities. They retain importance for this reason.

What is really valuable are claims on the future cash flows of companies that make new high-tech products and services. Stock markets propagate that message and the high valuations that go along with it. They propagate the high valuations wherever conditions permit.

Income Growth and Propagation

The usual prerequisites for income growth are natural resources, techniques, and human capital. People move beyond subsistence agriculture when techniques improve and when trade allows them to specialize. The prerequisites for social organization are not so often stated; the prerequisites are apparently so simple, or so obvious, that they can be satisfied with a social organization as simple as a small village. The social organization only has to exert enough control to permit the geographical scope of the market to expand. Income growth takes off when the size of the market expands enough so the production facilities can be large enough to take advantage of economies of scale. Long-distance trade requires a more highly organized society, with a strictly enforced code of commercial law, highways, ports, banks, and universities.

Once income grows enough, it tends to keep growing and to propagate to other countries. The propagation mechanism by which income growth spreads from one country to another has been the subject of intense scrutiny and acrimonious debate. Who was right—Alexander Hamilton, David Ricardo, Vladimir Lenin, Josef Stalin, Augusto Pinochet, or Lee Kwan Yu? Trade is a powerful genie that brings both prosperity and economic enslavement. It has been a magic wand and at the same time one of the prime movers behind gunboat diplomacy. How, or whether, a country should use trade to catapult itself to prosperity is also controversial. A country either must keep its frontiers open, or it must close them, or it must close them first and then open them later.

Whichever is the correct policy, whole countries were the conventional focus of analysis when the debate began. Whole countries gained from trade or they did not. The focus of analysis then narrowed to sectors of a country's economy, and to single industries. The debate still raged over whether free trade or protection benefited entire countries; but there were new controversies over more targeted assertions about the benefit and harm that trade brings to specific sectors of the economy, regions, or strata of the labor force. But through the long years of debate, one constant held true: The financial channel was the banking system. Trade was about goods. Beginning with the infant-industry argument and the wine and the cloth, the raison d'être was production: sourcing from the relatively cheaper place, or intentionally buying locally to build competitive capability.

Trade in services was retrofitted to the theories and models about trade in goods. The theories still worked as long as the services were just goods that did not have mass and physical form and did not come in cardboard boxes. Trade in stitching up garments seemed to follow the same rules as trade in garments. Outsourcing could be treated as an export of goods in process followed by an import of the finished goods. The familiar arguments about comparative advantage still worked to explain outsourcing.

International trade propagated higher incomes, but its propagation mechanism was disruptive. Goods from abroad would come into a market and compete successfully. Local consumers would get the goods for a lower price, and local producers would adapt or go out of business. When the local producers could not adapt, workers had to find new livelihoods, and machinery and factories were idled. Meanwhile, new resources would be deployed in industrial sectors where there was growth and competitive advantage. The economic transformation would be harsh. Factories would remain idle for years and whole towns would lose their livelihoods. The average standard of living in the entire country would rise because both labor and capital would gravitate toward activities where they had comparative advantage.

International trade also propagated innovations in production techniques. The effect of an innovation would be to give an advantage to the people who first put it into effect. The advantage would not last very long because the new technique would spread. Other producers would copy it, license it, or steal it to maintain their viability. The innovation would be fully propagated when trade, employment, and output had reached their new, higher equilibrium levels. At the new equilibrium there would be more output or more dollar value, but the distribution of that output could be more skewed than before. The winners would gain enough to pay the losers but often did not pay them.

At the new, higher equilibrium level, the market value of productive assets would presumably be greater, but the theories did not highlight this point. To an economist who thinks that value is tightly bound to production, the point would be both obvious and uninteresting. It would be like saying that when an ice crystal grows larger, it contains more water molecules, or its length and width increase.

Financial Wealth: Its Growth and Propagation

Financial wealth grows until something stops it or destroys it. Its nature is to grow. No innovations are required, and nobody has to teach anybody a new way of making a product. All it needs is for a few fairly obvious conditions to be met. Then it piles up, slowly or quickly. Particularly since 1945, the conditions have all been met in more and more places for longer and longer time periods. One condition is that the holders of financial assets have to set aside some of the income they earn from the assets and reinvest it. Another condition is that the interest rate net of taxes has to be higher than the inflation rate; otherwise, the nominal value of financial assets increases, but their value relative to current output does not. A final condition is that there cannot be wars or natural disasters that wipe out too much of the income-producing properties and human capital that collateralize the financial assets. In the decades and centuries prior to 1945, there were frequent wars, hyperinflations, expropriations, and conquests, so financial wealth grew sporadically and had to recover from frequent setbacks.

The natural predisposition to grow is a major difference between income and financial wealth. Financial wealth increases unless something goes wrong. And as soon as the disturbance is over, wealth begins piling up again. Income increases only when somebody does something proactive to make it increase. As soon as new investment stops, income stops growing and starts shrinking. For income to remain the same, the annual rate of investment has to be just high enough to maintain the installed capacity.

Stock market wealth propagates across national boundaries when investors buy stock on foreign bourses. They need inducements to do so, because it is risky and they fear losing the money. In every investor's mind there is a risk premium associated with investing in each foreign country. Two different inducements can overcome an investor's fear. One is the rate that is being offered on the foreign bourse. If that is high enough, it will pull money across borders. The other inducement is diversification. The foreign bourse does not have to offer a high rate if its fluctuations offset the volatility of the home-country bourse. To see how persuasive the diversification argument can be, consider a simple example.

Suppose an investor in a rich country is considering investing all his or her money in the home country's stock market for the next five years. Alternatively, the investor is thinking of investing one-tenth of the money in each of 10 rich countries' stock markets for the next five years. To make the two alternatives as stark as possible, suppose that the outlook for the stock markets of all the rich countries in the example is the same. Each stock market will, each year, either go up 54% or go down 18%. Each stock market has a 50-50 chance of doing one or the other each year, and all the fluctuations are independent of each other. That is, if a stock market goes up 54% in one year, there is no higher or lower probability that any of the others will also go up or down that year; and there is no higher or lower probability that the 54% gain would be followed by a decline.

In this simple world of stock markets, the investor who keeps 100% of the money at home will probably make an annual return of around 18% per year. The reason is that the expected value each year is $54\% \times 0.5 + (-18\% \times 0.5) = 27\% - 9\% = 18\%$. Some years the investor will make a 54% gain, and some years the investor will make an 18% loss. During most five-year periods there will be some up years and some down years, so considering all the possible sequences of up years and down years and averaging them all, there is a probability of about 60% that the investor's average annual gain will come out between 15 and 21%. The probability of an extremely favorable outcome, or an extremely bad outcome, is surprisingly large. The investor has a probability of $0.5^5 = 3\%$ of making 54% every year, and he or she has the same probability of making −18% every year.

Now consider the strategy of investing one-tenth of the portfolio in each of 10 countries. Also suppose that the outlook for the stock markets of all 10 countries is the same. Each one has a 50-50 chance of going up 54% each year, or falling 18%. In this example, the foreign bourses do not offer a higher rate of return to overcome the investor's fear of investing abroad. All 10 countries are rich industrial countries with well-organized financial systems, millions of local investors, and full legal protection for foreign portfolio investors. How different is the outcome with the international diversification strategy? The investor still has an expected annual rate of return of 18%, but now a much higher percentage of the possible outcomes are clustered in the 15 to 21% range. The tendency is for some countries to have good years while others are having bad years, because the probability that all 10 countries would have good years is 0.5^{10} or less than 0.1%. With the large number of countries, and a five-year horizon, an average annual rate of return outside the 15 to 21% range is very unlikely. To see why, consider that there are 50 possible ups and downs, one for each of 10 countries times 5 years. To have a result far from 18% on average would be like tossing a fair coin 50 times and getting more than 40 heads or more than 40 tails. There are many paths the portfolio could take, 2^{50} different ones, and the great majority of these would include many up and downs. The good outcomes would be partially offset by the bad ones, and the ending performance for the portfolio would probably be close to the average of 54% and −18%, which is 18%. To see in another way why it would not deviate from 18% by very much, consider what would have to happen for the investor to make 54% a year for all five years. Each of 10 stock markets would have to go up 54% every year. The chance that all 10 would do that for one year is less than 0.1%. And the probability that the investor would make 54% each year for five years is 0.5^{50}, a probability so small, 0.000000000000009%, that the investor would be more likely to be hit by a meteorite.

In this example, the key point in favor of diversifying internationally is that it gives results closer to the mean of 18% a year. The example assumes that all the stock markets in the example have the same outlook, both in terms of expected return and volatility. It also assumes that their annual returns are not correlated with each other. If these assumptions describe how the world really is, the investor gives up the possibility of making a much higher return but also avoids the bad outcome of making a much lower return. This is the rationale for diversification in general and diversification across national boundaries in particular. Expressing the argument in terms of the annual performance of each country's economy and stock market, the economy of a country can have a bad year. When a bad year happens, it can drag down all the stocks in that country's entire market, but a bad year in one country does not necessarily cause the economies of other countries to have a bad year. So in this example, diversifying within one single country would not be as effective as diversifying across many countries. Euroland, the United States, and Japan might fall into recessions individually, but it is likely that in a given year at least one of the three would avoid the recession, or go into it later than the other two.

Diversification therefore is a rationale for investing across national boundaries even if the foreign stock markets do not offer higher expected returns. A diversified portfolio gives a more stable rate of return, and that can be more satisfactory than the spectacular, boom-or-bust results from investing in a single country. Compare making a steady 18% per year to the more nerve-wracking experience of losing 18% in each of the first two years and then making 54% in each of the last three years. A beginning amount of $100,000 invested each way turns into $228,776 with the steady, boring 18% a year and $245,578 with the roller-coaster series of plunges and leaps. For most people, there is not enough more money at the end of the five years to compensate for the sleepless nights that come with the high-risk, undiversified portfolio. Also, the diversified portfolio is ahead until the fifth year. The undiversified portfolio overtakes the slow but steady one only in the final year of the five-year period. This is important because investors sometimes have to sell sooner than they had intended.

This example shows the rationale for cross-border portfolio investing in its simplest and most persuasive form. U.S. investors embraced the rationale in 1985 and 1986, and it worked well for them in those years. International mutual funds distributed by U.S. mutual fund companies like Fidelity and Scudder had excellent years at that time. Foreign countries that were rich and stable attracted portfolio investment from the U.S.

without having to make a special effort. Those countries had stock markets whose outlooks were as favorable as Wall Street's, and their ups and downs did not seem to track Wall Street's. These facts were enough to motivate U.S. investors to send money to those foreign bourses.

Portfolio investors send money abroad for other reasons besides diversification. Foreign markets sometimes offer higher returns than the home market. There are other reasons too, including altruistic ones, but this illustration considers only purely self-interested reasons. The foreign stock market can be more than a useful hedge against a disappointing year in the home stock market: It can be an opportunity for trading profits when the home market is sagging. There are investors who try to move money into a country before its stock market rises, and take the money out just as the foreign stock market peaks. These *market timers* are not trying to stabilize their returns. They are trying to beat the performance averages. Some succeed, but for one investor to do better, another has to do worse than the average. The key points are that there are several motivations for international portfolio investment, and internationally diversified portfolios should be more stable than portfolios that are entirely invested in any one country.

The Propagation Mechanism in Its Simple and Inadvertent Form

U.S. investors inadvertently enriched European and Japanese stockholders during the 1985 to 1986 time frame. The dollar had peaked in February 1985. At that moment an American who bought European or Japanese common stocks could have made a profit on the stocks and on the foreign currency. The American's combined profit in dollars was much greater than profits at home on U.S. investments of comparable risk. European and Japanese stocks were going up in their home markets for local reasons, and their currencies were rising vis-à-vis the dollar. The combination of currency gains and share price increases made many Americans sit up and take notice, and they followed the lead of the brave few who had bought European and Japanese common stocks earlier in the year. Their purchases added to the local buying and pushed up the prices of European and Japanese stocks. Wealth propagated from one rich country to another, traveling from one stock market to another.

At that time all industrial countries benefited from wealth propagation as money flowed from one stock market to another. When shares in one country went up, they pulled shares in the other countries up with them. Some industrial countries benefited more than others, and some stocks were more favored than others. Big companies in Europe and Japan with strong consumer franchises were obvious choices for investors, and their share prices went up accordingly.

There was a secondary effect also. Suppose that U.S. investors concentrated their buying in only one stock in the United Kingdom. For purposes of this example, suppose that the company was Glaxo. Americans would buy so much Glaxo that the price of Glaxo shares would be pushed up. Then other stocks in the United Kingdom would look undervalued. This created a disparity and led to spillover buying of other U.K. stocks and other pharmaceutical stocks on the Continent.

There is another kind of secondary effect that spreads wealth. Portfolio managers *rebalance* their portfolios after the proportions they want to maintain have been skewed by some event. There was a good example of this rebalancing effect in 1999. Finland was the beneficiary, and shareholders of Nokia in particular. During 1999, Euroland common stocks did well, and Euroland telecommunications stocks did especially well. Americans put money into international mutual funds that invested in Euroland stocks, and the rallies had self-reinforcing spillover effects. Consider what would happen when an American put $1,000 into a Euroland fund at the beginning of the year. Nokia is a prominent supplier of mobile telephony hardware and is also the largest company on the Helsinki Stock Exchange. The manager of the mutual fund would invest part of the money in Nokia shares. Suppose that the market capitalization of the Helsinki Stock Exchange at the beginning of 1999 was 2% of the total for Euroland, and Nokia's market capitalization was 60% of the total for the Helsinki Stock Exchange. The manager would probably direct 1.2% of the $1,000 to buy Nokia stock (2% × 60% = 1.2%).

Now suppose that ItalTelcom, the largest telephone company in Italy, is suddenly the target of a takeover battle. Deutsche Telkom and Olivetti are each trying to take it over. Its share price skyrockets. This creates a disparity. The mutual fund suddenly finds itself "overweight" in Italian stocks. The manager of the mutual fund has to make a move. The mutual fund might underperform if other markets in Europe subsequently do better than the Italian market. Suppose the manager of the mutual fund has no reason to think that the Italian stock market is going to keep rising; on the contrary, it is vulnerable to a decline after the takeover battle ends. So the manager of the mutual fund rebalances the portfolio by selling some ItalTelcom shares. Now the mutual fund is no longer overweight in Italy. Now this cash has to be allocated elsewhere—that is, everywhere else in Europe. Some of the cash will be invested in Finland, and some of that will go into more shares of Nokia. The result is that Nokia rises, as do other stocks on the Helsinki Stock Exchange. Any ripple in one part of the European stock markets spreads to other parts.

Stock market wealth spread from one industrial country's stock market to another during several time periods. The years 1985 and 1986 were good years for U.S. investors who diversified internationally. The period from 1994 to 1998 was a slow period for international diversification. U.S. investors did so well at home that many of them forgot about diversifying across borders. 1999 was a year when cross-border portfolio investment came back into vogue. The rationale for the diversification was valid, and the strategy worked. The U.S. investors did not all have a very precise idea of what they were doing. They might have neither liked nor disliked the countries they were investing in. The day-to-day fine tuning of country weights and industry sector weights was in the hands of professional portfolio managers, who were trying to deliver high returns with low volatility. If the portfolio managers moved money into or out of a country, they did not think of the impact their decisions would have on the country. Their overriding considerations were return and volatility. Their actions propagated stock market wealth, but the propagation was an accidental side effect.

Emerging Markets Coming into Vogue

International portfolio diversification stopped working at the time of the 1987 stock market crash. All the stock markets in the world went down at the same time. Internationally diversified portfolios suffered almost as badly as the ones that were entirely invested in a single country.

After the stock markets of the world all went down at the same time, and then all came back up again after the crash, investors had to reexamine their diversification strategies. They had to discard the view that stock markets of industrial countries all fluctuated independently of each other. The new view they adopted was that the industrial country stock markets were one big group of stocks that were all priced relative to each other, and all went up and down together.

Investors then looked for a new way to earn stable returns by diversifying internationally. Their attention turned to the emerging markets. These small, volatile stock markets had previously attracted little attention. After 1987, they gained credibility as the new vehicles for international portfolio diversification. They still retained the key virtue that developed country stock markets suddenly lacked: Their fluctuations did not track the ups and downs of the industrial country stock markets. American investors bought emerging market shares, and for the period from 1988 to 1993 the strategy worked.

Emerging markets were much more volatile than industrial country stock markets, so investing in just a few of them did not give enough diversification. Their year-to-year fluctuations were dizzying. Several recorded one-year gains in excess of 300% in dollars during the 1988 to 1993 period.

An example will show how emerging markets could be used to diversify a portfolio of common stocks. Suppose a U.S. investor had $100,000 invested in stocks. Of that amount, $50,000 could be invested in U.S. stocks, $30,000 in stock markets of other industrial countries, and $20,000 in emerging markets. The emerging markets component could be invested in 20 countries, in the amount of $1,000 each.

The emerging markets carried a risk premium to compensate for the greater risk of investing there. To put the emerging markets into the same framework used before, suppose that each year each emerging market had a 50-50 chance of going up 66% or falling 22%. The expected rate of return would be $66\% \times 0.5 + (-22\% \times 0.5) = 22\%$. This is 4% higher than the 18% expected rate of return used for industrial country stock markets in the preceding example.

Also make one more assumption: Suppose that the emerging markets did not go up or down as a group; instead, each jumped and fell according to its own internal rhythm. This assumption—that their fluctuations were independent—completes the view that many U.S. investors accepted in 1988. The emerging markets, at the beginning of 1988, were cast as the new foot soldiers of international portfolio diversification. The expected return on the portfolio, using the figures given before, would be 18% × 80% + 22% × 20% = 14.8% + 4.4% = 19.2%. Investing 20% of the portfolio in emerging markets would raise the expected return from 18 to 19.2%. Investors hoped that they would earn high returns without having to experience too many ups and downs.

As U.S. investors poured money into emerging markets, the markets rose, and the rise snowballed. The rates of return were high and volatile. The emerging markets lived up to their billing in terms of volatility, but U.S. investors did not mind, because as a group the emerging markets did very well. In 1993, the watershed year, the International Finance Corporation's composite index of emerging markets returned 67% in dollars for the year. A buyer who was lucky enough to invest $100 at the beginning of 1993 could have cashed in at the end of the year and collected $167.

During the 1988 to 1993 period, it appeared that the risk premium for emerging markets was higher than it needed to be. The risk premium is how much more yield the riskier security offers as an inducement to investors to buy it instead of the safe security. The easiest place to observe the risk premium is in the bond market. Corporate bonds have to offer higher yields than U.S. Treasury bonds or nobody will buy them. The extra yield is to compensate for the risk of default. U.S. Treasury bonds have no default risk. Bonds issued by the strongest corporations have to yield only a bit more, usually around 1% more, because the risk of default is very low. Bonds issued by weaker companies have to yield much more, sometimes as much as 4% more, to attract buyers, because the risk of default is greater.

In the example, emerging markets securities offer 4% more expected yield than industrial country securities, and during the period from 1988 to 1993 that was much more than enough extra yield to attract investors, and more than the investors needed to compensate them for the very few defaults that occurred.

Emerging Markets Basking in the Glow of Prosperity

Many emerging countries achieved huge gains in market value of wealth in the 1988 to 1993 period. They moved forward rapidly in securitizing their prime quality properties. It looked as if their stock markets would soon become large relative to the size of their underlying economies. This is one of the indicators that observers track. A typical industrial country has stock market capitalization equal to 60% or more of GNP. Many emerging countries have stock markets that approach this threshold. Taiwan, Turkey, Argentina, and others appeared to have crossed the threshold and been on their way to joining the ranks of the rich countries. Mexico and Venezuela also did well; for a time each country had market watchers expecting continued growth and prosperity.

U.S. investors believed that the extra yield they were earning on their investments in emerging markets was a good bargain. They were taking on risk, but they were spreading the risk across many different emerging countries. Each country was risky, and that was why its securities carried such a large risk premium. But the entire group of countries was not risky, because internal conditions in 20 or 35 countries would not all blow up at the same time, so U.S. portfolio investors were going to earn high returns by channeling money to countries where capital was scarce.

Prosperity was propagating from rich countries to poor countries at last. It was propagating through financial markets, and through stock markets especially. Capital was flowing to the places it needed to reach. Every river that needed to be bridged was going to have a bridge across it, every highway that needed to be built was going to be built, and everybody that could pay a reasonable monthly fee was going to have a telephone. Propagation would not stop until it reached everywhere.

The middle-tier countries were the first to benefit, but the wealth-creation process would eventually reach all countries that wanted to join in. Countries that were too poor to be reached at first would be invited to join for the later rounds. These countries were labeled *preemerging*. Intrepid investors were looking for ways to invest in these countries, to get in before the stampede that was going to come later.

The money was moving, valuations were rising, and every country was going to ride the wave of portfolio investment to wealth, or at least to a more adequate middle-class standard of living.

A Delay in Propagation

The money did not keep moving. The five-year period from the beginning of 1994 to early 1999 was a long series of cold showers for investors in emerging markets and for anyone who thought the spread of prosperity was quickly going to reach every country on earth.

Emerging market indexes reached a peak in February 1994 and had not surpassed that peak by December 31, 1999. For the period from January 1, 1994, through December 31, 1998, the annual rate of return on emerging markets stocks was −6%. Investors continued to earn interest on bonds and dividends on stocks, but the cornucopia of capital gains dried up almost completely. Individual emerging countries surged, private pension plans sprang up in many countries, and state-owned companies continued to be privatized, but the excitement was gone. A series of setbacks laid bare the shortcomings of many emerging countries. Behind the facade of modernism they were still traditional societies. There were habits and practices left over from bygone eras. A few years of stock market prosperity had not been enough to push aside those old habits.

The Russian default in August 1998 was a crippling blow, just as emerging markets were struggling back from the Asian crisis that began in mid-1997, so the emerging markets ended 1998 lower than they had been at the end of 1993. Surprisingly, the Brazilian devaluation in early 1999 did not cause much further damage. The markets recovered quickly, and within six weeks had marched upward again.

Then, for the rest of 1999, the emerging markets roared. They had an excellent year despite setbacks in Pakistan, Ecuador, Colombia, and other countries. Particularly toward the end of 1999, the tone of the market was like that in 1993, when investors shrugged off bad news and kept on buying. The year 2000 began with a breathtaking $21 billion offer from Telefónica de España to buy all the shares it did not own of its South American affiliate companies in Argentina, Brazil, and Peru.

Emerging markets investing was growing up. Investors differentiated between countries, instead of downgrading or upgrading the entire asset category. Investors were also getting tired of waiting for better performance. They were getting flint-eyed, cynical, and selective.

At the same time, however, investors everywhere were bidding up the prices of stocks on the industrial country bourses. High-tech companies headquartered in industrial countries were the new darlings, and investors paid steep prices for their shares. As the high-tech companies like Cisco Systems were skyrocketing, investors were refusing to pay very much for stocks listed on bourses in emerging countries. Telefónica de España and its Ar-

gentine affiliate are an excellent example of the divergent pricing that eventually led to the buyout offer. In 1991, Telefónica de España was a slow-
growing, overstaffed, quasi-state-owned company, and most investors only
bought its shares for the high dividend they paid. The shares were trading at
10 times earnings on the Madrid Stock Exchange. Telefónica de Argentina,
its affiliated company across the Atlantic, was trading at 25 times earnings
on the Buenos Aires Stock Exchange. It was a fast-growing company with
years of growth ahead of it. By 1999, however, the valuations had reversed.
Telefónica de España was trading at 27 times earnings, and Telefónica de
Argentina was languishing at 12 times earnings.

The buyout offer was an immediate success in the eyes of investors.
Shares of both companies boomed. Investors evidently thought that Telefónica de Argentina would be worth more as a 100% owned subsidiary of
Telefónica de España. That is the clear verdict of the price action in both
stocks after the buyout was announced. Stock market investors in both
countries had their reasons for being in favor of the buyout. Their reasons
go a long way toward explaining why emerging markets fell out of favor
starting in 1994. Here are some of the reasons they gave:

- The Argentine company was always going to be vulnerable to a
  currency devaluation, and as part of the Spanish giant it would not
  be. The Spanish company hedged its Latin American currency exposure, so part of the valuation difference was that after the buyout
  cash flows would be denominated in euros, whereas before the buyout they were denominated in pesos.
- The Argentine company was never going to get a takeover offer.
  The Spanish company had enough shares to block a takeover by
  anybody else.
- The Argentine company was never going to be able to spin off its
  Internet properties. Instead, it was going to have to sell them to the
  Spanish company. After the buyout, the Spanish company planned
  to spin off its Internet properties. In that case, the shareholders of
  the Spanish company would benefit. The minority shareholders of
  the Argentine company would not have benefited as much.
- The Argentine company was never going to be completely independent from the influence of its Spanish affiliate. Although the

Spanish company owned less than 50% of the Argentine company, it had effective control.

- The laws of Argentina do not protect minority shareholders, and particularly foreign minority shareholders, as thoroughly as the laws of Euroland emanating from Brussels do. A foreign portfolio investor had more protection buying a Euroland stock than an Argentine stock.

These concerns are all good reasons for paying less for Telefónica de Argentina as a separate company and more for it when it is part of the Spanish giant. Thoughts like those would not have been so much in the forefront of investors' minds during the golden years of emerging markets investing. In 1991, investors would not have wanted the Argentine company to combine with the Spanish company. The Argentine company was growing much faster, and investors would have wanted it to remain separate so that they could see its growth and pay a high multiple for it. Now, after scandals, banking panics, currency devaluations, suspensions of convertibility, and defaults, investors are wary of emerging markets. They are inclined to think that the country risk premiums for many emerging markets are high because the risks really are large. They also know from experience that the risks are impossible to avoid by diversifying among many emerging countries.

The stock markets of the emerging countries did not live up to their potential during the period from 1994 to 1998. Instead of attracting more and more investors, they drove away many of the ones who had come in earlier. These markets were supposed to get much bigger as more investors and more companies got involved. But the investors did not do well enough. The U.S. stock market was on the greatest bull run in history, and that made the poor performance in the emerging markets even harder to stand. The poor performance had to have an explanation. Because many investors did not know very much about the countries they were investing in, they jumped to the conclusion that they had been victimized by local plutocrats. There were many investors who believed that well-connected local oligarchs had cooked the books, siphoned off the profits, or embezzled the money that should have gone to the small shareholders.

The poor performance and skepticism started a vicious circle. One of the most damaging consequences of poor performance was that the flow of new listings slowed down. For some emerging stock markets, the new listings were too few to replace the companies that were being bought out. The number of buyouts was large enough to threaten the survival of South American stock exchanges. Spanish banks and electric utilities bought many of the South American companies that had been the blue chips of their local stock exchanges. Buyouts like those are routine, healthy events in the life of a stock exchange. Buyouts and takeovers are good because they usually give traders and investors an extraordinary gain, and that can be what keeps the investors interested. The problem is that many new South American companies are now seeking to list directly in Madrid, London, or New York. They are bypassing the local stock exchanges, so it is not clear whether local stock exchanges will continue to play the central role in the economy that they played in the 1988 to 1993 period. During that time they were catalysts and harbingers of the new wealth-propagation dynamic. They gave an outlet for shares of companies that were being privatized, and for family-controlled firms that were selling stock to the public for the first time.

The rebound that began in 1999 may be a new dawn for the emerging markets. These stock markets face a real threat of being leapfrogged, but they can use the 1999 rally to regain their relevance. They need to make sure that they are well-policed channels to high-yielding, prudent investments. Then, after they have made sure that they are as transparent, even-handed, and efficient as the stock markets in the industrial countries, they need to communicate that message to investors. Many investors, after the disappointing experiences they had from 1994 to 1998, think that emerging stock markets are feudal fiefdoms where inside information and local clout are prerequisites. The impression that many foreign portfolio investors have is that they shoulder more than their share of the risk and get less than their fair share of upside potential.

The Propagation Mechanism: Working Again, or Spinning Its Wheels?

Stock market wealth will continue to grow and propagate over more and more of the earth's territory. Wealth went through a period when it was growing fairly evenly in many parts of the world at the same time. Then it piled up in a few places in the United States, namely Silicon Valley, Seattle, and eastern Massachusetts. Then it started to spread once again, to bourses in Euroland and Tokyo.

There is nothing looming immediately on the horizon—no world war, no ecological disaster, no great depression—that will derail stock market growth. Financial wealth may sustain the growth rate it has achieved in the recent past. Buyers have good reasons to continue buying, and to increase their purchases. Issuers have every reason to exercise as much restraint as they have in the recent past, so the shortage of high-quality securities should persist.

The question is which countries and which geographical areas investors will choose as their favorites in future time periods. Which industry sectors will be the new winners? The choices investors make seem capricious, and they turn into self-fulfilling prophecies as millions of investors pile into the latest favorite. Investors are guilty of herding, following some opinion leader who later may be discredited, cast aside, or tossed into jail.

In defense of investors, their madness often has reason to it. They may seem to be lulled by a simplistic story, but the story may not be what is causing them to buy. Take, for example, the tech-stock mania. Older observers who have seen stock market cycles rise and fall are warning that these stocks have risen too far. But investors have to buy something with their savings, and the other asset classes all have something questionable about them. Tech stocks are headquartered in places where shareholder value creation is accepted as management's top priority. High-tech companies give stock options to employees, and they control how many shares are outstanding and how many come to market. In short, they try to deliver high returns and protect investors against downside surprises. Other asset classes do not do that so assiduously.

Will industrial countries other than the United States benefit from stock market wealth propagation? It appears that they will, but to varying degrees. They are courting investors and making the right motions. But some of them are unable to show enough growth potential to attract inflows of portfolio investment. Those countries will underperform until their common stock valuations are too cheap, and then investors will buy and push them up. Their companies will be attractive takeover candidates.

The answer for the industrial countries is quite positive. Financial wealth will propagate to them, as it has done already. The countries that do not successfully attract portfolio investment in the first instance will attract some later. So the worst fate they will suffer is to lag behind. Foreign companies will come in and buy the local companies whose shares are too cheap because of being out of favor. Foreign portfolio managers will buy blocks of shares in the unloved but valuable local companies. These cross-border buyouts and purchases will spread wealth by delivering higher prices to local shareholders for the shares they held.

For the emerging markets, the answer is also positive, but the timing may be delayed a long time. The main unanswered question is how long high-tech investments in the industrial world can keep yielding outsize returns. If technology companies can absorb all the available investment dollars and return 30% a year or more, the emerging world will have to make do with tiny amounts of investment each year. The emerging world can compete with investment opportunities in the industrial world that yield 12%, but cannot compete with investments that yield 30%.

Emerging countries might get more inflows if returns in technology fall back into the normal range—that is, 9 to 12%. There is still hope for the emerging countries if investment returns in technology remain at abnormally high levels. In that case, emerging countries will be able to attract spillover investment. The technology boom will spin off so much extra profit that investors will be looking for diversification. Emerging markets offer diversification, and asset prices in many of them are low, so they are likely to get more inflows of investment.

The emerging markets will not become the darlings they once were. Middle-class Americans will need to forget the debacles of early 1995 and 1998. Instead, a wary trickle of money will tiptoe back in, aware that disaster may be lurking, but attracted by the high returns and the lack of attractive alternatives in other asset categories.

Whether the emerging stock markets come back onto center stage or not, the propagation mechanism can keep raising wealth in the poor countries. State-owned companies in the emerging countries continue to be privatized, and new businesses continue to launch initial public offerings. The poor performance of emerging markets from 1994 to 1999 will probably not be repeated. Commodity prices may continue to stagnate, but market participants are not going to be surprised, because they are already accustomed to price stagnation for traditional export goods. Many emerging countries have found new ways of raising exports. They have also developed their infrastructure and their internal markets. U.S. investors have paid little attention because the brilliant performance of high technology has dazzled them. The stampede into technology stocks has pushed the emerging markets to the sidelines.

The combination of stagnant commodity prices and soaring technology stock prices has created an enormous valuation disparity. At the end of 1999, the stock market capitalization of Microsoft alone was greater than the combined stock market capitalizations of Argentina, Chile, Brazil, and Mexico. Those four stock markets were relatively depressed, and had never achieved a high degree of coverage over the economies where they are located. Most Latin American businesses are not listed on any stock exchange. Still, the valuation disparity is so striking that some money will surely flow.

Consider an investor who has $500,000 worth of a U.S. mutual fund that invests in high-technology shares like Microsoft, Sun, and Oracle. This holding was worth only $300,000 one year earlier. The investor is nervous, because the $200,000 gain came so suddenly. The investor decides to sell $100,000 worth of the mutual fund and invest the money in U.S. Treasury bills.

The Treasury bills belonged to a person whose portfolio is worth $1 million. This person now has $100,000 in cash, and will have to invest the cash. The portfolio already holds other safe investments, so this person takes a risk and buys $50,000 worth of shares in a mutual fund that invests in emerging markets. This is one way the gains in the U.S. stock market can propagate to the emerging markets.

This scenario for emerging markets is guardedly optimistic. There is a likely sequence of events that will benefit the emerging markets. Many of the events in that sequence, however, happen in the rich countries, or at the level of all the emerging countries as a group. Emerging market stocks are still lumped together as a single asset category. Emerging market stocks come into favor when other asset categories fall out of favor, or after other asset categories have already risen. Some emerging markets rise on their own individual merits, but most of them fluctuate with the tides of money flowing into or out of the asset category. When any one emerging market sins, the punishment falls on all of them, as if they were all guilty but only one was caught.

The frustrating reality for the emerging markets is that each one has to strive to separate itself from the group. Each one has to follow the rules scrupulously, and hope that no disaster happens anywhere. If a country can stay compliant for a long enough period, it achieves its own identity in the financial markets. Analysts then view it as a postemerging country. The country can then swiftly grow its financial wealth. The next lurch downward for the emerging countries no longer hits it so hard.

Stock market wealth propagation is a new and demeaning game that the emerging countries have to play. It is new because what stock market investors think is at least as important as what the real situation is. The distorted rumor has more effect than the true story. The new game is demeaning because the emerging countries have to justify their actions to people who are capricious and uninformed. Yet the countries cannot refuse to play the game. If they refuse, financial wealth passes them by. Meanwhile, it piles up in other places. Soon so much of it has piled up that foreigners can come in and buy local trophy assets.

Conclusion

The stock market wealth-propagation mechanism is much more powerful than its earlier predecessors, international trade and the spread of higher incomes. It can create financial wealth much faster than those older mechanisms. Both international trade and stock market wealth propagation are controversial. There is a long history of policies aimed at reaping the benefits of international trade without suffering the disruptions it can bring. The stock market wealth-propagation mechanism has intensified the controversy and pushed it to the fore. The stock market wealth-propagation mechanism operates according to simple principles. Investors seek high returns and shun volatility, and those two motivations lead them to diversify internationally. Consequently, when stock prices rise in one country the rise tends to spread to markets in other countries. It does not spread equally, but it does spread rapidly. Emerging markets participate sporadically in the spread of stock market wealth. For short periods of time they benefit from massive inflows of capital and dizzying rises in asset prices. They are vulnerable to massive and devastating outflows. They try to separate themselves from the rest of the emerging countries by performing well. When they succeed, they quickly increase their financial wealth and distance themselves from the roller-coaster volatility that was their fate before.

Chapter 8

Multinational Companies as Issuers of Securities

Multinational companies are not yet creating financial wealth to the fullest extent of their capability. As issuers of securities, large multinationals whose names are well known, and whose credit ratings are strong, have immense advantages that they have not fully exploited. Many multinational companies are aware of their potential as issuers; so far, however, very few have configured themselves to emphasize issuing securities. Most of them continue to develop the same strengths they have always emphasized. They identify themselves as producers, marketers, or traders, and not as issuers of securities. Their core expertise is in chemistry, geology, logistics, electrical engineering, or consumer marketing, but not in finance. For most multinationals, finance is a support function. Multinationals have excellent finance staffs, that perform pivotal roles in day-to-day operations and in strategy formulation. But for most multinationals, finance is not preeminent. Mission statements center around adding value in the goods and services markets. Doing well at that set of tasks is how the typical multinational still intends to create value for its shareholders.

An earlier version of this chapter appeared under the title "The Multinational as an Engine of Value." Reprinted with permission from *Business Horizons*, July–August 1995, copyright © 1995 by the Board of Trustees of Indiana University, Kelly School of Business.

The Opportunity

For many multinational companies, the route to creating value for shareholders can be more direct. The opportunity is very large and is immediately at hand. In order to take advantage of it, most of these companies would have to reorganize themselves once again. They have already reorganized several times, and now they would have to put themselves through that turmoil once again. Their recent restructuring has been to respond to falling trade barriers and falling transport costs. To be successful in a world of open trade, they have sought to become global instead of multiregional. They have already reconfigured their production, assembly, and marketing to suit the new, specialized roles they are best suited to play. They have outsourced production and installed information systems to coordinate their far-flung factories, warehouses, and transport operations. As they have done so, they have discovered new strengths, and have renewed their viability, while at the same time many of their traditional strengths have faded or disappeared altogether. They have not, however, carried their transformation to the stage advocated here. They have not turned themselves single-mindedly into issuers of high-quality securities.

The implications of the shift proposed here affect the range of activities these firms should engage in; how they should be organized; how their managers should be motivated and rewarded; how their internal communications systems should be set up; and how they should handle their relationships with suppliers, with customers, and with the financial markets.

The world is facing a chronic shortage of high-quality securities. This is evident because the prices of securities keep rising. There are not many issuers who can create securities that will qualify for high credit ratings and that will appeal to buyers. Large multinational companies are issuers that can meet the criteria. They have assets, cash flow, strong brand names, excellent market shares, and standing in the business community. They have expertise in finance, law, and accounting. They can work with investment banks to design, issue, and place securities successfully.

This chapter describes how multinational companies can rearrange their securities offerings and organizational emphasis so as to maximize their clout as issuers of securities. It gives numerical examples showing the advantages they could gain from systematically issuing securities.

Strengths Contrasted with Self-Image

Multinational firms have been communications-intensive since they first appeared in the Middle Ages. They were trading firms that handled long-distance trade in goods and needed up-to-date bulletins about market conditions. They used couriers, carrier pigeons, and secret codes in a top-priority effort to stay abreast of events. They were among the earliest and heaviest users of the telegraph, the telephone, the communications satellite, the modem, and fiber optics. Today they are as communications-intensive as ever. They have transactions-based financial reporting systems that operate in real time. They have internal cash management and treasury management systems that operate around the clock, with the "book" being passed from one regional headquarters to the next as the workday ends in one time zone and begins in another. They have leased lines, dedicated circuits, and conference calls, and are large users of videoconferencing services.

Multinational firms have also been finance-intensive throughout their history. They have moved gold, handled bills of exchange, opened letters of credit, and given guarantees, and they were among the first issuers of stocks and bonds. They move money across boundaries and trade foreign exchange: They swap it, lend it, borrow it, and bounce it off satellites.

Multinational firms have also been able to organize and manage far-flung operations. They have excelled at logistic coordination: procuring in one country, processing in another, and marketing to final users in all three. They have been able to set up vertically integrated businesses and keep all the installations operating close to capacity, with a minimum of slack.

But surprisingly, most multinationals do not see themselves as information managers, as financial intermediaries, or as masters of logistics. Instead, they see themselves as manufacturing firms, as marketers, or as technology implementers. Information-gathering and -processing activities, financial activities, and logistics management are seen as subordinate.

The Changing Mix of Activities: Dragging Self-Image along Behind

For most large multinationals, the organization's self-image has changed more slowly than its pattern of actions. Companies' statements about themselves reveal glimpses of the transformation, but lag behind the day-to-day changes. The financial press has caricatured the modern large corporation as being "hollow" or "virtual," well on the way to becoming a mere shadow of its former self, and still obsessed with remaking itself. The financial press has used dieting as the metaphor: Firms are "slimming down," or "shedding" all sorts of things—layers of management, factories, whole divisions. They are "flattening" the organization, to bring the top closer to the market, be more in touch, be more agile. The words betray a tinge of condemnation, a veiled criticism that large corporations have abdicated the social role they used to play. That role, which is now outmoded, was to strengthen the economy of the nation where they happened to be headquartered. They were supposed to hire the middle class of the country where they were headquartered, and strive to make the national economy strong. Multinational corporations of today are less imposing than their muscular, fully integrated megalithic ancestors of the 1950s. A corporation that is "hollow" or "virtual" has put distance between itself and its earlier very solid and tangible incarnation, when it was a protean creator of jobs, generator and harnesser of new technologies, and builder of sprawling industrial complexes.

The conventional wisdom still links the fortunes of a multinational corporation too closely to the economic strength of its headquarters country. In times past, the two were closely linked, to the extent of seeming to be alternate manifestations of one another. Years ago, it would have been absurd to disassociate the German economy from German chemical companies, the Japanese economy from Japanese trading companies, or the U.S. economy from General Motors and IBM. The companies were multinational, but tightly associated with their nationalities in the popular imagination.

The conventional wisdom was behind the times. Ownership of the large multinational companies had already spread across national boundaries as investors in many countries bought the shares, and the multinationals had begun to diverge from their national economies, becoming more global and less national.

The Global Anorexic in the Driver's Seat

The caricature of the slimmed-down firm, striving to become yet leaner, has a grain of truth to it. Multinationals indeed are remaking themselves, not to lose weight, but to reposition themselves into activities where they have advantages that are growing. As the modern large multinational corporation transforms itself into an ever-smaller core, with more and more activities pushed out to the periphery, it becomes more powerful and influential in the domain of abstractions, while it becomes harder to locate and pin down in the domain of tangible reality. It ceases being the brawny machine of production and international commerce, and evolves into a ghostly force in the network, a neural net of commercial intelligence perched atop an eminence of information, organization, and financial clout. The new corporate form creates more value than the old form. Its securities are worth more in financial markets. Condemning it or caricaturing it does not help to understand it. What follows is an attempt to describe the new corporate form and to show how the new form is a better springboard for issuing securities. After that, the next topic is how multinational companies can move proactively toward achieving and implementing the new form.

Nodes, Business Units, and Companywide Networks

Most large companies are described using block diagrams. The labels inside the blocks might be factories, controlled corporations, affiliates, suppliers, or distributors. If the block diagram is an organization chart, the block labels are job titles and the names of the people who hold those jobs. If the block diagram is intended to represent strategy, the blocks may contain the names of business units or the links in the chain of value. These block diagrams are useful, but three more diagrams are needed. The first is the diagram of the company's *communications network*. The second is the diagram showing the company's *financial linkages*. And the third is the company's *logistic setup*.

The communications diagram has to show each node, the directions of communication, the sources of information, the processing points, and the targets. It should show the density of communication, and if possible it should give approximate error rates. The discussion accompanying the diagram should include an assessment of the reliability of the commercial intelligence the firm collects, and it should also describe how decisionmakers in the firm use that information, and how they can cross-validate the information they receive.

The diagram showing the company's financial linkages should show much more than the consolidated financial position of the entire multinational company. It should group the firm's total financial resources by country, by line of business, by currency, and by trading bloc, and it should show the finances of each legal entity in the group as a stand-alone. It should show how much money the organization has moved from each node to another, or from each bank account to another. It should show the locally granted lines of credit that each national office has available to it. It should show the assets that each subsidiary has available as collateral. It should include an estimate of the market value of every investment that one company in the group has made in another. It should show the stock market value of each affiliate that has a public listing on any national stock market.

The diagram showing the company's logistic setup should be multidimensional. There will be no diagram as such. Instead, it will be a relational database. Two-dimensional views of it will be easy to show on sheets of paper. It should show the company's physical movement of goods from different points of view. It should allow the user to look at the company's entire world system, or zoom in for closer views of regions, provinces, or cities. For example, one image should show the amount of freight shipped from each point to each other point, with the width of the lines varying according to tonnage moved between points. Another view of this image would show the dollar value moved from each point to each other point. Another view would show the frequency of shipments, with heavier lines representing greater frequency. Another view would show the mode of transportation: trucks, ships, and planes. Another view would show the perishability or time-sensitivity of the merchandise being moved. Yet another view would show the movement of goods according to the stages of production: raw materials, work in process, and final goods.

These diagrams would not be reported to shareholders. They would be used internally to show the managers of the multinational company what its capabilities are in three areas: first, its ability to collect, filter, organize, and transmit information, and then to take profitable actions based on it; second, its ability to raise money, move it, and allocate it to profitable activities; and third, its ability to gather goods, move them to points of production, and then move them to markets.

These diagrams would help managers to see their corporations in a new light. Managers are already familiar with their corporations' prod-

uct lines, customers, organizational structures, legal entities, and buildings. These diagrams would give them new and useful ways of seeing their
corporations, which they would be able to use to develop new sources of
profit.

Packaging Cash Flows and Spinning Them
Off to Shareholders

For most multinational companies, a key issue is how much of an industry
sector, or what stages of a production process, they really have to control in
order to make a high and enduring rate of profit from it. Centuries ago, mar-
itime empires seized monopoly control over production and marketing of
spices, tobacco, and sugar. Later came attempts to lock up the supplies of diamonds, quinine, rubber, bananas, nitrates, and a lengthy list of other goods
that commanded high scarcity value. The quest for market power and commercial dominance continues. Nowadays, it is research and development
spending, or marketing, or horizontal and vertical integration that give high
returns—or, at least, that are thought to give high returns. To that list we
now add issuing securities.

Multinationals have always gathered cash where it is abundant and
allocated it where it is scarce and productive. They have gained the benefit of this from year to year, but have usually not captured the value that
comes from packaging these profit streams and selling them as securities.

The hallmark of the old corporate structure was that only the parent
company's common stock was publicly listed. The multinational may also
have had some publicly quoted bonds, but most did not have any other
publicly quoted securities. In consequence, the stock market could price
only the consolidated earnings stream of the multinational. All the income streams and financial advantages that the multinational encompassed were reported to shareholders at the parent-company level. There
was no attempt to design and issue securities covering only specific subsets
of the multinational's cash flows, nor securities targeted to specific groups
of investors. There were old-fashioned, plain-vanilla common stock and
old-fashioned bonds. There were occasionally separate classes of common
stock, or preferred stock, or securities convertible into common stock. But
these were not designed to appeal to any narrow segment of the investing
public. They were issued at different times, in response to market condi-

tions at those times, to raise amounts of money that were needed at those times. The market price of the headquarters company's stock could not transmit accurately all the information about the myriad income streams encompassed within the multinational. It had to clump together the information and send a simple signal that did not give details about the individual streams nor include all the nuances.

Packaging cash flows and issuing many different securities is justified because the headquarters company's stock may not move as much as the size of the profit stream would justify. An example will illustrate how losses in one subsidiary can partially mask the value being created in other subsidiaries of a multinational. Suppose there is a multinational called Global Enterprises Incorporated (GEI) headquartered in a rich country, say Switzerland. GEI's product lines are consumer goods, including toiletries and housewares. GEI has only three subsidiaries, and all are in rich countries, say Sweden, Canada, and the United States. Each subsidiary is large and all are the same size in assets and historical earnings. Each subsidiary is 100% owned by the parent company. The parent company's shares are the only ones that are listed on a stock exchange. Recently, the earnings of the subsidiaries have been diverging. One is now making $100 million a year, the second is making $25 million a year, and the third is losing $50 million a year. Now the most profitable subsidiary has an opportunity to make $10 million a year by borrowing $200 million in Switzerland for 8% per year and investing it in riskier countries at 13% [(13% × $200 million) − (8% × $200 million) = $10 million]. Investors would duly note the increased profit, and that would incline them to bid up the price of GEI's stock, but they might also downgrade GEI's common stock slightly because the deal borrowing $200 million and relending it adds slightly to the risk that GEI might go bankrupt.

GEI's simple legal structure commingles earnings streams and gives lenders access to collateral in excess of what they might have required as security for the loans they made. The firewalls in GEI's ownership structure might be inadequate to separate the claims that a security holder might assert. Investors therefore have to assume that any claim might be enforced against any GEI asset or income stream. GEI has four different earnings streams, and with the simple structure it has at the beginning, the first claim on profits is to offset losses in the subsidiary that is losing money. Let us change that priority by spinning off the shares of the subsidiary that is losing money. This will distance the affairs of the subsidiary with losses. There are two stages to this spinoff transaction. First, GEI has to split the shares of the losing subsidiary so that their number corresponds to some fraction of the number of shares in the parent company. This facilitates paying out the shares of the losing subsidiary as a stock dividend to the parent company's shareholders. If the parent company has 500 million shares, the subsidiary's shares could be split to make their number equal to 50 million. Then the stock dividend to GEI shareholders would be 1 share of the losing subsidiary for every 10 shares of the parent company. A GEI shareholder who owned 4,000 shares of GEI stock would get 400 shares of the losing subsidiary's stock.

The losing subsidiary's shares would not be distributed immediately, however. The second stage of the spinoff is to do a road show preparatory to an initial public offering (IPO) of the losing subsidiary's shares. The road show would tout the shares to be issued and would build demand for them. For example, the road show might attempt to place 10 million newly issued shares. If the subsidiary had 50 million shares after the split just described, and if the road show succeeded in placing 10 million more, the subsidiary would have 60 million shares after its IPO. The proceeds from selling the newly issued shares would go to the subsidiary. This way, the subsidiary would start out its independent life with some cash. After the initial public offering there would also be a public market for its shares, so GEI's shareholders could sell the shares of the subsidiary that they receive when it is spun off. The public market demand for the subsidiary's shares might be quite strong. The reason is that the road show would distribute the newly issued shares to investors who are not shareholders of GEI, so the shares of the subsidiary might be dispersed enough that nobody would have control of the subsidiary after its initial public offering. A takeover battle might break out to win control of the losing subsidiary. The takeover battle would drive up the price of the losing subsidiary's stock, so GEI shareholders would have a chance to get a good price for the shares they receive in the spinoff.

After the spinoff transaction, the losing subsidiary has been cut away from GEI, and its losses are excluded from GEI's consolidated earnings. GEI no longer owns the losing subsidiary, so the subsidiary—henceforth called the *losing company*—turns into a company that is farther removed legally from GEI. The losing company's shares are now quoted in the stock market, and they trade every day.

Why should GEI go to so much trouble to do a spinoff transaction? The whole exercise may seem more trouble than it is worth. But the spinoff might create much more value for shareholders than liquidating the losing subsidiary or selling it for cash, or operating it unprofitably for several more years. The losing company is fairly large; it also may have some other appeal. Selling the entire subsidiary to a single buyer in a cash transaction may not create as much shareholder value as spinning it off. Doing a road show, then an initial public offering, then distributing the losing subsidiary's shares to GEI shareholders may get more money for the shareholders if any of several circumstances apply. For example, the subsidiary may be valuable to a competitor, but the competitor may not be willing to pay very much. Alternatively, the subsidiary may have liquidation value, and its liquidation value may be highest if it is liquidated soon. As part of GEI the subsidiary may stumble along for years, and its liquidation value may deteriorate. After the spinoff, whoever wins control of the losing company will liquidate it faster.

After the IPO, the losing company's stock cannot have a price lower than zero. Even if the losing company is completely worthless and has no attraction to any buyer, its shares will not trade for less than zero. But while the losing company was part of GEI, it lowered the stock market value of GEI. Its losses lowered the profits of GEI, so in effect its stock price was below zero. Its assets may have added something to GEI's market value, but if this is the case, the losing company's stock will trade for a price greater than zero. So after the spinoff, GEI shareholders should have two securities worth more in total than the one they had before. The two would be shares of GEI and shares of the losing company.

To see what these two securities would be worth, let us consider what GEI shares were worth before the spinoff. Let us begin by summing the multinational's consolidated earnings from its three subsidiaries. The figure is $75 million a year ($100 million + $25 million − $50 million = $75 million). Suppose that its price/earnings (P/E) ratio is 20. Its stock therefore would have a market capitalization of $75 million × 20 = $1.5 billion before the spinoff. After the spinoff, GEI stock should be worth more because the losing subsidiary has been cut off and can no longer lose the profits of the two profitable subsidiaries. GEI's consolidated earnings from the two subsidiaries that remain are $125 million, and if its P/E ratio is still 20, then its stock market capitalization will be $125 million × 20 = $2.5 billion. This is an increase of $1 billion. In addition, GEI shareholders will have shares of the losing company. They may not get much for those shares, but any value they get for them increases the gain in shareholder wealth that the spinoff achieves.

In this example, the spinoff was probably worth the extra paperwork. It probably got more for the losing subsidiary than selling or liquidating it would have brought, and the spinoff delivered that value to shareholders immediately. The spinoff sent the clear signal to shareholders that GEI was really getting rid of the loser, instead of dithering while it continued to lose money. The spinoff also signaled that GEI was not going to keep the proceeds at headquarters. Instead, GEI showed clearly that it was going to dedicate the proceeds to benefiting shareholders immediately.

The Borrowing and Lending Transaction: Deal Structure Affects Shareholder Wealth

GEI's management saw how effective spinning off its losing subsidiary was, and now is going to structure the borrowing and lending transaction. Its objective will be to raise shareholder wealth. GEI's most profitable subsidiary is its Swedish affiliate, which has been making profits of $100 million a year. The opportunity to invest $200 million in riskier countries arrives at the Swedish affiliate's office. The assets to be acquired are car loans, and the car owners are in Finland, Latvia, Poland, and Estonia. The car owners make monthly payments, and when they have finished paying for their cars they renew the loans to get new cars. The average yield on these car loans is 13% net of administrative costs and allowances for bad debt. GEI's Swedish affiliate has lines of credit with Swiss banks for more than $200 million, and the interest rate on these lines of credit is 8%.

It appears at first glance that the Swedish affiliate should go ahead and borrow $200 million, then use the $200 million to buy the car loans. This would add $10 million to the Swedish affiliate's earnings. That $10 million would be consolidated with the $125 million that GEI is already making from its Swedish subsidiary and the other one that remains after the spinoff. If GEI's P/E ratio remained at 20, the earnings increase of $10 million would add 20 times as much to shareholder value.

The real effect, however, would not be that good, and might be negative. The Swedish affiliate would be much riskier after the transaction. It would have used its borrowing capacity and so would not be able to get as much cash in event of need. Also, it would have gone outside its range of expertise and would have blurred its image in the minds of shareholders. They might question whether GEI's strategy is still on track. Consequently, they might downgrade GEI's stock and lower the multiple they would pay for it from 20 to 17, for example. In that event, the transaction would have destroyed shareholder value. Earnings were $125 million before the transaction, and earnings are $135 million after the transaction, but the P/E multiple has fallen to 17, so GEI stock is worth only $2.295 billion instead of $2.5 billion.

GEI can do the transaction, but it has to take care to create a separate corporate entity to hold the $200 million of car loans. The car loans should not be mingled with existing businesses. The separate corporation that holds the car loans should have its own financial reports, and those should be prepared each year by outside auditors. The separate corporation should obtain its own financing, instead of using the Swedish affiliate's lines of credit. The separate corporation, Central European Automobile Finance (CEAF), should raise most of the $200 million by selling bonds. The bonds would be secured only by the car loans, so they would be junk bonds. Neither the parent company nor the Swedish affiliate would guarantee the bonds.

The separation has to be complete, or investors will probably downgrade GEI's stock. The risks of car loans are different from the risks of GEI's existing product line, and GEI shareholders probably will not want to shoulder those risks.

The car loans do provide an opportunity for GEI to reward its shareholders. Here is a way to do so without blurring GEI's image or compromising GEI's finances with guarantees. Suppose that GEI headquarters has budgeted $25 million to reward its shareholders, and has been planning to use it to buy back shares, when the car loan opportunity comes along. Instead of buying back shares, suppose that GEI creates CEAF, the car loan holding company, and invests the $25 million in shares of CEAF. GEI's investment bankers then arrange a road show to sell $175 million of junk bonds issued by CEAF. In this fashion, CEAF gathers $200 million and uses it to buy the car loans.

CEAF is now up and running as an independent legal entity. The junk bonds have a 10% yield because they are not guaranteed. CEAF makes 13% per year on $200 million of car loans and pays $17.5 million a year interest on the junk bonds. This gives a net of $8.5 million per year before taxes. This is a good return on the $25 million of equity that GEI put in. CEAF then applies for its shares to be listed on the Swedish and Swiss stock exchanges. After the listings have been obtained, GEI distributes all its shares of CEAF to GEI shareholders as a dividend.

GEI shareholders now have shares of CEAF. In a perfect world, the CEAF shares would be worth $25 million in the aggregate. That is the cash investment that GEI put into CEAF. If that is all the shares are worth, then GEI should not have gone to the trouble of creating CEAF. But there are several reasons why CEAF's stock market value might be greater than $25 million. One reason is that its expected earnings before taxes are $8.5 million per year. Applying a low multiple—for example, 11—to those earnings gives CEAF a stock market value of $93.5 million. Another reason is that CEAF can grow. Yet another reason is that CEAF shares may find a natural niche in the stock market. The shares appeal to investors who understand the risks and rewards of the car loan business. GEI stockholders would probably sell the shares of CEAF after receiving them. The typical GEI shareholder would probably not be interested in owning shares of CEAF. Every different common stock has its clientele, and CEAF shares would find their own natural clientele of new owners. CEAF is a simple company to understand, and it would quickly attract a following of shareholders and analysts who would be happy to own it as long as it performed up to expectations.

This example shows that GEI can probably use the car loan opportunity to create value for its shareholders. GEI can also structure the deal incorrectly and blur its image, complicate its finances, and make itself look riskier and befuddled. The key to creating shareholder value is to separate risky cash flows, package them, and target them to the segments of the investing public that want those particular cash flows. Listing only the common stock of the headquarters company does not accomplish this. The headquarters company is a catch-all that mingles too many disparate businesses and guarantees the liabilities of each individual business with the assets and cash flows of the others. Sophisticated investors prefer to see each separate business in isolation. Then they can buy what they want and leave the rest for other buyers who want different things.

An Example Involving Emerging Countries

So far this chapter has considered a multinational that had subsidiaries only in rich countries. The examples have shown how the multinational could create or destroy shareholder value by structuring its offerings of shares and distributing them to its stockholders. This section now looks at an example of a multinational that has subsidiaries in emerging countries and considers what the company can do to create value for its shareholders.

This company is called Worldwide Products (WP), and it produces and sells branded consumer products in many countries, including emerging countries. WP is based in London and has a 100% owned subsidiary that operates in Indonesia. This company is called WP Indonesia and is a strong and well-known player in the local economy. Its products are widely known in Indonesia and are closely identified in consumers' minds with WP Indonesia. It has 20 years of successful operations in Indonesia, and has been advertising its products on local television and radio for 15 years. Its annual sales are the equivalent of $100 million, and its annual profit for the most recent year was $4 million after paying local taxes. WP's stock trades at 15 times earnings in London, and WP Indonesia's earnings are consolidated into the parent company's income statement. WP's stock trades at only 15 times earnings in London because of WP's history of fluctuating earnings and high exposure to emerging markets. The total market value of WP's stock in London is presumably $60 million higher because of WP Indonesia's earnings. This figure assumes that investors apply the same P/E ratio to all of WP's earnings.

Now suppose that WP offers 20% of the shares of WP Indonesia on the Jakarta Stock Exchange. There would be costs and taxes to pay; assume that WP Indonesia pays those out of the proceeds of the offering. Suppose the shares are placed at 12 times earnings, a lower multiple than the 15 that investors pay in London for the shares of the parent. The gross revenue from selling the shares would be 20% of $4 million × 12 = $9.6 million. Costs of the flotation and taxes due to the Indonesian government consume $2.9 million of the proceeds, so the remaining amount is $6.7 million. Technically, this money belongs to the parent. Suppose the parent leaves this money with WP Indonesia to invest locally on behalf of the parent. Suppose that WP Indonesia does not invest this money in new factories, machinery, or marketing, but instead invests this money in shares of other Indonesian companies. It buys shares of companies that are well run but little known abroad. Suppose also that half of these companies' shares are listed on the Jakarta Stock Exchange, and the other half are not yet listed but are going to be listed in the future. The shares that are listed are trading at 9 times earnings, and the ones that are not yet listed are purchased at 6 times earnings. These low multiples reflect the scarcity of capital in Jakarta and the companies' lack of name recognition.

How much will this series of transactions benefit WP Indonesia and WP's stock price in London? At first glance, the effect would appear to be negative because WP Indonesia pays so much in taxes and fees to raise the $6.7 million. After floating 20% of the stock of WP Indonesia in Jakarta, WP owns only 80% of WP Indonesia's income stream. So WP Indonesia's contribution to WP's consolidated income statement has declined from $4 million to $3.2 million. The other $800,000 per year belongs to the investors who bought the shares of WP Indonesia. The income from investing the $6.7 million, however, will more than replace the $800,000 income stream that investors bought. Consider that half the $6.7 million, or $3.35 million, is invested in companies that are priced at 9 times earnings, and the other half is invested in companies that earn 6 times earnings. The earnings stream from these investments is

$$\frac{\$3.35 \text{ million}}{9} + \frac{\$3.35 \text{ million}}{6} = \$930,556 \text{ per year}$$

In this example, WP Indonesia would have sold 20% of its income stream, worth $800,000 a year, and used the net proceeds from the sale to buy income streams worth $930,556. The difference in these annual income streams is $130,556. This difference would accrue to the parent company's consolidated income statement. If investors in London continued to apply a P/E ratio of 15 to WP stock, the increase in shareholder value would be $1,958,340, or 15 times $130,556.

Where does the value creation come from in this example? This is not simply a case of bringing cheap capital to a place where it is dear. On the contrary, the example has been constructed using capital from investors who buy shares of WP Indonesia when the shares are floated on the Jakarta Stock Exchange. Neither does the value creation come from evading taxes. WP pays $2.9 million in fees and taxes to raise $9.6 million, so it keeps only $6.7 million to invest. The value creation comes from WP's franchise. WP has name recognition and credibility with investors. It steadfastly seeks to reward shareholders, gives stock options to its managers, and operates with full financial disclosure in accordance with the rules of the London Stock Exchange. Investors pay more for shares of WP Indonesia than they would for the shares of local companies that are not subsidiaries of multinational companies. They buy shares in WP Indonesia in full knowledge that the parent company retains majority control. They are confident that WP Indonesia has the expertise to select investments well and the incentives to deliver the profits to investors.

How Will Multinationals Create Value in the Future?

The examples just given are only a few of many that can create value for shareholders. Multinationals, especially the ones headquartered outside the United States, have scarcely begun to restructure their securities offerings. There are more designs, more transactions, and more innovations that this chapter could survey, but it will suffice to mention just one more.

Many multinationals have subsidiaries in countries where stock prices are high. It would benefit them to sell part of the shares of those subsidiaries and use the proceeds to repurchase the shares of the parent company. For example, consider a company headquartered in London that has a 100% owned subsidiary in Japan. For simplicity, suppose that the company has operations only in London and in Japan. In London it makes $200 million a year, and in Japan it makes $100 million a year. All the Japanese earnings are consolidated into the London company's income statement, and so the combined earnings are $300 million a year. The London company's shares are listed on the London Stock Exchange, where they trade at a multiple of 23 times earnings. Consequently the combined company's stock market capitalization is $6.9 billion, or $300 million times 23. Meanwhile, however, the average P/E multiple in Japan is higher. For this example, suppose that the Japanese subsidiary would trade at 45 times earnings if it were listed on the Tokyo Stock Exchange. This indicates that all by itself it would be worth $4.5 billion. So the London company should sell a partial interest in the Japanese subsidiary and then use the proceeds to buy back the London company's shares on the London Stock Exchange. Suppose that the London company sells 50% of the shares of the Japanese subsidiary for $2.25 billion and then uses the money to buy back its common stock on the London Stock Exchange.

This transaction creates a money machine. The stock price of the London company would rise spectacularly. To see why, consider that half the Japanese subsidiary has been sold, so the consolidated earnings of the London company now are only $250 million. If its P/E multiple is still 23, the London company's stock should be worth $250 million $\times$ 23 = $5.75 billion. This figure, however, is only $1.15 billion lower than the $6.9 billion the London company was worth before it sold half its Japanese subsidiary. Yet the proceeds of $2.25 billion from selling half the Japanese subsidiary have been used to buy back common stock on the London Stock Exchange. Because there was $6.9 billion worth in the first place, the remaining stock should be worth $6.9 billion − $2.25 billion = $4.65 billion. Instead, it is worth $5.75 billion, so the stock price must have risen. The amount it rose in this example is 23.6% (5.75/4.65 − 1 = 23.6%). So shareholders benefit if headquarters sell subsidiaries that are operating in countries where P/E multiples are high.

These examples all point to the same general method of creating value: issuing securities, and structuring those securities to be worth as much as the markets permit. The transactions described here may seem like distractions from the real business that most multinationals engage in. These transactions do not add any productive capacity or develop new technologies. But they definitely do add value, by making shareholders wealthier.

The argument here is that if a multinational company is to earn more than 12% per year on average for its shareholders, it will not consistently be able to do so by investing in plants and equipment. Investing in human capital and in packaging and selling cash flows will consistently yield more than 12% for shareholders.

New forms of controlling the value chain are now adequate. Previously it was necessary to control and monopolize every step from production to marketing. Vertical and horizontal integration continue to be strategic objectives, but in most industrial sectors they are tempered by other objectives. To have effective control of an industry sector, it may be enough to have an advantage of market share, technology, or access to shelf space in retail outlets.

Business advantage in an industrial sector has always diminished with time. Imitators and substitutes always encroach, and the high profits always fade into mediocre returns. The shortening product life cycles make the high profits fade quicker than they used to. The question is what, if anything, multinationals can do to postpone the inevitable.

The classic strategy was to keep investing in improvements to the design, the production process, the packaging, the positioning, and the distribution. This involved large expenditures in production facilities and large work groups that included designers and marketers. This product-focused strategy prolonged the high-profit phase of the life cycle, but it did so by raising fixed costs and reducing flexibility. There was also the tendency to keep on making new investments in the same lines of business after the high profit phase had already ended.

Investors feared that the high costs would go on longer than the high profits. Top managers heard their fears. Their responses have been to restructure, when a more sweeping and proactive reexamination of the sources of high profits would have indicated the need for a more sweeping reorientation. The sources of high profits are no longer found in control of geography, nor are they found in control over raw materials. Now they are found in control of information, in the form of technology, patents, or proprietary processes; or commercial contacts, brand-name recognition, or knowledge of consumer tastes. Or they are found in financial advantages, in the form of cash, low cost of capital, or the ability to mobilize cash in different places to achieve an objective. Skill in designing and placing new issues of securities is now a key advantage. There are also logistic advantages, in the form of warehouses, shipping capabilities, freight forwarders, knowledge of customs regulations, and fleets of delivery vans. In short, the sources of high profits are exactly what the multinationals have had all along.

The Hierarchy of Production Units

The multinational can gain the most advantage from its distinctive competences by acting as a catalyst. It should place the keystone in the arch, not build the whole arch. Its contribution to a deal or to a production and distribution process should be only to put in the ingredients that its smaller, less-known collaborators cannot supply. It should not own assets or have employees unless they are crucial to maintaining its dominant position in the hierarchy. The hierarchy is as follows, expressed in terms of the credit ratings of the participants in a coordinated production arrangement:

Entity	Credit Rating
Multinational, known worldwide	Credit rating A
Local prime contractor	Local credit rating good
Local subcontractor; small firm; low overhead	No local credit rating

This separation of entities in the production and distribution process follows the pattern of the Japanese *keiretsu* but is set up multinationally and not all within one country.

The chain of production is controlled from the top, but the local contractors and subcontractors have the land, buildings, machinery, warehouses, and production-line employees. The multinational controls the whole chain by contracts and by market intelligence, database design, and superior telecommunications.

Managing in Virtual Reality: Autonomy with Strictly Controlled Risk

Firms that accomplish vertical integration via contracts tie up less capital and have fewer direct employees, potentially greater flexibility, and less control over production and distribution. Though they are smaller in physical dimensions, they are financially stronger because their assets are composed of relatively high amounts of accounts receivable, inventories, and cash equivalents, and relatively low amounts of plant and equipment. For this reason their asset turnover will be faster, so they will be able to reposition assets more quickly. They will also have higher debt capacity because they will be able to keep their cash flow more stable than if they owned fixed assets that are susceptible to cyclical downturns.

Managing by contracts instead of by owning facilities means that the firm operates more in the commercial sphere and less as a technology creator or implementer. To operate in this style requires a corps of managers to originate, monitor, maintain, and renew or discontinue the contracts. These people are like foreign exchange traders or bond dealers, but they deal with goods and services. They need to be managed in the same way as foreign exchange traders. They are assigned trading limits; their trading limits are tracked carefully and are raised or lowered according to their performance.

This chapter intentionally portrays an extreme vision of the multinational. It advocates turning every multinational into an investment bank and a playground for financial consultants. It implicitly advocates jettisoning factories, employees, and traditional relationships, all to levitate shareholder wealth. There are many who will balk at this prescription. There are also multinationals that cannot make themselves into puppetmasters of financial wealth creation. Nevertheless, the market is rewarding the ones that manage to do so. All multinationals, even the small ones, will be able to execute some of the maneuvers described here, and if they do not do so, then the market's fickle but opulent rewards will go to the ones that do.

Treasury Management and Hedging

After a multinational decides to become an issuer of high-quality securities designed to appeal to preidentified groups of investors, the treasury management and hedging roles take on greater importance. The treasury managers will track cash collections and disbursements, foreign exchange risk, capital structure, cash flow by business unit by currency, and the market prices of the firm's securities. Treasury managers will enter into swap deals to smooth the volatility in the firm's underlying cash flow, which will continue to be more erratic than the financial markets want it to be.

Hedging has always been important but now will have a broader objective. Its old objective was to hold raw material or foreign exchange risk within acceptable bounds. Now its objective is to buy as much stability as investors are willing to pay for. This objective is easy to state but hard to achieve in practice.

Hedging instruments are like insurance policies. There are many different kinds of hedging instruments that cover against most of the damaging events that can happen to a company. They have different price tags depending on how much coverage they give. The skill is in buying the right amounts of the right ones.

Hedging is important because the multinational's cash flows are no longer going to be clumped together and reported only in consolidated form. More and more securities are going to be issued that give claims on selected cash flows, so those are going to be disclosed. There will be less and less hope of burying a loss or an embarrassingly high cost in the company's consolidated accounting statements. Pet projects, white elephants, and padded payrolls will all be in the spotlight. Each dollar saved will add a multiple of itself to shareholder wealth.

Conclusion

Multinational companies are already formidable issuers of securities, but most of them can improve their performance as issuers. They can systematically reconfigure themselves to become more effective in creating shareholder value by issuing securities. Historically, they have gone along with the view that their role as value creators through financial markets is subordinate to their role as value creators through technology implementation. The alternate view, namely that they have been paying too much attention to their historical core competencies and not enough to their power to create value through financial markets, is given in this chapter. There are examples of using spinoffs, franchises, and buybacks. All the examples hinge on disaggregating consolidated cash flows or taking advantage of disparities between national capital markets. Multinationals are ideal raw material for financial engineers. Now, with middle-class savers demanding more securities that are highly rated, the multinationals can redefine their primary mission as being engines of value creation through financial markets. They are the obvious players to respond to the market's appeal.

Chapter 9

Tracking Ownership: Transparency, Sovereignty, and the Level Playing Field

The capacity now exists to record and track all economically relevant attributes of every productive asset on earth. To a technologist, this statement is too obvious to be worthy of comment. The cost of storing a megabyte of data has fallen steadily, as Moore's law predicts, and has already fallen enough for the statement to be true. To a civil libertarian, the feasibility of collecting and storing that much data puts privacy into jeopardy, and evokes images of Big Brother looking into everyone's affairs. To a nationalist, the statement is a threat to sovereignty, because the people who collect the data will not necessarily be local nationals, and they will disseminate it everywhere, all over the earth, to anyone who is willing to pay for it, or is interested in seeing it. That dissemination quickly will lead to foreign buyers finding out how attractive local assets are. Then it is only a small step to foreign buyers trying to buy assets that have always been in local hands.

One of the meanings of sovereignty is that countries can make rules about ownership of assets within their borders and apply those rules in accordance with local procedures. Foreigners are allowed to investigate what these rules are, but if they attempt to subvert them, it is a violation of sovereignty. Foreigners would not take the trouble to subvert local sovereignty unless there was enough money to be made. Accurate, highly detailed data will tell them how much money might be made. But data about properties and rules of ownership are hard to obtain in many countries. Inaccurate data and opaque rules of ownership are so often the norm that many writers have settled on an explanation: Murky rules serve the interests of local elites. Where rules are murky, local knowledge and connections are valuable. If this is the case, it follows that local rich people have no incentive to push their own governments to put clearer rules into effect. For the same reason, local rich people have not pushed for more accurate data, and they have especially not pushed for equal treatment for foreigners in local disputes over money.

The advantages that local rich people obtain from opaque rules and spotty data are numerous. Local well-connected people can sometimes assert ownership over parcels of land they never acquired by grant nor paid for. This benefit is obvious, but there is a more subtle benefit that is more important: The cost of capital in many countries is very high. Consider a poor country, where wholesale and retail trade are very fragmented and inefficient. Local rich people who invest in wholesaling and retailing are earning, for example, 60% a year on their working capital. This high rate of return is feasible in countries where there are many tiny retail outlets, each with a small inventory of high-turnover items. The retailers charge high markups but provide a service for their customers because they will sell goods in tiny amounts—200 grams of rice, two or three cigarettes, and a small measure of cooking oil. The local rich people do very well in an environment where returns are so high. With working capital of $200,000 they can make $120,000 per year without much risk. They can keep each retailer on a very short leash, giving only three to five days' inventory, and firing the ones that do not perform. Other low-risk, high-return investments are buying grain after the harvest, drying it, storing it, and selling it before the following harvest, or buying used cars and leasing them to taxi drivers.

All these high-return businesses would turn into low-return businesses if too much foreign capital came pouring in. This is the usual explanation of why local rich people do not take steps to level the playing field for foreign investors. This explanation, however, has now been overtaken by events. Local rich people now suffer when rules are opaque. Rising world financial wealth will benefit them if it flows into their countries and raises the market prices of capital assets. Local rich people living well on high-turnover working capital investments will suffer, because their annual returns will go down, but local rich people who own land and buildings will benefit. The net result of clearer rules and equal treatment for foreign investors would be strongly positive for local rich people.

Opaque Land Ownership Records

For an example of data that is hard to access and of uneven quality, consider land ownership records in most countries. These records are essential to the smooth functioning of any economy, but in most countries they fall far short of the standard of precision and accessibility that is now technically feasible. In many jurisdictions, land registries are inexact and the information can be accessed only at the registry offices themselves. Deed records are still on paper and have not yet been scanned and digitized. Expensive title searches are required to ascertain exactly what the boundaries of a parcel of land are, who the owner is, and what liens and other claims are outstanding against the parcel. Local lawyers and title examiners conduct these searches. A person who lacks expert training probably cannot do a reliable title search, and a person from another country would be a fool to try. Local experts earn fees for issuing title reports. They sometimes make mistakes, because the job of tracing land ownership is difficult. Mistakes are frequent enough that buyers and title examiners buy insurance that pays when they make a mistake.

In comparison, consider ships, another important asset category. It is easy to find out who owns a ship and what liens there are against it. Ship mortgages are safe investments for this reason. With so many ports in the world, such big oceans, and so many pirates, it would seem that sailing a ship away and selling it under another name would be easy. But in fact it is difficult to evade a lien on a ship. Even modifying the ship and repainting is not always enough to disguise it. Creating a new identity for a ship and extinguishing its old one is hard to do. Surprisingly, it is hard to fake a sinking and still keep the ship. Pirates and unscrupulous merchants usually get only the cargo, and then sometimes have a hard time selling it without getting caught. Sometimes they go to the extreme of sinking the ship. This gets them nothing, because the insurance money goes first to the mortgagee, and the legal owner gets any money that is left over.

The contrast between these two asset categories is striking. Ships seem harder to track, but good data about them has always been collected and maintained, so tracking them is in fact easier. Land ownership should be easier to track, and perfecting liens on land should be a routine and unremarkable exercise. The purpose of drawing the contrast is to show that there must have been opposition to clearing up land titles. The surveying and tracking would not have been difficult half a century ago. Now, with global positioning satellites, computers, video cameras, and networks, the task is straightforward. If a parcel of land has an owner who has proof of ownership, and if the owner is allowed to give a mortgage on the land to a lender, the lien should be easy to enforce. But enforcing a lien against a parcel of land is difficult, and is especially difficult if the lienholder is a foreigner. One possible reason is national preference—that is, the view that local owners should have the advantage in disputes with foreigners. Whatever the reasons are, local preferences are now damaging to the interests of local rich people. When local preferences are eliminated, or clarified, the value of assets in many countries will go up, and the world's wealth will be spread more evenly across countries.

There are many productive assets on earth and many claims on them. Some claims are financial, some are ecological, and some are traditional. Some cultures give paramount standing to use rights; other cultures give top precedence to ownership rights. Setting land-tenure policy is a collective decision that every country makes. Sometimes the policy is stated in the country's constitution, or is set by acts of a parliament, and is promulgated in legal codes; other times the policy is unwritten and opaque to outsiders, but well understood locally. Quite often, the policy favors one group over another; in particular, it sometimes favors local citizens over foreigners. Mexico's constitution, for example, prohibits foreigners from owning land that is within 50 kilometers of the border. Mexico lost parts of its territory to the United States between 1830 and 1848, and it did not want North Americans to buy land near the border for fear that the North Americans might try to move the border farther south once again.

Many countries around the world have policies that restrict who can buy some category of asset. Apart from land, mineral resources are often restricted to local owners or are inalienably the property of the state. These policies are a prerogative of sovereignty. The policies are usually grounded in the country's history.

These policies have always lowered the value of assets by restricting the pool of eligible buyers. Less obviously, these policies have also raised the value of assets elsewhere that all buyers are eligible to buy. There is a gap between what an asset is worth in a country that allows anyone to buy and what the same asset is worth in a country that restricts who can buy. Now, after the rapid rise of financial wealth, asset prices in most places have risen, and the gap has gotten wider. Nationalism and favoritism have always lowered the prices that local owners get when they sell. In the past, owners were not aware of how much more they would get if foreigners could buy, or they did not press their case for giving equal treatment to foreigners. Now, however, the costs of restrictions and favoritism have gotten more expensive and more noticeable. The costs are still hard to see, because they are in the form of higher prices that would have been paid but were not.

The Cost of Restrictions and Favoritism

To make the costs of favoritism visible, the following example discusses the prices of farms that are all the same except that they are located in three different countries. Consider a simple world in which there are three countries. One country allows all buyers to compete for any asset that an owner is selling. In this example, let us call this country the United States. The second one allows only local nationals to buy assets that are for sale. For convenience, let us call this second country Malaysia. The third one publishes that anyone can buy assets that are for sale, but gives preference to local nationals in lawsuits and regulatory rulings. Let us call this third country Indonesia. These names are used because they are easier to remember than invented names.

In each country there are 1,000 savers. The savers in the United States have an average of $10,000 each, the savers in Malaysia have an average of $5,000 each, and the savers in Indonesia have an average of $3,000 each. In this simple world there are no savings accounts and no stock markets. The only assets that these savers can buy are farms. There are 1,000 farms in each country. All are of the same size and fertility. Each farm produces 500 tons of grain per year and needs no inputs to do so. The farms are all for sale. The savers have no location preference. They are considering the farms only as investments and will take into account how much a farm might be worth in the future. None of the savers is going to live on any of the farms.

Total buying power is $(1,000 \times \$10,000) + (1,000 \times \$5,000) + (1,000 \times \$3,000) = \$18$ million. All this money is going to be spent buying all the farms. How will the money be allocated, and what will be the equilibrium prices of the farms in the posited regulatory environment? Each farm produces the same amount of output, so from that point of view they should all be worth the same. Because there are 3,000 farms in total and $18 million to be spent to buy them, each should cost $6,000. But that is not what the farms will cost.

The most obvious point is that there is at most $5 million available to buy the 1,000 farms in Malaysia. The $5 million is the $5,000 that the 1,000 local buyers each have. The other $13 million of buying power is excluded from competing for these farms. So the maximum price that the farms in Malaysia could be worth is $5,000 each. But the equilibrium price in the market might be lower than that.

Some of the savers in Malaysia will know that the United States does not restrict foreign ownership and does not exhibit favoritism toward locals. So they might buy in the United States, thinking that they are more likely to make a capital gain there. Suppose that this siphons off $1 million of the $5 million. So the price of farms in Malaysia could be $4,000 each.

Now there remains $14 million to allocate to buying the farms in the United States and Indonesia. The $14 million consists of $10 million belonging to savers in the United States, $3 million belonging to savers in Indonesia, and $1 million belonging to savers in Malaysia. There are 2,000 farms remaining to be bought, but the price will not come out to $7,000 in each country.

The opaque rules of ownership in Indonesia will discourage most savers in the United States. Suppose that they send only $2 million to Indonesia to buy farms. Their $2 million would be added to the $3 million in the hands of savers in Indonesia. This would give a total of $5 million.

But not all of the $3 million in the hands of savers in Indonesia would be dedicated to buying farms in Indonesia. Some of those savers would be worried about losing a lawsuit or an administrative ruling. Some of them would be members of the wrong political party, or ethnic group, or from the wrong part of the country. So they would not buy in Indonesia. Instead they would channel their money to the United States. Suppose that the amount they channel is $500,000. The result would be $2 million + $3 million − $500,000 = $4.5 million for farms in Indonesia. The price of a farm in Indonesia would be $4,500.

Knowing how much of the grand total of $18 million was spent buying farms in Malaysia and Indonesia, it is easy to infer how much was spent buying farms in the United States. The answer is $18 million − $4 million − $4.5 million = $9.5 million. So the price of a farm in the United States would be $9,500. This is approximately double what the farms cost in the other two countries.

In this example the farms are all the same. The difference in prices is due to the different regulatory regimes. The savers in the United States had more money on average, and although they had no location preference most of them invested it at home. They would have invested more abroad, but in Malaysia they were prohibited, and in Indonesia the opaque rules and local favoritism discouraged them.

Increasing World Financial Wealth

Now suppose that world financial wealth increases. All the savers now have much more money. The savers in the United States have $100,000 on average, the savers in Malaysia have $20,000 on average, and the savers in Indonesia have $6,000 on average. These new amounts have been chosen to represent the unequal accumulation of financial wealth that has happened in the recent past. The savers in the United States are 10 times as wealthy as they were before, the savers in Malaysia 4 times as wealthy, and the savers in Indonesia twice as wealthy.

Suppose that once again all the farms are for sale. What will be the new prices of the farms? Again, it is easiest to start with Malaysia, because only Malaysian savers are eligible to buy. This time, however, more of the money they have saved will go to buying farms in the United States, because that strategy worked the last time. Consequently, more of Malaysia's buying power will find its way to the U.S. market. Although U.S. farms were more expensive before wealth went up, they appreciate more, both in absolute and percentage terms, when wealth rises. In this second part of the example, the price of farms in the United States will rise by approximately 10 times after all the savers in the three countries have allocated their larger amounts of wealth. The higher price for farms in the United States, which plausibly might turn out to be $91,000, will come about because buying power from all three countries, and especially from Malaysia, converges on the U.S. market.

Farms will cost so much in the United States because its savings cannot spill over into Malaysia, and its savers will be wary of flowing money into Indonesia. Plausible new prices for farms in each country will be $91,000, $13,000, and $22,000, respectively. To produce that result, $17 million from the United States would flow to Indonesia, $7 million from Malaysia would flow to the United States, and $1 million from Indonesia would flow to the United States. Total buying power in the United States would be $100 million − $17 million + $7 million + $1 million = $91 million. Total buying power in Malaysia would be $20 million − $7 million = $13 million. Total buying power in Indonesia would be $6 million + $17 million − $1 million = $22 million.

Note that the country that prohibits foreign buyers suffers relative to the country that allows foreign buyers but has opaque rules. Its farms were worth $4,000 and after the surge in financial wealth are worth $13,000, a bit more than 3 times as much. This sounds like a spectacular increase, and it is, but it is also a relative decrease. Indonesia, which does not prohibit foreign buyers but occasionally penalizes them, benefits from $17 million of capital inflow from the United States, so its farms rise in value by about 5 times. And finally, in the United States farm prices skyrocket. Its farms rise in value by about 10 times. Its savers have 10 times as much money as before, so the increase in price is commensurate with the increase in savings of U.S. citizens. An important result of the money flows is that farms in the United States increase in value more than the total amount of buying power increases. The total amount of buying power increases from $18 million to $126 million, only about 7 times.

The increased buying power piles disproportionately into the country whose assets were already the most expensive. Remember that the farms in this example are all identical regardless of which country they are in, and each produces 500 tons of grain per year. Remarkably, the rate of return on investment in the United States is low if one considers only how much it costs to buy an income stream of 1 ton of grain per year. The cost is $91,000/500 tons = $460 for 1 ton per year. This is 7½ times more expensive than the 1 ton per year income-stream costs in Malaysia and a little more than 4 times as expensive as the 1 ton income stream in Indonesia. Yet the capital gains yield from the investment in the United States is much greater, even after adjusting for the higher initial cost.

Capital Gains Yields

United States
$$\frac{\$91,000 - \$9,500}{\$9,500} = 858\%$$

Malaysia
$$\frac{\$13,000 - \$4,000}{\$4,000} = 225\%$$

Indonesia
$$\frac{\$22,000 - \$4,500}{\$4,500} = 389\%$$

The investment recommendation, in view of this example, would be to buy farms that are located in the country that has the most transparent and egalitarian policy toward foreign ownership.

The most striking conclusion of this simple example is that savers in Malaysia and Indonesia do best when they put their money into the United States. If a saver in Malaysia had put money into the United States at the beginning of this example, that saver would have made enough on the investment to buy more than twice as many farms in Malaysia at the end of the example.

The Wealth Transfer

These calculations so far have focused on the rate of return that each saver would make under the simple conditions of the example. Now let us consider what the effects of ownership restrictions and favoritism are on the aggregate value of farms in each country. In the first part of the example, the 3,000 farms are worth $18 million in total, or $6,000 apiece on average.

Using the assumptions that are given, the farms in Malaysia are worth $4,000 each. This is $2,000 per farm less than the global average of $6,000, so it follows that Malaysia's restrictions on foreign ownership reduce the value of its farms by $2,000 per farm × 1,000 farms = $2 million. Malaysia's decision to exclude foreign buyers has two effects. It makes the farms in Malaysia worth that much less, and it makes the farms in the rest of the world worth that much more. This is a wealth transfer. Farm owners in Malaysia have lost value to owners in the other two countries. Some owners might not care, or even notice, but the loss is real. It is important if the owners sell, or if they use the farms as collateral for loans.

The farms in Indonesia are worth $4,500 each in the example. This figure could have been higher or lower, depending on how much favoritism there was for local owners—and particularly for local owners who are from the favored region, ethnic group, or political party. In the example, the fear of unfair rulings keeps the prices $1,500 per farm lower than the $6,000 world average. This is a total of $1,500 per farm × 1,000 farms = $1.5 million. This $1.5 million is the cost of favoritism.

The owners of farms in the United States are the beneficiaries. Farms there are worth $9,500 each, or $3,500 more than the world average. This is a wealth transfer of $2,000 per farm coming from Malaysia and $1,500 per farm coming from Indonesia. The total amount of the wealth transfer is $3,500 per farm × 1000 farms = $3.5 million.

These amounts may not be large enough to cause farm owners in Malaysia and Indonesia much discomfort. But in the second part of the example, which considers what happens to the total values of farms after financial wealth has increased, the magnitudes of wealth transfer become much larger.

The Wealth Transfer after Financial Wealth Has Increased

After financial wealth increases, the total amount of buying power has increased to $126 million, or $42,000 per farm on average. This is 7 times the average price at the beginning. The average capital gain is $42,000 − $6,000 = $36,000 per farm. What happens is a more exaggerated version of the wealth transfer illustrated by the beginning set of numbers. Farms in the United States go up to $91,000 each, for a capital gain of $91,000 − $9,500 = $81,500 each. Farms in Malaysia experience a capital gain of only $13,000 − $4,000 = $9,000 each. Farms in Indonesia experience a capital gain of $22,000 − $4,500 = $17,500.

The wealth transfers are much larger after total financial wealth has increased. The United States benefits in the amount of ($81,500 − $36,000) × 1,000 = $45.5 million. This is how much larger its total capital gains are under the assumptions in the example.

The wealth transfers are also proportionately larger. The United States gained ($9,500 − $6,000)/6,000 = 58% over the world average before financial wealth increased. After the increase, its gain is ($91,500 − $42,000)/$42,000 = 118% over the world average.

The implication of this calculation is that as world financial wealth increases, the magnitude of wealth transfers increases, and under most sets of assumptions the magnitude grows disproportionately.

The Value of Leveling the Playing Field

In the example, the savers in the United States send money to Indonesia to buy farms. They do not send enough to equalize the prices in the two countries, because they fear that locals in Indonesia will have the advantage in legal and administrative disputes.

Now suppose that Indonesia reaffirms its policy of allowing foreign investment and announces that it is determined to guarantee equal protection under the law for foreign investors. They will not be deprived of their property unless they have really done something to deserve such treatment.

If investors in the United States take this announcement seriously, some of them will sell farms in the United States and take the money and invest in buying farms in Indonesia. The price gap will narrow. Malaysia will not receive any inflows because in this example it still prohibits foreign investment. Malaysia might suffer more capital outflows after Indonesia's announcement, but to keep the example simple, suppose that prices of farms in Malaysia are unaltered. In that case, the question is how much money would flow from the United States to Indonesia.

The amount will be small at first, because all observers will view the announcement skeptically at first. The flow from the United States to Indonesia may later increase, but if it does not, Indonesia may take a further step to convince U.S. savers of its sincerity. Indonesia's government could set up a fund to pay the damages and legal costs that foreign investors might incur. As part of the same act, Indonesia could stipulate that commercial disputes be mediated by arbitrators known for their impartiality. The arbitrators could be internationally recognized teams of judges and technical experts, and the venue for dispute resolution could be The Hague or Switzerland. Indonesia would, in effect, bypass its legal system to attract foreign investment. Indonesia would not be acknowledging that its courts are biased in favor of locals. It would only be making a practical response to outsiders' fears of bias. The impartial arbitrators would control disbursements from the legal defense fund. They would have full discretion to pay foreign investors' damages and legal costs, if they found that the foreign investors were injured.

Once this dispute-resolution and compensation arrangement is in place, and U.S. investors know it, money should move into Indonesia.

The fund to compensate foreign investors would not need to be very large. Investors would compare the size of the fund to the amount of foreign investment in the country, but they would look more carefully at how the fund was replenished.

For example, suppose that the initial amount in the fund is 1% of the value of the farms in Indonesia. This amount might seem too small to neutralize foreigners' fears. But consider that foreigners would not buy all the farms in Indonesia. If they bought 5% of the farms, the compensation fund would look large from their point of view, because it would hold an amount equal to 20% of their aggregate investment (1%/5% = 20%).

Therefore, the compensation fund does not have to be very large at first. It would work very well from the beginning, because of being large relative to the amount of investment. It would work especially well after the first test case that a foreigner won. If the arbitrators decided a case in favor of the foreign investor, and promptly paid the judgment, the fund would be validated. Foreign investment would flow quickly after that.

At that point foreign investors' attention would focus on how the fund grows. A tax on land transfers is the obvious way to replenish the fund and make it grow fast enough to cover the rapidly rising amount of foreign investment. Local elites should favor creating a fund and building up the amount in the fund, because the larger the fund, the more foreign investment will come in. They should be willing to pay a tax on land transfers in order to keep the fund growing. To see why they should favor such a tax, consider a rich person in Indonesia who owns 10 farms. The Indonesian sells one of them to a foreign investor. Then a local dispute breaks out and the foreign investor's claim is attacked. The dispute goes to the international arbitrators in The Hague.

If the arbitration procedure does not exist, the Indonesian landowner's other nine farms are less valuable. They can be sold only to locals. No foreigner will pay very much for them. Also, if the arbitration procedure exists but the compensation fund does not have enough money in it, foreigners will lower their bids to protect themselves against the risk. If the fund has enough in it and has a track record of paying when a foreigner's case has merit, then foreigners will bid more.

A numerical illustration will show how much local landowners would gain. The farms in Indonesia start out being worth $4,500 each. After financial wealth increases, they rise in value to $22,000. If the bias against foreign investors has been completely eliminated, they rise further, to at least $42,000. Now consider the Indonesian landowner who begins with 10 farms. These are worth $4,500 each, for a total of $45,000. The landowner sells one farm for $4,500. Of this amount, suppose the landowner has to pay 1%, or $45, into the compensation fund.

What does paying this tax buy the landowner? The value of the nine remaining farms goes up as the compensation fund gets larger. The market value of the remaining farms rises from $4,500 each toward $6,000 each. Suppose that the payment into the fund is too small to make the value of the landowner's farms rise very much. Suppose their value rises only to $4,600 each. The increase in value is still very large compared to the amount of tax the landowner paid. The increase would be ($4600 − $4500) × 9 = $900. This is 20 times the tax paid.

After financial wealth increases, the effect of paying a tax into the compensation fund is much greater. After wealth has risen, the landowner's farms are worth $22,000 each. If foreigners trust the guarantee mechanism, the market value of the farms would be higher, potentially as high as $42,000 each. Again, suppose that the payment into the fund is too small to make the value of the farms rise very much. Suppose their value rises only to $23,000 each. The increase in value is now immense in comparison to the amount of tax the landowner paid. The increase in value is ($23,000 − $22,000) × 9 = $9,000. This is 200 times the tax paid.

Conclusion

This chapter notes that it is now technically feasible to track ownership of all income-producing assets and questions why tracking systems have not been thoroughly modernized everywhere. The discussion reviews a conventional answer, namely that local elites benefit from opaque rules of ownership.

Opaque rules keep foreign capital out. Local rich people have no reason to clarify the rules unless they want to sell their properties. If all they want to do is operate their properties, they keep the rules murky and discriminate against foreign investors. These policies maintain the high returns they earn on their capital.

The new reality is that the market values of the properties matter much more than the annual yield an owner can earn from operating them. The massive increase in financial wealth has showered capital gains on property owners everywhere. Local landowners now have a very compelling reason to favor clear rules of ownership and equal treatment for foreigners. These policies raise the market value of their properties.

A simple numerical illustration shows how much a landowner's capital gains can be, and how much effect ownership restrictions can have on property values. The illustration shows how much a country can suffer and how much a country can benefit. The illustration shows how much a country can gain by leveling the playing field so that foreigners participate to their fullest potential.

The computations also show that sovereignty can have a cost. Local owners can get more for their properties if sovereign prerogatives are set aside. This sobering result is not surprising in the context of the numerical example. Some may be disturbed, however, by one result of the calculations: Rules that favor local owners in disputes with foreign investors hold property prices down. This is obvious, but the magnitudes are greater than many readers might guess. At the beginning, before financial wealth increases, favoritism holds local property prices down by about a quarter. Later, after financial wealth has increased, favoritism hurts more; it holds down local property prices by almost a half.

What is perhaps even more distressing is another result of the calculations: Favoritism raises property prices in the country that gives equal treatment to foreigners. Favoritism in one part of the world showers greater capital gains on property owners in another part of the world where foreign investors receive equal treatment.

To put the most salient result succinctly: Favoritism reduces the wealth of the group it tries to benefit and enriches the group it tries to injure.

Chapter 10

Nation-States Come to Terms with the World Capital Market

The worldwide debate over international portfolio investment has become heated and polarized. Every informed person is suddenly feeling the pressure to take a position: Are the economies of the world to be opened to financial inflows and outflows? Or are they somehow to be insulated from these awesome waves of money, which roll in and then capriciously roll out again? Mainstream media correctly give high priority to the issue, but incorrectly portray it as bipolar.

The New Prodigy Intrudes

Portfolio investment used to be important only to a few experts who debated its arcane controversies among themselves. Economic theory did not rate portfolio investment very highly as a prime mover. Portfolio investment was *accommodating*, meaning that it balanced out the deficits and surpluses that trade in real goods and services left. A country with a trade surplus would invest its surplus cash in a country with a trade deficit.

Then, suddenly, portfolio investment arrived on the scene as the new prodigy. It tiptoed to center stage, then elbowed aside older geopolitical

John Marthinsen coauthored this chapter.

and macroeconomic prime movers. Indeed, its power has apparently been great enough to redefine the main objective of economic policy in the United States. U.S. economic policy has lately aimed to raise the value of financial assets. This objective has not been stated explicitly, but has nevertheless been achieved.

The challenge for nation-states is to take advantage of the new prodigy's power to create wealth, while keeping their autonomy and their own priorities intact. The threat for nation-states is that they might fall under the control of the new prodigy and lose control of their policy agenda. This chapter summarizes the arguments for giving unfettered welcome to portfolio investment, and the arguments for restricting its entry, or blocking it completely. It also assesses the feasibility of each set of policies. It then proposes a set of policies that uses financial engineering to bring the benefits of openness to countries while holding at bay the volatility that it usually brings.

United States as Shining Exemplar— and Lender of Last Resort?

The United States's success in raising the market value of its bonds and common stocks has become the new metric of economic performance. Countries that are not performing well economically are exhorted to enrich their citizens through share ownership. The United States's claim to legitimacy as an exemplar of economic policy has been its long stretch of real growth, propelled by its ever-rising financial wealth. The United States's resurgence has been driven by the high returns that its companies deliver to the holders of their securities. The investments in new production facilities and equipment, and the corporate restructuring and downsizing, did not themselves generate prosperity. Corporate profits went up, but the payrolls of the Fortune 500 went down. The payoff came in the stock and bond markets. Every dollar of after-tax corporate profits went from being worth $9 in 1982 to being worth $25 in 1999.

The trick of multiplying financial wealth does not look difficult, now that the United States has shown how to do it. Consequently, other countries are trying it, though not so wholeheartedly. Some are trying to grow the old-fashioned way, and hoping that their stock markets will go up only as much as the country's accomplishments merit. Every country fears a bubble and its aftermath.

Before countries are willing to take the leap, they have to feel sure that there is a safety net. They forego the golden dream of new inflows of portfolio investment if there is no lender of last resort. Panic selling happens too often, and bailouts are too hard to get. Too many countries have needed a bailout and could not get one. The International Monetary Fund (IMF)'s resources are not large enough to meet the need, and that leaves only Uncle Sam's massively thick checkbook. Countries are aware that Uncle Sam does not like to do bailouts—and they are painfully aware that after a panic a country's gleaming new office towers, showpiece factories, and five-star resorts fall into the hands of vulture investors—so they hesitate before embarking on the new path to riches. It looks too much like a high-speed expressway with no guard rails.

Reasons to Hesitate

In countries outside the United States, the chorus of opposition to opening financial markets has grown. There are convincing reasons to hold the prodigy at the gates: The wealth is paper; it accrues disproportionately to the rich; and investors turn a blind eye to destruction of the environment, circumvent and subvert democratic institutions, demean traditional cultures and trades, and displace native peoples from their homelands. Some examples of countries that have rejected full openness include Chile, Malaysia, China, and India. All have achieved high, or at least respectable, growth rates without opening their financial markets completely.

Meanwhile, protagonists of openness are banging the drum. Every country has to be for or against; they assert that there is no Third Way—in fact, that there is no Second Way—countries either must embrace economic openness or fall into obscurity, isolation, poverty, and backwardness. At the other extreme, protagonists of autonomy assert the value of traditional cultures, and talk of preserving the dignity of work and of keeping workers in contact with the finished product; they reject elitism and American triumphalism and advocate keeping local autonomy; and they seek to insulate the local economy from the financial market raiders, the gnomes of Zurich, and the caprices of speculators half a world away. Both sides deride anyone who does not want to take a side. But is it so untenable not to decide? Is the issue such a stark either-or? Is there no way for countries to get the benefits of portfolio investment while insulating themselves from the volatility?

Points in Favor of Opening Financial Markets

The main point in favor of opening markets is that it creates wealth. Countries open up to portfolio investment and attempt to attract it, because when it comes in, it raises the market value of all the income-producing properties in the country. Its arrival raises the market prices of common stocks and bonds directly, by adding to the local demand. The value of other assets rises because for some investors they are substitutes for the stocks and bonds that already went up. Also, local interest rates go down, so buyers can pay more for income-producing properties. For a numerical illustration, consider a country whose annual gross national product (GNP) is worth $15 billion. Prior to the inflow of foreign portfolio investment, the country's capital stock is 20% securitized. The unsecuritized portion of the capital stock is worth 2 times the annual value of its output, and the securitized portion is worth 3 times the annual value of its output. So the unsecuritized assets have a market value of $24 billion (80% × $15 billion × 2), and the securitized portion has a market value of $9 billion (20% × $15 billion × 3). Assume that before foreign portfolio investment comes in, all the securities and unsecuritized assets belong to local citizens.

Now suppose that $1 billion of foreign portfolio investment comes into the country's market. This new money buys part of the outstanding securities, pushing their value up. Suppose that the original $9 billion of securities consists of bonds with a market value of $6 billion and common stocks with a market value of $3 billion. And suppose that half of the $1 billion of new money goes to bonds and half goes to common stocks. How much would this buying drive up the prices of stocks and bonds? Assuming that the sellers of bonds used the money they got to buy other local bonds, the $6 billion of bonds would now be worth $6.5 billion. The foreign investors would own $0.5 billion of bonds, and the original local owners would own bonds worth $6 billion in the market. The price of the average bond would have risen ($6.5 billion/$6 billion) − 1 = 8.33%. So a local owner who did not sell would have experienced a 8.33% windfall gain.

The gain for common stockholders would be greater, because part of the common stock is held in control blocks, so less than half of it is available in the free float. The foreign buyers would be spending $0.5 billion, and no more than $1.5 billion of common stock would be available. Again assuming that the sellers of common stock used the money they got to buy other common stock, the $1.5 billion of free float would rise in value to $2 billion. This is a 33% increase in the market value of common stock. A local owner of common stock who happened to be asleep when the foreign money arrived would awaken to find that his or her holdings had become 33% more valuable.

The effect that this upvaluation would have on the market prices of unsecuritized assets depends on how suitable they are as collateral for securities that might be issued in the near future. Prices of farmland might not go up as much as prices of luxury hotels or television stations, but all asset prices would rise. If all of them rose as much as 10%, it would bring a total increase in wealth of $2.4 billion + $0.5 billion + $0.5 billion + $0.5 billion = $3.9 billion. This is $3.9 billion/$15 billion = 16% of annual GNP. The increase in wealth is also, in this example, 3.9 times the amount of the inflow of foreign portfolio investment.

This simple example illustrates the power of international portfolio investment. No additions to capacity have been built, nor has there been any increase in output. There has been no belt-tightening, no forced savings, nor any improvement in human capital. Nevertheless, owners of assets have received a windfall worth 16% of annual GNP. A country in the midst of an old-fashioned economic miracle would not achieve an increase in real output this large. Indeed, an increase half as large would be impressive, if it were obtained the old-fashioned way.

Other points in favor of opening need to be noted, but they are less dramatic. Allocation of savings becomes more efficient; local entrepreneurs get more access to capital; jobs trickle down; and U.S., Euroland, and Japanese Boomers earn higher returns, solving their retirement-income dilemma. Local citizens get greater access to information.

The Main Sticking Point against Opening Financial Markets

The biggest reason to stay closed is that boom is followed by bust. Violent swings in the value of local financial assets and local currency happen frequently and suddenly, without prior warning, and often without the country itself having done anything to deserve the dispossession it suffers. The prosperity is real while it lasts, but so is the cold, nauseous feeling of helplessness after a crash. That is when the regrets and recriminations come forth. The country realizes it has lost local autonomy and sovereignty. Foreigners second-guess its economic policies and loudly query why the country does not dollarize completely.

After a crash, local technocrats look like stooges. Demagogues berate them for trying to remake the country in the image of the United States. The wealth gap remains wide, but now everyone is poorer, and the poor fall deeper into misery. The job market dries up, and the few jobs on offer are demeaning. Young graduates emigrate.

The Feasibility of Blocking the Entry of Portfolio Investment

Countries have achieved high real economic growth without inflows of foreign investment. There are numerous cases of countries that have achieved growth rates of output in excess of 5% per year without inflows of capital from abroad. These "bootstrap" cases have common elements: a high savings rate, sometimes imposed by the state; a mechanism for assigning these savings to productive uses; restrictions on travel; and effective controls to prevent capital flight. Savings need to be applied to developing human capital and building factories and infrastructure, and capacity-building needs to be balanced at every level, from extraction to production to distribution. The task is difficult, but many countries have been able to do it for decades at a time.

Countries trying to grow without inflows of portfolio investment will not experience astronomical rises in the market prices of income-producing properties. Prices of income-producing assets will not rise spectacularly, because huge increases in the demand for them will not occur. Indeed, asset prices may stagnate if savings cannot be held within the country. Keeping local savings within a country has always been difficult and now is harder than ever. Telecommunications advances make it easier to evade or to arbitrage any restrictions on cross-border transactions that a government may impose. But again, it can be done.

The key question is not whether a government can bootstrap its country's economic growth. Clearly, a determined government that is in firm control of all economic activity in its territory can do so. The key question concerns the relative growth rates: not relative growth rates of real output, and not growth rates compared across countries. Those are not very different in the countries that restrict access and in the ones that do not. The key question concerns the relative growth rates of financial wealth owned by the middle class, upper class, and wealthy class in each country. In the countries that allow cross-border portfolio investment, asset owners gain. The poor do not become worse off in absolute terms, but in relative terms they definitely suffer. So the key question is political: In economic policy decisions, will the owners of income-producing properties be able to outweigh all the groups who will lose? If the wealthy have more clout and are able to push open the country's capital markets, they will soon be wealthier, and they may have enough new wealth to influence the economic decision-making process yet further. The losers will have to respond quickly, to regain the upper hand in setting economic policy, or their economic clout will fall farther in relative terms.

Now suppose that a country has decided to prevent capital from entering or leaving; it is attempting to grow economically by producing and trading goods instead of financial assets. This decision brings the country face to face with a classic dilemma: What goods will the country produce that can deliver enough growth in added value? The amount of growth has to be enough to compete with the wealth creation that international portfolio investment offers. Commodities do not meet the need, because commodity prices have been stagnant since 1979. The country cannot produce low-technology manufactures and hope to achieve enough growth. In the wake of the capacity-building boom of the 1980s and 1990s and the Asian slowdown, the prices of low-technology manufactures have been under pressure.

So the country would have to produce high-technology manufactures or services. Otherwise, it would not be able to deliver enough real growth. And it would have to be very successful, because even a country that does only moderately well at attracting foreign portfolio investment can deliver more wealth to property owners. So even moderately successful real growth, as a substitute for financial wealth creation, would gradually lose credibility and legitimacy.

The conclusion may be unpleasant, but it is hard to escape, because the capital markets are like a volcano that keeps spewing out money. Countries can keep portfolio investment out and still bootstrap their way to economic growth. This path, however, was never easy, and with each passing year it becomes more difficult. There were always many ways to fail on this path. Now there is a new one: All a country has to do now to fail is have a recession, or a year of slow growth. Then people will ask why the country went to so much trouble to keep out foreign portfolio invest-ment. The bootstrap path has to prove itself over and over again. As soon as it falters, the pundits will be calling for a switch to openness. So the dif-ficult choice grows more difficult. The temptation to choose the easy route is always there, and it gets stronger as world financial wealth grows. The easy route to wealth is the quick route. The next section questions whether the quick route has to be so dangerous.

Getting the Inflows without the Volatility

The deterrents to taking the quick and easy path to financial wealth are the panics and the loss of sovereignty. With the market arrangements that now exist, panics are too frequent and capricious. Countries lose sover-eignty without getting enough prosperity to compensate for it. The fol-lowing sections propose a simple modification of market arrangements that will go a long way toward preventing the panics.

Most countries seek capital inflows and are usually willing to take whatever money comes in, without restricting the terms that private par-ties can agree to. The foreign portfolio investor usually expects to be able to liquidate and repatriate on one to five days' notice. Volatility, from the foreign portfolio investor's point of view, is the shrinkage that can occur if the investor sells during a panic.

The suggestion here is to design securities and trading protocols that can accommodate a wave of selling without draining all the central bank's foreign exchange holdings. The arrangement proposed here buffers the cen-tral bank's foreign exchange holdings from runs. It does not seal the central bank's reserves off completely. Those reserves can still deteriorate, but only if the country's economic policies cause a chronic shortage of foreign ex-change. The designed securities and trading protocols will not prevent a sudden, groundless wave of panic selling. Nor will they protect the country from investors' wrath completely. But what they will do is partially shield the country from the market's unpleasant tendency to overreact.

Defects of the Current Design

Most of the securities that foreign portfolio investors currently buy have a serious defect: They allow *flowback* to occur. That is, when the foreign portfolio investor sells, there is an immediate drain on the country's for-eign exchange holdings. There are several types of securities that have this defect. The infamous Tesebonos of the 1994 "tequila shock" case are the most obvious example. These bonds offered a high yield, but they were denominated in pesos and were linked to dollars at a fixed exchange rate—so, in effect, they were dollar liabilities of the Mexican Treasury. When foreign investors panicked and insisted on cashing them in, the entire amount of Tesebonos outstanding had to be paid promptly in dollars. The Mexican Treasury did not have enough dollars to honor all of the Tesebonos. The total outstanding amount of dollar-denominated obligations had often been greater than the Mexican Treasury's foreign exchange holdings. Prior to the devaluation of 1994, this had not been a problem, because most investors would, in effect, trade their expiring Tesebonos for new ones that would expire later. But when the holders panicked, they all wanted dollars at the same time, and the Mexican Treasury could not cope. Since 1994, governments have paid much closer attention to the due dates before selling dollar-linked bonds, and many have sworn off issuing this type of security.

The most widespread designs today are open-ended mutual funds and American or Global Depositary Receipts. Each has the same flowback defect. When the foreigner redeems shares of a mutual fund or sells an American Depositary Receipt (ADR), it triggers a sale of the issuer's stock on the issuer's home stock exchange. The local-currency proceeds from that sale then have to be converted to dollars, and the dollars repay the foreign investor.

With these mechanisms in such widespread and rapidly growing use, any country is vulnerable to a run on its currency. For a country to be bulletproof against a run, its central bank has to have foreign exchange holdings greater than the total amount of claims that can be presented for payment in foreign exchange. Most central banks do not have that much foreign exchange. When financial writers compare the amount of foreign exchange that a central bank holds to the bonds that are due for payment in the next 12 months, the disparity is disturbing. But the true amount of the disparity is even worse than the figures that skeptics bandy around. The true amount of dollar-denominated claims that can be presented is larger by the dollar value of outstanding ADRs and the value of shares that foreign open-ended mutual funds own. Technically, all these shares could be liquidated, and payment for them could be demanded in foreign exchange.

A numerical illustration shows how disturbing these magnitudes can be. Consider an emerging country that owes $40 billion to banks, including the IMF and the World Bank. It also has sold dollar-denominated Eurobonds totaling $10 billion. Its central bank has $14 billion of foreign exchange reserves. The usual coverage ratio that experts would cite is as follows:

$$\text{Coverage} = \frac{\$14 \text{ billion}}{\$40 \text{ billion} + \$10 \text{ billion}}$$

This indicates that the country has a safe amount of foreign exchange, because the maturity dates of the debt extend over several years, and the amount falling due in the next year is less than $14 billion.

The situation is more precarious than this calculation indicates, however. Suppose that all the country's local investors are comfortable with their holdings and will not panic. Also suppose that the total value of listed stocks on the country's stock exchange is $60 billion. Foreigners own 40% of this stock, or $24 billion worth. They hold this stock in the form of ADRs that they bought on the New York Stock Exchange and via U.S. open-ended mutual funds.

Now suppose the foreign stockholders panic and the local investors do not. The foreigners sell. Their selling automatically generates sales of local currency for dollars. The total amount of dollars the foreigners could demand is $24 billion. They will not get that much because their selling will quickly drain the central bank's foreign exchange holdings. Their selling will also cause a local stock market crash, because local investors will not be able to buy all the common stock that will be sold, except at lower prices. So the emerging country's stock market will crash and its exchange rate will also weaken or collapse. The coverage ratio calculation should look like this:

$$\text{Coverage ratio} = \frac{\$14 \text{ billion}}{\$40 \text{ billion} + \$10 \text{ billion} + \$24 \text{ billion}}$$

This more realistic coverage ratio is obviously much more precarious.

This refines the earlier description of the dilemma that central banks face. The types of securities and trading protocols that allow flowback force central banks to deal with an impossible dilemma. If they allow money to come in via ADRs and open-ended mutual funds, they will have to decide what to do with the foreign exchange. If they let private individuals have it, the central bank's holdings of foreign exchange will fall below the amount of potential claims. The central bank can keep the foreign exchange and give the local private individuals its equivalent in local currency, but this will destabilize the country's money supply. In either case, the country will lose a big part of the advantage of having attracted the money from foreigners.

The fault lies in the trading protocol that gives the foreign investor instant liquidity. Liquidity has a cost, and the current trading protocol masks that cost. For open-ended mutual funds, it masks the cost by mingling relatively liquid securities with others that are much more vulnerable. U.S. middle-class savers know that in every country there are blue-chip stocks that will hold up better in a panic, but they do not have an easy way of judging how well each of the stocks that are in an open-ended mutual fund's portfolio will fare in a panic. For ADRs, the current trading protocol masks the cost of liquidity because the investor does not routinely find out how much of the free float is held by foreigners. So a U.S. middle-class saver investing in an emerging country does not get an accurate impression of how vulnerable those holdings might be to a broad decline in the country's stock market.

The offer of instant liquidity combines with the uncertainty about how vulnerable the holdings might be. The result is an explosive combination. Foreign portfolio investors know that if there is a panic, every security in a country's market has the same right to grab foreign exchange. Whoever sells first gets local currency and then rushes to convert it to dollars. Then when there is no foreign exchange left at the central bank, all the rest of the sellers get only local currency, or they buy dollars in the street at worse and worse rates.

The cost of instant liquidity can consequently be very high. The high cost falls on the investors, who demand high returns for bearing the cost, and it falls on any country that suffers a panic. How many investors really insist on instant liquidity? How many of them really do need to be able to sell and force the conversion of the proceeds back to dollars on a moment's notice? Today's trading protocol implicitly assumes that all investors insist on being able to get back to dollars on short notice.

There should be no masking the cost of liquidity and no illusions about how liquid each security is. In an emerging country's stock market there should be securities that offer guaranteed instant liquidity, convertibility, and repatriation. There should also be other securities that are identical to the ones with guaranteed liquidity except that they offer lesser degrees of liquidity. Foreign portfolio investors then would weigh the cost of liquidity against their individual needs for it. They could then make an intelligent allocation among securities that have guaranteed liquidity, partially guaranteed liquidity, and no guarantee of liquidity.

Securities Engineered for Liquidity and Clarity

The types of securities and trading protocols that allow flowback do not have to retain the dominant position they have in the markets of so many countries. They can be replaced by securities that control flowback and make the liquidity-versus-return trade-off more explicit. The securities proposed here are engineered to put the cost of liquidity clearly in front of the investor's eyes. They are only slight modifications of the securities that currently exist. They are intended to be superior to the ones that currently exist. They are intended to meet the needs of investors, issuers, investment bankers, and other intermediaries. They are a slight reengineering and repackaging of the existing securities. Countries and issuers can easily adopt the design proposed here, and the issuing country should then be less vulnerable to financial panics and runs on its currency.

These engineered securities will be the same as the stocks and bonds that already exist in the stock markets of most emerging countries, with one added document: a liquidity guarantee that comes in four variants. These four variants would be like credit enhancements, but they would be explicitly aimed at giving four levels of assurance that there will always be a liquid market for the security.

Market participants are already familiar with enhancements. Credit enhancements are widely used, especially in the municipal bond market. An issuer who is weak or unknown buys a credit guarantee from a strong outside party, such as a Swiss insurance company, and then is able to place bonds without having to pay a very high interest rate. The credit enhancement says that if the issuer does not pay the security when it is due, the guarantor will.

The enhancement proposed here is different. It is only a guarantee that there will be a liquid market for the security. The liquidity guarantee says that if the market for the security is suspended because of a foreign exchange crisis, the guarantor will buy the security. Later, the guarantor will sell the security back to the owner for a prearranged price.

Here are some distinctions between a credit enhancement and a liquidity guarantee. A credit enhancement bolsters the weak issuer; it does not insure against any set of macroeconomic conditions that would close an entire country's securities market. A credit enhancement enters into effect if the issuer's finances have deteriorated so much that the issuer is unable to make payments due on the security. It attracts investors who question whether the issuer will be solvent in the future; they rely on the guarantor's strong balance sheet. A liquidity guarantee bolsters the shaky, erratic local securities market; it does not ensure that the issuer's affairs will go well enough to pay the security. A liquidity guarantee enters into effect only if the local supply of foreign exchange dries up, local regulators place new restrictions on convertibility, or local securities trading volume dries up. A liquidity guarantee provides a temporary market for the security.

In its pure form, the liquidity guarantee says that the guarantor will buy the security, hold it for some agreed length of time, and then deliver it back to the owner. For example, suppose there is a bond with a liquidity guarantee. The bond trades at $1,000 every day for several months. Then there is a crisis, and the owner of the bond wants to sell but cannot find a buyer. So the owner invokes the liquidity guarantee, which states that the guarantor will buy the bond for 90% of its average price during the previous three months. Accordingly, the owner sells the bond to the guarantor for $900. Then, four months later, the crisis has ended, the market has reopened, and the bond is once again worth $1,000. The owner now calls up the guarantor and buys the bond back for $900. The owner then sells it for $1,000 as he or she had originally intended to do. Alternatively, suppose that the crisis goes on longer than the period the liquidity guarantee covers. When the time period has elapsed, the owner has to buy the bond from the guarantor for $900.

This example should make clear that in its pure form the liquidity guarantee only provides continuity to the market for the security, and not credit enhancement to the issuer. In the example, if the market had reopened but the bond were only worth $700, the owner would have had to buy it back from the guarantor for $900.

Having seen what a liquidity guarantee is and how it works, let us move on to the details of the proposed design. Every time an issuer in an emerging country sells securities, the issuer should package the securities with four different liquidity guarantees. Each security would exist in four variants. One of the guarantees would be very strong, the second one would be weaker, the third would be weaker still, and the fourth would be the weakest. Investors would buy the security with the liquidity guarantee that they want at the time when the securities are issued. The four different liquidity guarantees would have different price tags. The strongest guarantee would be most expensive, and the weakest would be cheapest. The strongest guarantee would be provided by an external guarantor with a strong credit rating—for example, a Swiss insurance company. The weaker types of guarantee would not offer the same certainty of instant liquidity, but they would not cost as much.

The four different liquidity guarantees would be letters and associated documents that the buyer would get along with the stock or bond itself. Each set of documents would describe how the plan assures that the owner can convert the security into dollars.

Example of a Bond Issue with Liquidity Guarantees

Suppose that an electric utility company in Brazil wants to issue five-year Eurobonds in the amount of $500 million. Current practice is that the issuer will wait until the market has an appetite for the paper, and will then place it. The buyers may not intend to keep the paper long, or they may be optimistic about Brazil's prospects, so they do not insist on a bulletproof scheme for liquidating the paper. In particular, they analyze the issuer's prospects carefully and convince themselves that the issuer will easily be able to repay the bonds, even though they are denominated in dollars. They also analyze Brazil's capacity to repay foreign-currency-denominated liabilities. Then they demand a risk premium large enough to cover the risks that the issuer will default and that the Brazilian Central Bank will have no foreign currency available when the bonds mature.

The change proposed here is to divide the $500 million issue into four tranches and package each tranche with a different guarantee. Here are examples of four guarantees:

- One tranche would be packaged with a guarantee from a strong third-party guarantor—for example, a Swiss insurance company. This guarantee would be expensive because it would allow the holder of the bond to sell it to the guarantor whenever the market for the bond is illiquid. The guarantor will buy the bond for 90% of its face value, keep it for one year, and then sell it back to the owner for the same price.

- A second tranche would be packaged with an inferior guarantee from a strong third-party guarantor. For example, the guarantor would buy the bond for 80% of its face value and hold it for only six months before selling it back to the owner.
- A third tranche would be packaged with a guarantee from the Brazilian Central Bank that foreign exchange would be available on scheduled dates. For example, the Brazilian Central Bank would arrange a standby letter of credit guaranteeing that dollars will be on hand to honor those bonds on those dates. That is, if a local Brazilian investor wants to buy those bonds on those dates, the Brazilian central bank will exchange the local investor's local currency for dollars, so that the foreign investor can sell to the local investor and get dollars for the bonds. The guarantee would cover only the specified dates—for example, May 1 and November 1 of each year. If a liquidity crisis occurs at some other time of year and the holder wants to sell, the holder would not get any relief until the date when the guarantee is scheduled to allow the conversion into dollars.
- The fourth tranche would be packaged with no guarantee, only a letter from the Brazilian central bank saying that it is aware that the bonds exist. The letter might also say that the Brazilian central bank will attempt to provide dollars when the seller happens to demand them.

These four tranches would obviously have four different levels of liquidity risk. The safest are the tranches packaged with third-party guarantees. The fourth tranche is the riskiest because there is no assurance that there will be dollars to convert it, only a "comfort letter" saying that the Brazilian central bank acknowledges that the bond exists and will try to have dollars available to honor it.

Each tranche would have a different yield to the buyer. The issuer would have to pay for the guarantees, and would also pay the Brazilian central bank for the cost of the standby letter of credit. The total cost of the issue could be lower, because the buyer's risk is reduced. The cost of the liquidity enhancements can be lower than the risk premium that would have to be paid to place the bonds.

To see what each tranche would yield, suppose that the Brazilian electric utility pays 11% per year to borrow the $500 million. Suppose also that five-year U.S. Treasury bonds yield 6%, so the Brazilian issuer is paying 5% per year more than the U.S. Treasury to borrow dollars. This 5% is the risk premium; it covers the risk that the Brazilian utility will fail, and also the risk that the Brazilian central bank will not have enough dollars for the utility to buy to make payments to bondholders. Suppose that the fees for each guarantee scheme are as follows:

- The strongest guarantee costs 2% per year, so the tranche with the strongest guarantee yields 9% to the holder (11% − 2% = 9%).
- The lesser guarantee costs 1% per year, so the tranche with the lesser guarantee yields 10% to the holder (11% − 1% = 10%).
- The standby letter of credit costs 0.5% a year, so the third tranche yields 10.5% to the holder (11% − 0.5% = 10.5%).
- The comfort letter costs nothing, so the fourth tranche yields 11% to the holder (11% − 0 = 11%).

This four-tranche design takes much of the pressure off the Brazilian central bank's foreign exchange holdings. Consider what happens if foreign portfolio investors totally lose confidence in Brazil. Assume that no foreign buyer is willing to buy the bonds for dollars at any price. With these liquidity guarantees in place, the entire bond issue would not flow back into the hands of local Brazilian investors, and the Brazilian central bank would face immediate demands for foreign exchange for only a half or a quarter of the face amount of the issue. The guarantees would spread the demand for foreign exchange over a longer period of time, and the Brazilian central bank would be able to cope with the total demand more easily.

Let us see tranche by tranche how the holders would react, and see how the liquidity guarantees would buffer the pressure on the Brazilian central bank's foreign exchange holdings. Assume that before the panic, all four tranches were trading in the market at 100% of face value. Also assume that the panic affected only the availability of foreign exchange and did not cast doubt on the Brazilian utility's survival. When the panic began, the market prices of all four tranches would fall by different amounts. The bonds with the third-party guarantees would continue to trade, and their price would hold up well. The tranche supported by the standby letter of credit would also continue to trade, and its price would hold up well unless panicky investors doubted that the Brazilian central bank would use the stan dby letter of credit to honor the bonds. The fourth tranche would be ravaged. The holders of the fourth tranche, who are presumed to be panicked, would cash out at any price, selling for local currency, then take a second haircut when they converted the local currency to dollars. The fourth tranche, which has only the comfort letter as its guarantee of liquidity, would flow back into the hands of local Brazilian investors; by assumption, they would be the only buyers as long as the panic lasted. But they would pay in local currency. The prices they would pay would be very low, so a foreign holder who insisted on selling during the panic might suffer a loss of 80% or more in dollars depending on how severe the panic was.

The important point is that investors have protection, so they do not dump huge blocks of bonds into a market where there are only a few bidders. Trading does not come to a halt. There are buyers who are willing to take the gamble that the Brazilian crisis will pass. Sellers can cash out if they need to, and they lose much less because the guarantees work. The Brazilian central bank also benefits because sellers will take refuge in the third-party guarantees. If those guarantees expire and the crisis is still going on, then selling will cause local currency to be presented to the Brazilian central bank for conversion into dollars.

The liquidity guarantees described here do not remove all the risks that foreign portfolio investors face in emerging markets. The Brazilian electric utility could still fail. Management might choose to locate generating plants where there was not enough demand for electricity, or fail to collect from its customers. These guarantees do not protect against that kind of risk. And they do not protect against a really prolonged market paralysis. They are not all-purpose palliatives, but they do isolate and illuminate the cost of liquidity.

In sum, the proposed design would allow the Brazilian issuing company to obtain the use of $500 million, without exposing the Brazilian central bank to the possibility of having to pay out $500 million on short notice.

Liquidity Guarantees for Common Stocks

There are advantages to putting in place similar guarantees for new issues of common stocks. Suppose that a Brazilian company is going to sell $100 million worth of common stock. The shares are denominated in Brazilian currency, and their primary listing is on the São Paulo stock exchange. Foreign buyers, however, figure prominently from the beginning. Eighty percent of the issue is going to be placed abroad, and foreign buyers will hold the stock via ADRs. The remaining $20 million will be placed with Brazilian investors.

If the stock is popular with foreigners, they will buy more ADRs. Brokers in São Paulo will buy shares from local investors to collateralize the ADRs. Those brokers will get dollars from the foreigners and will use the dollars to buy Brazilian currency to pay for the shares. This is the benign face of foreign portfolio investment.

What if there is a panic, and the foreign holders all want to sell? When they sell the ADRs, Brazilian brokers sell the underlying shares on the São Paulo stock exchange. Brazilian investors buy the shares at knocked-down prices, paying local currency. The brokers then take the Brazilian currency and try to get dollars for it.

What shock absorbers can prevent the panic selling from putting immediate pressure on the Brazilian central bank's holdings of dollars? A similar set of guarantees can be created for this hypothetical issue of common shares. To show the many types of guarantees, these are slight variations from the ones for the bond issue.

One quarter of the issue, or $25 million worth, could be packaged with a put option from an outside underwriter—for example, a Swiss insurance company. The guarantor would buy the ADRs for dollars at a prearranged price and would keep them for a prearranged length of time. The prearranged price could be 100% of the average market price for the preceding 30 days, and the prearranged length of time could be one year. After that, the outside guarantor would not sell the stock back to the previous owner. The guarantor would own it, and would be free to sell it in the market or hold it longer. Another quarter of the issue could be packaged with a put option that is not as good. The prearranged price might be only 90% of the average market price of the preceding 30 days. The length of time could be shorter. A third tranche could be packaged with a forward contract guaranteeing conversion of an amount of local currency into dollars. And the last quarter of the issue would have no guarantee.

Now with these guarantees in place, consider what happens if there is a panic. Assume that the panicky foreign investors all sell. The Swiss insurance company buys one-quarter of the $100 million issue at 100% of the prepanic price, and another quarter at 90% of the prepanic price. The Swiss insurance company then keeps the ADRs for the required length of time. Then, if the market has not recovered, it liquidates the position. This may involve selling the underlying shares on the São Paulo stock exchange and using the local currency to buy whatever amount of dollars it can. The ADR holders who have the forward contract also sell. They liquidate the underlying shares on the São Paulo stock exchange and then use the forward contract to convert the local currency into dollars. By assumption, the panicky investors who hold the tranche of ADRs that has no guarantee sell at distress prices to Brazilian investors for local currency, then use the local currency to buy dollars. The holders of the riskiest tranche lose most of their investment.

This shock-absorber mechanism provides some relief. Brazil takes in $80 million from foreign investors when the shares are placed. When a panic occurs, Brazil loses foreign exchange, but much less than it would have lost without the guarantees. The demand for foreign exchange is also staggered over a longer period of time.

The cost of these guarantees to investors might be low. Investors would give up some prospective return in exchange for greater safety. This scheme does not give much protection on the downside. Only one half of the issue has a guaranteed conversion to dollars at a stated price. Nevertheless, investors might be so comforted by the guarantee that they would be willing to accept a much lower expected yield. The issuing company in Brazil might find that the cost of using $100 million is lower when the issue is structured this way. The issuing company can pay the Swiss insurance company for the put option, and pay the shareholders their required return, and the total cost might be less than what shareholders would require if there were no guarantee.

Making the Transition

If all the securities offered by Brazil were structured in this fashion, it is clear that Brazil would be able to obtain the use of more foreign portfolio investment, while exposing itself less to financial panics. Foreign portfolio investors would also benefit, because they would earn lower returns in the aggregate, but would not have to tolerate the violent swings in yields that have plagued them. They would have a wider array of securities to choose from, ranging from securities with a third-party guarantee to securities as risky as the ones they now reluctantly hold.

Individual issuing companies can make this transition on their own. They can arrange the third-party guarantees, or ask their investment bankers to do it. Governments in emerging countries can also make the transition, by packaging their Treasury bonds with guarantees and urging local issuers to do the same. There is no need for unanimous compliance by all countries, nor by all issuers in a country.

To see why, consider two companies, one in Brazil and one in Mexico, each large enough and strong enough to place five-year Eurobonds in the amount of $500 million. Investor sentiment is positive enough that investors do not demand the design proposed here. Nevertheless, one of the companies goes to the trouble of issuing four tranches as proposed. The other issues a single tranche with no guarantees. Both bond issues are placed in the market at the same time. Other things being equal, the three guaranteed tranches of the four-tranche design will be bought in preference to the one-tranche design. The bonds that have guarantees are superior to the ones that do not.

The bonds with guarantees will be easier to sell unless investors think the guarantee is too expensive for the amount of protection it provides. Investors will probably prefer the guaranteed bonds. The reason is that insurance companies are good at assessing risk, and they compete with each other to write guarantees. Investors do not have as much time or expertise, and they have to be wary of risk, so the bond with no guarantee that yields 11% looks too risky to many investors and they do not buy it. They try to assess its risk, but they have to be risk averse. Then insurance companies look at the bond with no guarantee and compete to offer a liquidity enhancement. The price of the enhancement is 2%, creating a bond with a guarantee that yields 9%. The yield of 9% is 3% more than five-year U.S. Treasury bonds pay, so investors look at the bond once again. This time more of them buy it because the guarantee outweighs their wariness.

In the secondary market, the bonds with guarantees will probably maintain a price and quality advantage vis-à-vis the tranches that have no guarantee. As the amount of bonds with some guarantee increases, the outstanding issues that lack enhancements suffer. In effect, they become inferior goods, because their only claim on foreign exchange is the central bank's unstable holdings.

Pressure from investors will push issuers to refinance all outstanding securities, both bonds and stocks. The old-style securities will be cashed out and replaced with issues offering explicit degrees of insulation from the ups and downs of the central bank's foreign exchange holdings. The investors who want the risk of the old-style securities can still find them, and some small amounts may continue to be issued.

Conclusion

Countries are ambivalent as to whether they should open up to portfolio investment or fend it off. Defects in the current market arrangements for cross-border portfolio investment are a cause of their ambivalence. The easy path to prosperity is not through production; it is through revaluing the capital stock. Countries that open up to foreign portfolio investment can expect immediate windfall gains to owners of income-producing assets. Countries that remain closed to portfolio investment can grow their real economies but cannot obtain a dramatic increase in the market value of their capital stock. Countries that fend off portfolio investment face a relative decline in financial clout. They can produce goods and can deliver an adequate standard of living to their citizens, but their relative ranking in ownership of financial wealth will inexorably decline.

The current mechanisms of cross-border portfolio investment have worked well in one important respect, because they have made it safe for middle-class savers in the rich countries to invest abroad. But they have a major defect: They give investors the illusion of instant liquidity, and promise them they can sell and have dollars in a money-market fund at a moment's notice. This promise has inadvertently become an engine of destabilization. Two forms of cross-border ownership in particular are excessively potent as transmission mechanisms: open-ended mutual funds that invest in international stocks and bonds, and ADRs. Both can unwittingly precipitate sudden and enormous demands on a central bank's foreign exchange holdings. Those demands surge up too fast, propagate too easily to other countries, and do too much damage. Countries that import foreign portfolio investment must, in the present arrangement, import instability along with it. The financial press tracks each central bank's holdings of dollars and compares that figure to the amount of dollar-denominated debt that has to be refinanced during the upcoming time interval. The figures usually look disturbing, but the true situation is worse than the figures show, because all the common stocks that are held by foreigners via open-ended mutual funds and ADRs can potentially lead to demands for dollars, and no emerging country's holdings of dollars can be enough to meet these demands when panic breaks out.

To put the current dilemma in extreme terms, a country can import foreign portfolio investment, but if the country then uses the foreign exchange to finance growth and expansion, the foreign exchange will move out of the monetary authorities' reach. The country would then be vulnerable to a foreign exchange crisis later on. If the country does not use the foreign exchange, and instead holds it offshore in "sterilized" accounts, the country's central bank will be able to meet the demand for it if the foreign investors want it back on short notice. But the country would gain little benefit from having imported it.

Countries can obtain the benefit of foreign portfolio investment without importing as much instability as they do currently. Private insurance companies with strong balance sheets can create and sell enhancements for securities that are vulnerable to panics. This chapter describes one type of enhancement, namely liquidity guarantees of several sorts. These could be attached to stocks and bonds that companies in emerging countries issue. These liquidity guarantees would broaden the appeal of these securities and also keep panics from putting pressure on the central bank's holdings of foreign exchange. Issuing companies could buy these outside guarantees to make the securities they are selling more attractive. The guarantees would interpose a strong private insurer's credit between the demands of holders for foreign exchange and the central bank's reserves of foreign exchange.

Companies that issue securities, portfolio investors, financial institutions, and governments of emerging countries can all benefit from this transition. Any issuer of securities in a country that has a high country-risk premium can begin the transition. The issuer can ask for quotes for guarantees of the sort described in this chapter. Insurance companies and other financial intermediaries with strong credit ratings will reply with offers. The issuer can then test how easy it is to sell securities with and without the guarantees. For the issuer, the cost of issuing the securities with guarantees will often be lower than the cost of issuing them without the guarantees. After there are enough securities with guarantees in the market, market participants will become familiar with these types of securities and enhancements, and issuers that can benefit will start using guarantees. More capital will then move into the emerging countries.

Chapter 11

Potholes on the Road to Prosperity?

Not everyone is convinced that the world is on the express bus to prosperity. There are many who believe fervently that the bus is heading for a pileup. There are others who are dissatisfied because they feel that the rising wealth is worsening the quality of life for the great majority of the world's poor. Many also believe that world economic growth is destroying the environment so rapidly that we may already have passed the point of no return.[1] These critics have solid arguments on their side, and their arguments explain why the world has not moved even faster in the direction of financial wealth creation.

Controversies

Every new growth path has its disruptive and damaging side effects. When agriculture replaced hunting and gathering, humans had to tolerate and adapt to major changes in their routines of daily life. When the Industrial Revolution devoured the Midlands of England and sucked up the landless agricultural labor supply, it forced whole villages into oblivion and black-

Mark Potter coauthored this chapter. An earlier version appeared in *Marketing Intelligence and Planning*, vol. 17, no. 1 (U.K.: MCB University Press, 1999).

ened the skies with the belching of a thousand smokestacks. The present phenomenon, a growth path based not on raising output but more on increasing the market value of productive assets, does not apparently provoke destruction of a new sort. Instead, it intensifies and hastens the kind of damage associated with the growth path the world was previously on. That growth path was known as *industrial* or *postindustrial,* and its damaging effects are constantly in evidence. The new path has its own rhythms and forces, and it is important not to mistake it for its older cousin. The new path has more power and geographical reach than the earlier one had. Its power may contain the potential to do both good and evil. The new growth path does provoke polemics and controversy. For example, it generates inconceivable paper wealth, but keeps that wealth out of the reach of people who would like to redistribute it. The new prodigy also brushes away defenses that groups have set up against it, and at the same time ignores the appeals of people who are trying to attract it. This chapter touches on topics in the controversy, shows the compelling wealth-creation and signaling mechanisms that are fueling the controversy, and discusses how much difference there is between the new path and the earlier one.

The first point that must be noted is that the distribution of wealth is rapidly becoming more skewed. This accompanies and intensifies the widening gap in incomes. Data showing that the distribution of wealth and income is becoming more skewed abound. Data for the entire world show that the top quintile earned a higher percentage of total income in 1995 than in 1990. Data for the United States show a faster widening from 1995 onward. The widening of the income gap shows over longer time periods as well, but the spread has been accelerating in recent years. A few economic regions may buck the trend, but at larger levels of aggregation the pattern is quite robust. The United Nations found that in the United States the richest 1% of the population increased its share of the wealth from 20 to 36% from 1975 to 1990; since then the gap has continued to widen.[2]

The second point is that poor people all over the world are being drawn into the world trading economy. Some of them are working long hours in unhealthy conditions to produce goods that are consumed thousands of miles away. Evidence of child labor and exploitation of prisoners, women, minorities, and indigenous peoples is surfacing frequently. Many critics believe that access to markets in rich countries has worsened the lives of these people. Trade has strengthened the links and the incentives to recruit them, without creating any protections for them. Remote areas in the Third World used to be ignored but are now pulled into the supply chain. Previously these indigenous peoples lived in subsistence or were exploited by local elites. Long-distance exploitation is now feasible.

The third point is that environmental degradation is happening and may be accelerating. Scientific controversies on this point are ongoing, and the debate about them is on the front pages. The stakes are high, because some experts believe that the planet's capacity to sustain human life is quickly coming to an end.

This chapter addresses these three points. There are other controversies about the world's current growth path; for example, cultures are being undermined and overridden. This chapter does not touch on these other controversies directly. It addresses the first three points and seeks to put them into the framework of the world's current growth path of financial wealth creation. It shows how the current growth path encompasses each of the controversies, affects the parameters of each controversy, and creates the potential to remedy the disparities and destruction.

This chapter begins with a discussion of the growth of financial wealth held in tax-deferred, internationally diversified portfolios, to explain why the wealth and income gaps are widening. The discussion first lays out the forces that are causing the widening, then shows a mechanism that is causing further widening. The widening wealth gap is self-propelling and self-propagating. It also creates rising absolute living standards for the poor and for the emerging nations. This chapter shows that the cost of raising living standards for the world's poor is small compared to the magnitude of wealth creation. This chapter touches on the scientific controversy and discusses how much difference the stock market–driven wealth process makes in decisions about resource use or conservation. The stock market penalizes some acts that destroy future potential; it values future output, not just current output. It is also selective in awarding premiums.

The message of this chapter is hopeful but realistic. Financial wealth creation has gained strength very rapidly and has become self-reinforcing. It has widespread and growing support, and has the capability of remedying the three ills that this chapter addresses. The financial wealth creation process is charting its own course and is not seeking to remedy those three ills. It may remedy some or all of them, but before it does, it may worsen some of them. This chapter shows mechanisms and magnitudes and thereby tries to shed light on these three controversies.

Trends in Financial Markets and Their Role in Widening the Gap

The rapid growth of stock markets all over the world and the growth of cross-border portfolio investment are the new prime movers. Members of middle-class households, and those of the Baby Boomer generation in particular, have made saving a high priority. They have been willing to sacrifice current consumption during their working years. It is important to them individually but also to successive generations that they succeed in saving enough to pay for their retirements. If too many of them fail, younger generations will need to support them. The cost of supporting them would be, in some scenarios, too a heavy burden on the smaller Generation X and subsequent generations.

The higher the return they earn, the less they will need to save to achieve their objectives. A person who wants to spend $5,000 per month from ages 65 to 80 and leave a legacy of $100,000 has to save $1,371 per month from ages 40 to 65 if the real rate of return is 3% per year. If the rate of return is 6% per year, the person has to save only $882 per month. These figures are all in constant dollars. The heaviest savings years for the average middle-class worker are ages 40 to 65; Boomers are in the young end of that age range, as the first ones are just turning 54 in 2000. The cohort from the peak birth year, 1957, turns 43 in 2000. Individually, more than half of them are still not saving enough to pay for an adequate retirement. In the aggregate, however, their savings already are awesome, and rising. Their collective accumulation will probably peak between 2007 and 2012. If only half of the Boomers save an average of $1,000 a month and earn 8% a year, their savings would reach $55 trillion (in 1997 dollars) by 2012. This is an amount equal to almost 6 times the U.S. 1999 gross national product (GNP). If all the Boomers save an average of $1,000 a month and earn 14% a year, their savings would reach $159 trillion by the end of 2012. This is an amount equal to about 16 times the U.S. 1999 GNP.

Portfolio Investment Spilling Over into Foreign Stock Markets

This amount is obviously so large that it could not all be credibly invested in claims on the United States. Conventional valuation yardsticks use 5 times annual output as an upper limit for plausible valuation. If the role of the corporation in society has changed and is now primarily as a vehicle and repository for financial wealth, a higher multiple, for example 10, may be feasible. For that valuation to be attained, however, the social contract would have to be rewritten, and corporate profits would have to rise and stabilize at a higher percentage of GNP. It is not clear how much the U.S. social contract has been rewritten, however, so this discussion uses the conventional upper limit of 5 times annual output. The accumulated savings of the U.S. middle class can continue to rise rapidly, as investors move money from one professional manager to another, chasing higher yields. Each month's new infusions can continue to pour into U.S. securities markets, buying claims on U.S. assets, until U.S. valuations exceed the plausible range. If all the savings of the Boomer generation were to represent claims on U.S. assets, then U.S. output would have had to quadruple from 1997 to 2012 ($159 trillion/$32 trillion = approximately 5 times; $32 trillion/$8 trillion = 4 times). Although this could happen, a much more likely scenario is that some of the U.S. stock market wealth would spill over into buying stocks outside the United States. International portfolio diversification—that is, North Americans buying stocks in companies headquartered outside the United States—has already been happening for many years, but has not reached the levels that would be implied if the $159 trillion level were to be reached.

If some of the U.S. stock market wealth spills over into foreign markets, the propagation of American-style wealth accumulation will spread to countries that it has not reached yet.

Effect of Tax Policy on Wealth Accumulation

In the United States, corporate tax revenues have declined both as a percentage of GNP and as a percentage of total tax revenues. Congress has given accelerated depreciation allowances and tax credits for new investment. Reasons cited include maintaining competitiveness and creating new higher-paying jobs. A consequence has been that corporate profits have risen faster than GNP (Figure 11.1).[3]

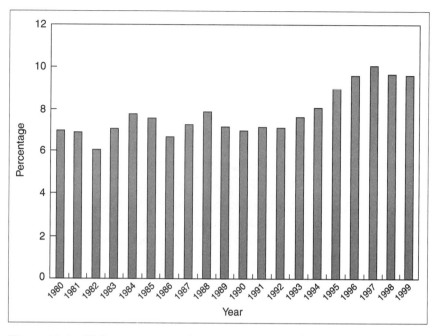

Figure 11.1   U.S. corporate profits as a percentage of GNP, 1980 to 1999.

This growth of corporate profits has helped support rises in stock prices. The rising stock prices have increased the rates of return on mutual funds and pension funds, prompting further individual investment in managed equity portfolios. America's Boomer savers have been enjoying a cycle of wealth creation that has become self-perpetuating.

Middle-class households have been given tax incentives to save. Tax-deferred annuities and Individual Retirement Accounts (IRAs) have been offered and accepted. European investors have put money in offshore funds in tax havens such as Gibraltar and the Channel Islands. Double taxation of corporate profits and dividend income still exists, but it has been partially circumvented. Stocks have delivered such mighty capital gains that investors no longer pay such close attention to dividend payouts.

U.S. federal tax collections from individuals have declined sharply as a percentage of the total value of pension funds and mutual funds. The tax burden on individuals is usually computed as a percentage of their annual earnings. Computing it that way gives the impression that the tax burden has remained steady and diverts attention away from the alternate view, that it has fallen sharply. The alternate view is more germane to understanding the widening income and wealth gap. Because the tax on savings for retirement is deferred or avoided, the individuals who save do not pay tax on the interest or capital gains that their savings earn in subsequent years. To see how quickly this divergence mounts up, suppose that two middle-class individuals each make $5,000 a month. Each pays federal taxes of 20%. One of them is putting $500 a month into a tax-deferred annuity, so the taxes are computed on a net monthly income of $4,500, and therefore are $900 a month. The other is not saving, so the taxes are computed on an income of $5,000, and so are $1,000 a month. After five years, the one who is putting $500 a month into a tax-deferred annuity is earning $240 per month on the accumulated savings in the tax-deferred annuity, so the total monthly income is $5,000 plus $240, and the monthly federal income tax continues to be $900. The federal tax burden as a percentage of total monthly income has fallen to 17%, well below the 20% his or her cohort is still paying.

Because upper-middle-income-class individuals take, on average, fuller advantage of tax deferral vis-à-vis lower-middle-income-class individuals, their income and wealth grow faster than salary data would indicate. A person earning $10,000 per month appears to be only 2½ times richer than a person earning $4,000 a month. However, if the higher-income person is saving $1,000 a month in tax-deferred schemes, his or her income after five years would be 2.62 times the income of the lower-income person.

To consider a more dramatic example, suppose that three individuals each have a different amount in retirement accounts. The rich one has $1 million and the two middle-class ones have accounts of $100,000 and $50,000, respectively. At the beginning, the rich one has 10 times as much as one of the middle-class savers and 20 times as much as the other. Now suppose that each earns 2% a month on their accounts. This rate corresponds to what common stocks have yielded in the five-year period commencing in 1995. Also suppose the rich one puts $5,000 a month into the accounts while the middle-class ones put in $1,000 and $200, respectively. After five years the wealth disparity among these three has grown enormously in numerical terms, and has also shifted in relative terms. The millionaire now has $3.9 million and does not have to pay tax on the increase because it is all in tax-deferred accounts. The middle-class striver who has put aside $1,000 a month has $442,155, more than four times the starting amount. Tellingly, the person who was poorest of the three is now poorer by a wider margin. The third person has accumulated only $186,861. This person saved least, and had the least at the beginning, so the account's accumulation has not quadrupled. The poorest person now has even less than one-twentieth as much as the richest. Interestingly, the gap has widened more between the two middle-class savers than between them and the millionaire. The wealthier one now has 2.36 times as much as the poorer, although he or she started out only twice as wealthy.*

Tax-deferred savings schemes have worked well to stimulate savings and to finance growth of productive capacity. They have also reduced the effective tax rate for savers. It is now clear that they have also played a role in widening the wealth disparity.

International Portfolio Investment in Developing Countries, the Wealth Gap, and Sustainable Environmental Practices

Portfolio investors' point of entry into a newly targeted developing country is generally the capital city, where the country's stock exchange is located. Foreign portfolio investors begin buying shares. Quickly they buy all the common stock held by local dealers. Their buying invigorates local businesspeople, and asset prices begin to rise. Immediately the distribution of income becomes more skewed. Local stockbrokers, shareholders, and entrepreneurs are enriched. The rest of the country feels the benefits later on, if at all. It is an accidental side effect of neoliberal policies that the distribution of income becomes more skewed. The educated, urban households gain first. The rest of the country gains later, and may not participate fully in the gains until much later. This fact is a consequence of the diffusion pattern and is part of the reason that income and wealth gaps are widening.

After a country makes its first steps toward neoliberal reform and sustainable growth, and experiences its first stock market rally, the process can halt and go into reverse. The country can revert to protectionism or

---

* These numbers are developed in a spreadsheet called Three Savers.xls. This spreadsheet, along with others referred to in this book, is posted on the author's Web site, www.faculty.babson.edu/edmunds.

to a preindustrial economic model. Foreign portfolio investors need the process to keep going forward. If it does not continue, they will lose part of the money they have already put in, and they will lose the opportunity to keep investing in the rising local stock market. They will have to invest at home, or in some other countries where expected returns may be lower.

The rates of return do not look very different at first glance (see Table 11.1), but compounding makes the differences enormous quickly. The rewards for chasing higher returns are rich when the higher returns come true. If individual middle-class investors can earn 16% on their savings, instead of 12%, the difference in the amount a person has to save to accumulate a given sum by age 65 is massive. For example, saving $1,000 a month, and earning 12% annually, a saver who begins at age 40 will have accumulated $1,879,000. To accumulate the same sum at a 16% rate of return, the saver would have to save only $480 per month. Consequently, middle-class investors in the rich countries have good reason to want a country that has just begun to adopt neoliberal policies to continue along that path, or any path that will allow high returns to investors. They benefit from it personally.

A country that begins along the neoliberal path will continue if results are good. The policy will produce good results if setbacks do not intervene. War, mass internal migration, natural disasters, ignorance, xenophobia, and epidemics all can derail the policy, as can corruption, capital flight, embezzlement, badly designed taxes, and monetary mismanagement.

Social Policy and Investment

What do countries need to accomplish to keep a neoliberal policy initiative going? There are several indicators that portfolio investors look at

Table 11.1 **Average Annual Returns for U.S. Dollar Investors 1945 to 1995**

Equity	Return
U.S. equities (Standard & Poor's 500)	11.7%
Other industrial country equities	13.2%
Emerging markets equities	16.9%

Source: Figures from Morgan Stanley Capital Markets International, cited in *Barrons*.

when they are deciding whether to put more money into a country. Steady improvement in each is helpful in attracting more incoming portfolio investment. Capital inflows help a government stay in power. Several indicators are described here.

Workforce quality has to be on a good trajectory. Public health, nutrition, and family planning must achieve broad coverage. In most preemerging countries, many children are born to families who are not able to provide a child with all the necessary nurture and investment required to make the child a productive, informed adult. Migrants to a capital city where prosperity is beginning to take hold can overwhelm the city's infrastructure. Unless the migrants get training they cannot find high-paying jobs, so their frustration threatens the continuation of the neoliberal policy.

Lower birthrates in rural areas lead to lower rates of migration, so discouraging childbearing helps to sustain a neoliberal growth policy. One way of discouraging childbearing is to push the costs of childrearing onto the families. Another way is to raise the amount of money that women can earn working outside the home. Foreign portfolio investors have reason to support both policies.

Telecommunications and rural electrification must reach every household directly. In 1980, the number of telephone lines in the world was 600 million, or one line for every 7.5 people. In 1995, the number was 1 billion lines, or one for every 5.7 people. At this rate complete coverage would not be attained before 2055, but it may be attained sooner because the rate of growth in lines accelerated from 1995 to 2000. People living in remote areas must be reached by telephone, video, and the Internet; they must receive enough information to know how to improve their quality of life and to learn what the consequences of their actions are on others in faraway places. When high-bandwidth telecommunications reaches a new area, the birth rate drops, infant mortality drops, education levels improve, income rises, and agricultural practices change. The influence of patriarchs who are antieducation and pronatalist declines. People's horizons are broadened, and they see scenes of daily life in faraway places, so they see how people live in foreign countries. Exposure to broadband communications makes it harder for demagogues to demonize foreigners.

Education and public health must reach everyone, and progress toward a sustainable equilibrium has to be monitored everywhere, even in remote villages. Accomplishments on this front are less satisfactory. More than 60% of the children in the world do not go beyond the eighth grade, and public health is still inadequate in most of the world.

The people who seek to protect the sustainability of the ecological niche have to prove that they have enough financial resources to be able to offer inducements to the target audience. They have to be able to offer a better way of living to peasants who are cutting down rain forest. A comfortable and glamorous lifestyle, including an adequate retirement, is the carrot they offer. The offer has to be backed by enough money, information, entertainment, and other quality-of-life inputs to make it credible.

It is too early to tell whether the influence of international portfolio investment will bring enough pressure to improve delivery systems in the emerging and preemerging countries. The carrot exists, but many people who need to be able to see it still cannot. In too many remote corners of the world, the full blueprint has not yet arrived. In other corners of the world, images of an attractive lifestyle have arrived, but not enough information has come along with the images for people to be able to attain that lifestyle.

The data from financial markets does not answer the big question of how or when an adequate living standard will reach all the people on earth. The data do allow calculating several figures that show some of the relevant magnitudes. These shed light on the big question, and the calculations are shown in the next section.

Affordability of Progress toward Sustainable Environmental Practices

The total cost of bringing everybody to an ecologically sustainable lifestyle with a standard of living high enough to satisfy most people has not yet been computed. It would be nice to put a price tag on that and to calculate how long it would take to achieve. The numbers cited in this section have a less ambitious objective. They show how easily the wealthy people in the world can afford to pay the poorest 40% of the world's population to stop some destructive agricultural practices. Such practices could include cutting down trees and growing crops on steep hillsides. These two practices are selected as examples because they are conspicuous, damaging, and not very profitable to the people who do them. Obviously, poor farmers are not the only ones doing things that should be stopped. The rich have their own ingrained bad practices, such as using too much energy, and those will be more expensive to stop. The numbers cited here only show how far the world has come toward being able to afford to pay the poorest 40% of the world's people to stop doing some things that damage the environment.

The affordability has improved markedly. Rich countries are castigated for dedicating such small percentages of their annual output to foreign aid. The dishearteningly low percentages directed to foreign assistance are only one view of the affordability ratios. There is another view that is more optimistic, and that is to look at the poorest 40% of the world as a market that can be developed. Looking at the prospects for the poorest 40% from this viewpoint, the outlook for them is brighter. This approach asks whether there is enough financing to turn the world's poor into a market for goods and services; then it looks at how the poor can be brought up to a level of purchasing power so that they can buy goods and services. To begin, let us look at an impressive measure of progress toward affordability, namely the stock market value of companies in consumer goods, telecommunications, entertainment, and media. These companies have been among the market leaders in the 1995 to 2000 leg of the long bull market, and would do better in the future if the bottom strata of the world's population had enough discretionary income to be able to buy some of their products. It may seem far-fetched to hope that the world's poor could ever reach that level of income. But many of them could do so if they were simply paid not to cut down trees and not to grow crops on steep hillsides.

The calculation that follows is simple and has a very limited objective. Its main purpose is to show how much the parameters of the debate on world poverty can shift as financial wealth accumulates. The dollar magnitudes make it feasible in principle for the wealthy to afford to pay incentives to the poor to stop cutting trees. This is a hypothetical calculation; the point is not that the world is about to implement a program of cash incentives, but rather that the world could afford to do it now.

The dollar value of all common stocks is now large enough to overshadow the cost of direct incentives to the world's poor. Direct assistance to the world's oxygen supply is affordable. In 1997, companies whose shares are listed on the New York, London, and Tokyo Stock Exchanges had more stock market capitalization than 12 years' annual income of the poorest 40% of the world's population. In 1987, the multiple was only 7 years. By 2000, the multiple had grown to 17 times. The stock market values have gone up partly because the companies have become larger. The companies have become larger because their products reach a higher portion of the world's population. The portion that can buy the companies' products has increased and will probably keep increasing as the world economy grows. The calculation here takes a more direct route to increasing that proportion. It assumes that the poor will be paid not to cut down trees.

Consider a scheme of paying $100 per year to the 2.4 billion poorest people in the world. They would qualify for the payment if, during a stated time interval, some trees in specified areas were left standing. Imagine for a moment that this program could be administered, and that the poor would leave the trees standing. The cost would be $240 billion per year. This is a large number compared to the U.S. GNP of $9 trillion. It is about 3% of the U.S. GNP and exceeds the entire U.S. foreign aid budget. But it is not such a large number compared to the annual increase in financial wealth that the world might achieve. World financial wealth could rise by as much as $20 trillion a year by the year 2003, for example. Part of the increase, happily enough, would be the price increases in the shares of companies that sell the products the poor would buy. Because those shares trade at prices between 2 and 4 times annual sales, the incentive scheme might add as much as $480 billion to $960 billion to the companies' stock market capitalizations!

Because the companies that would benefit are easy to identify, it is possible that their shareholders might vote to join a scheme that would use part of the increase in the stock prices to pay for the incentives. To see how this would work, consider a simple example that sidesteps the difficulty of figuring out how much each company benefits. Suppose that only one company sells products to people in the lowest income stratum; for convenience, call this company Unilever. All the companies that would benefit if the poor received checks for $100 are agglomerated under the name Unilever for the calculations in this example. Unilever would get the entire $240 billion as the poor spent the $100 checks buying soap and toothpaste. Also suppose that Unilever's share valuation was $300 billion before the scheme. This was 3 times Unilever's annual sales of $100 billion. Now, after the scheme, Unilever's sales would have risen to $340 billion, and its market capitalization would have risen to $300 billion + $240 billion × 3 = $1,020 billion. Unilever's shareholders would have capital gains of $720 billion. Suppose that they had agreed to give up $240 billion of these capital gains. They would hand over the $240 billion of gains, and keep $480 billion of gains.

This Alice in Wonderland example illustrates how surreal the stock market wealth process is. The example makes it seem that giving to the poor can be profitable! The earth would keep its trees, the poor would get soap and toothpaste, and the people who pay for the incentive would be wealthier than they were before. The reality is not quite that sanguine, and the example is a bit too good to be true. It pays for the subsidy for only one year, and to turn the $240 billion into cash there would have to be too much selling of Unilever stock. Nevertheless, the example does illustrate how the parameters of the world economy have shifted. The world is already able to afford incentive schemes like the one described here. In order to have much support, an incentive scheme would have to be more thoughtfully designed and cost-effective. But the point of the numerical example is that paying poor people to act in a stated way can be profitable to the shareholders of a private company.

More generally, the magnitudes of financial wealth are already in the correct proportions to lend credibility to the offer of a better lifestyle for everyone. The world has not yet made the offer, but can now begin to think about how to design the offer. The offer has already been made to some small groups, and there is now enough wealth to create and market an inducement to the bottom income percentiles of the world's population. The question of what the inducement will be, what mix of lifestyle inputs it will include, and what the people in the target group will have to do to qualify for the reward is being worked out in the marketplace. The question of how the message will be communicated to the targeted groups is also being worked out. Two large countries, China and India, are each finding ways of upgrading the quality of life for their populations. Because of their size, the world's attention is on them. There are other smaller countries that are working on the same task.

The Widening Income Gap as an Accelerant for Further Widening

The preceding numerical examples sketch the dimensions of a tantalizing prospect. Financial wealth is piling up to levels that will easily allow the owners of financial wealth to bribe the world's poor to behave in accordance with the wishes of the wealth owners. This is a startling fact that has never before been true. What is more, the owners of financial wealth can make themselves richer by paying the poor to join the money economy more completely and become consumers. Therefore, all humankind is now united in a symbiotic, synergistic wealth-creating process. The moment must be fast approaching when the selfish face of wealth accumulation will give way to the new alchemy of self-interested generosity. Fairly soon, the wealthy will gain more from being generous than from being selfish.

That moment has not yet arrived, however. Conditions in the stock market still favor selecting stocks in companies that sell sophisticated, expensive goods to rich people. The poor in the emerging countries are not yet a high-priority target market for the companies that are Wall Street's darlings. Although a few billionaires have made big donations to help the world's poorest people, their generosity stems from altruism, not from self-interest. Their stock portfolios may go up by an amount greater than what they have given away, but that happy outcome would be a lucky surprise, not a planned effect. Consequently, financial wealth will continue to pile up inequitably, and the gap between the wealthy and the poor will keep getting wider. The outlook is for more and more widening, with no narrowing foreseeable in the future. The moment that does appear to be arriving is the time when the wealthy will take the well-being of the entire world more explicitly into account.

Market Pressures

In the near term, pressures from stock market investors are aimed at improving efficiency and securing for shareholders returns that otherwise go to other stakeholders. The offer of capital inflows, and the threat of capital outflows, are quickly bringing many governments and corporate managers to pay closer attention to the stock market and to heed its signals. The signals can be delivered with crushing force. As of June 20, 1997, Brazil's stock market was up 72.3% from the beginning of the year; and Thailand's stock market dropped a dizzying 19.9% in dollars that week. By December 1997, Brazil's stock market had lurched down and was struggling its way back up, on track to close the year up 40%. Thailand's market was still reeling and had a steep slide ahead of it. These examples of the stock market investors' selective, manic-depressive style of overrewarding good performance and panicking and collapsing at the first signs of rough sledding contrast with the market's behavior in 1998 and 1999. In the latter two years, the market's reaction was to shun all emerging markets across the board, and then embrace them as the last frontier of undervalued stocks.[4]

The market sometimes delivers rapier thrusts, skewering only an unlucky few who have been classified as poor performers. Lately it has been delivering shotgun blasts, blowing whole categories of securities off the recommended list, into the limbo world where only bottom-fishers and grave-dancers find them. The latter pattern is disturbing because it tells issuers that their identity is more important than their actions. This is like condemning them for original sin. Market pressure works better when it is delivered selectively, to individual issuers, in response to its judgment of their actions.

A stock market boom is sustained by purchases of securities. The wealthy buy more securities than the middle class or the poor. It follows inexorably that financial wealth accumulates faster if the distribution of wealth becomes more skewed. At least for the short run, the financial engine will have more power if the income gap and the wealth gap widen. The voters in the aggregate must also become absolutely better off. Otherwise, they will vote to revert to a closed or premodern economy. A higher growth rate for portfolios of the wealthy builds more financial wealth to pull noncomplying nations and business owners into the fold. The reason is that if 10 people making $100,000 a year get another $10,000 each, they may use 40% of it to buy securities, but if a person making $1 million a year gets the extra $100,000, he or she puts a much greater percentage of it into buying securities. This builds financial markets faster.

The rationale for tolerating the widening wealth gap is that, at least for the time being, it is more important to remedy two social priorities that are more urgent. These are the cost of funding retirement for everybody on earth and the looming threat to the ecological niche that humans occupy. Of these two megaproblems the first is already partially solved, and the cost of solving it and the time horizon for solving it are well understood and calibrated. The retirement-funding dilemma is easier to solve than the ecological challenge for two reasons. First, individuals can calculate how much they need to save, and societies can work out a solution that will be in a self-sustaining equilibrium by 2050. Second, people will accumulate assets on their own behalf more readily than they will contribute to or support spending for protecting the environment. The extent of the damage to the niche we occupy and the cost of maintaining our niche in the biosphere are not so well calibrated, so the much bigger challenge is how to channel wealth and income into the effort to clean up the environment and protect it from damage.

Environmental Protection Signaled via the Stock Market?

The widening wealth gap may help discourage some forms of environmental degradation. The reason is that the stock market attaches more importance to future earnings than to current earnings. For most common stocks the annual dividend is less than 2% of the stock price, so investors are paying for future potential. Their best returns come when market participants reassess a stock's future potential upward. This reassessment has made capital gains a larger source of returns than dividends for much of the period since detailed record keeping began, and especially since 1990.

Stock market investors are focused on short-run profits. They try to make quick gains by trading stocks, and they prefer companies that maximize short-run profits. There is an important caveat to this get-it-now philosophy: Company managers try to protect the value of productive assets and to prolong the assets' productive lives. Some assets can be squeezed quickly or milked for long periods of time. Some oil wells, for example, will put out oil quickly or will put out much more oil slowly, depending on how they are operated. Corporate managers will usually choose the slower rate of production if it will give much more total output. This is especially true if the managers are responding to stock market incentives. There is a difference in incentives for corporate managers and private owners. For example, consider the decision to cut all the trees in a forest and sell them for cash, even if the cutting would damage the forest's ability to regenerate. The manager of a publicly listed corporation would be less likely to do that than a private owner who is not responding to shareholder pressure. The publicly listed company might cut as much of the wood as it could without permanently impairing the forest's recovery. But once it reached that point, it would not cut the rest of the trees, because if it did its share price would go down. Management would have delivered a large burst of earnings by selling all the wood in the forest. There would be no follow-up after the blip, however, and everybody would know it, because they would know that all the trees were already cut down. The stock market signals clearly that underutilized assets should be used; consequently, it signals that any trees that have stopped growing, and can safely be cut without damaging the forest's recuperative power, should be cut. But it does not signal that *all* the trees should be cut.

This difference in outlook and time horizon is pivotal. Individual owners may be selfish and grasping, and may not care what happens after they die. But well-managed corporations must successfully address the more subtle trade-offs between current income and future value. They do this by trying to maximize their share prices. The difference in behavior may not be enough to lead to an ideal outcome, but the difference exists and is exerting powerful influence.

For an example of the signals the stock market can send, and the pressure it can exert, consider the track record of mutual funds in two industry sectors related to health. These funds invest in companies in a single industry sector. These funds are launched when there is a sector that attracts investors and that performs differently from other sectors that are closely related to it. The two funds are Select Biotech and Select Health Care. For the five years ending December 31, 1999, the Biotech fund earned a 33.56% annual return, and the Health Care fund returned only 21.63%. Both rates might seem high enough, but the signal is clear: Investment in new "silver bullet" remedies is rewarded more than investment in bricks and mortar to supply more hospital beds. This signal was delivered with massive force in calendar year 1999. For that 12-month period, the Biotech fund yielded 77.72%, while the Health Care fund yielded –2.89%.[5] Confirming these startlingly divergent numbers are the industry sector performance figures tracked by Dow Jones. Health care providers yielded an annual return of only 11.1% for the 17½-year period from mid-1982 to the end of 1999. By comparison, the biotechnology industry group yielded 23.56% annually for that same time interval.[6] The reason for the difference in performance is not stated, but may simply be that although pills are expensive, staying in the hospital costs more, so patients are encouraged to treat their ills with pills instead of going to the hospital. The market's signal is even more specific than these data show. Market valuations of hospital management companies have been particularly depressed.[7] The inference is either that hospitals will be in a profit squeeze for years to come or that their shares are shunned for being on the front lines of the battle over health care expenditures. The signal does not say what causes it, but it does tell the money where to go in the future. Money will go into developing new drugs, not into building more hospitals.

Another example of the market's signaling power is the lackluster performance of tobacco stocks. These shares are risky to own because lawsuits to recover health care costs are going to continue for a long time. The magnitude of the liability is still unknown, and the possibility of getting new customers is unclear. Tobacco stocks yielded 13.53% a year for the 17½-year period from mid-1982 to the end of 1999.[8]

The industry sectors that did even worse include steel and coal, which yielded 2.95 and 1.77% a year on average for one of the best stock market periods on record.[9] They were not in the headlines. They just quietly lost importance as environmental costs and chronically low prices for their products sapped their profits. They lost protection, visibility, and sponsorship.

So the stock market can deliver selective signals, and some of the signals have a vaguely environmental aura to them. The information content of the signals is low, and the reasoning they are based on is not observed. There is doubt whether these signals are clear enough or accurate enough to guide resource allocation decisions.

Regardless of the clarity or accuracy of the signals, they are getting stronger. The stock market was not originally intended as an institution for delivering signals that have ramifications beyond the pricing of the company shares that are traded. Nevertheless, the financial wealth continues to pile up, so the signals will continue to get stronger; they may be targeted, but they may also be capricious and erratic.

The next section asks if these signals are clear enough for countries in the rest of the world to decipher them. Certainly the signals are loud enough; the question is if they are understandable. The section begins with the Americas and then asks what the effects of bringing more people into the stock market's orbit are.

The Signal in the Americas: Loud, but How Clear?

In the Americas, the power of the financial transmission mechanism and the demonstration effect are particularly strong. The United States is the dominant financial power, and its portfolio investors have large holdings in all the other stock markets in the hemisphere. The U.S. dollar is the dominant currency in the hemisphere, and the North American Free Trade Agreement (NAFTA), the Andean Pact, and Mercosur help transmit financial market signals from northern Canada to Tierra del Fuego. The Americas can serve as a test zone for effectiveness of the signaling. The Americas are a good test zone because they are so well endowed with natural resources and are not so densely populated as Eurasia. The Americas are adequately endowed with oxygen, fresh water, food, oil, gas, coal, iron ore, and aluminum. In terms of population indicators, the total for all countries in the Americas is only 800 million, and more than half the adults have been educated at least as far as the eighth grade. In terms of information, mass communication coverage is above 95%. Only four languages are needed to speak to the entire hemisphere. The Americas are separated by oceans from Eurasia and Africa, so mass migration from more densely populated continents cannot happen, and military threats can come only from high-tech opponents.

The North American zone, including Mexico, Central America, Panama, and the Caribbean, has at most 460 million people, with 302 million in the United States and Canada. The remaining 158 million are decisively in the U.S. orbit and are subject to influences of every sort from Washington, Hollywood, and Wall Street, from trade groups, and from pressure groups of every stripe. Most of the elite has been educated in the United States, and many Caribbean, Mexican, and Central American families have a family member living in the United States. The rapid annual growth rate in numbers of telephone calls between the Caribbean, Mexico, and the United States is an indication of the strengthening ties.

The campaigns emanating from the United States have been for human rights, family planning, public health, nutrition, rural electrification, universal education, equal protection under the law, free elections, political pluralism, open trade, protection of the environment, job creation, reduced migration from the countryside to the cities, and reduced migration to the United States.

These messages have been delivered through many channels. The stock market did not carry the message all by itself. Some parts of the message were accepted and acted on. Other parts were misunderstood or rejected. The message continues to be sent, louder than ever, if not more clearly. Telephone and television broadcasting monopolies have been privatized and broken up. The stock market continues to send its signals, but deciphering what they mean is not always easy to do.

Including More People in the Loop: A Further Accelerant to Widening the Gap?

After people gain access to telecommunications and rural electrification, their physical quality of life improves. They move above their previous level of subsistence and become more engaged in the world economy. They begin with very few financial assets, so they start at the bottom in the pecking order of financial wealth. Many do not move up that pecking order; instead, they remain at the bottom. Nevertheless, most of the world's population is being linked into the world telecommunications network quickly. One might think that shortages of capital are holding back the spread of rural electrification and telephony. Shortages of capital may have existed, and may still exist, but no longer are severe enough to hold back the spread. Technological change and the growth of the wealth pool have cut the problem down to size. To see what the required amount of investment might be, consider the figure $10,000 per capita for the 4 billion people on Earth who do not have full access to telecommunications and physical and social infrastructure. This is more than enough to pay for a cellular telephone, a television, a satellite dish, a personal computer, a modem, and 1,000 minutes of hookup time per month. The $10,000 per capita multiplies out to $40 trillion—for comparison, the dollar value of all financial assets in the world at year-end 1998 was just under $80 trillion—so the magnitude of money that has to move is well within the feasible range for securities markets. The world's stock and bond markets could move that much money in 10 years or less. Buyers would be forthcoming for newly issued securities in the amount of $40 trillion. This is less than eight years of buying power at the average absorption rates of the years 1995 to 1997. It is a daunting amount of money, more than 12 years of the combined annual savings of the Organization for Economic Cooperation and Development (OECD) countries for 1997. Nevertheless, it is feasible, because annual savings are not the only money that is available. Capital gains and interest on amounts saved in previous years can also be brought to bear through securities markets.

The $40 trillion of new securities would have to be adequately collateralized and legally protected against fraud, and would have to offer competitive rates of return. This means that the new cash would have to earn returns comparable to what telecommunications investments have returned recently. As long as the rates of return held up, new money would keep flowing in. The total of $40 trillion would be reached only if the return on each successive investment remained positive, and high enough to make new investments look attractive. Waste and fraud would delay the process, and then people would have to wait longer to achieve the boost to their standard of living.

The effect that wiring up the world has on the distribution of wealth is paradoxical. The faster the world gets wired up, the more the gap between rich and poor widens. The paradox is that each poor person who gets a telephone becomes better off immediately. So how does this widen the gap instead of narrowing it? The reason is that the people who obtain telecommunications and rural electrification come into the financial economy at the bottom. They enter with nothing, or with very little. At the same time, however, the fact they have subscribed raises the value of financial assets. In particular, the shares of the company that has signed them up should rise. Shares of telecommunications companies are priced in part according to how many subscribers they have. This is especially true of cellular telephone companies, and those are the ones signing up new subscribers fastest. The shares of the company that signs up the new subscribers belong to investors who are already relatively wealthy. So as more people sign up, the market value of the shares goes up, and the gap between rich and poor gets wider. Furthermore, each new zone that is wired up has to be profitable for the investors. If it is not, the money to wire up the next zone does not appear. So if all new investments are successful, and the entire world is wired up quickly, the shareholders of telecommunications companies will have profited from the increase in the subscriber base. The quicker the subscriber base grows, the richer they become.

In this fashion, the widening wealth gap serves as an accelerant for still further widening. As wealth accumulates, there is more financing for telecommunications companies to sign up more people who have never had a telephone. As more people get a telephone for the first time, the shareholders of telecommunications companies get richer. The market's signals grow louder and reach more people. The market's signals propagate faster and with greater intensity, sometimes coming down forcefully with great clarity and sometimes passing by without saying anything very clearly. The wealth-creation process, in order to be self-reinforcing, needs to pull people into the money economy who were not previously in it.

Stock market wealth is created when they buy toothpaste or when they sign up for a cellular telephone.

The stock market–driven wealth-creation process has a beneficial effect on wealthy people's motivation for helping the poor. The motivation was purely altruistic in the past. Now there are stock market profits to be made from raising the standard of living of the world's poorest people. This may not sound different from the motivations of the colonial traders who followed the flag of the colonial power to remote corners of the earth. But it is different in magnitude because the stock market works in terms of multiples. A trader would not give a poor person a cellular telephone and hope to collect from that person later. But a telecommunications company whose shares are listed on a stock exchange in a rich country would do so. The reason is that the future revenues from that cellular telephone are immediately valuable in the stock market. As soon as the poor person signs up for the telephone and carries it out of the store, the shares of the telecommunications company rise. The telecommunications company may never make a profit on that particular person, but the potential is worth money anyway. If the company signs up 1,000 new customers, enough of them will pay off in the future, so investors bid up the price of the company's stock immediately.

How general is this phenomenon? Is it profitable for stock-exchange-listed companies to push merchandise into the hands of poor people, especially poor people in emerging countries, in hopes that enough of the new customers will pay to make the gamble profitable? Clearly the phenomenon extends beyond cellular telephony: It extends to Internet access. In Brazil and Argentina, Internet service providers are offering free access to the Web.* They do it to gain market share, and they hope to earn enough from advertising to make the free access profitable. The next section considers how far this phenomenon can go.

Does the Stock Market Push the World toward Adequate Living Standards?

The financial system, and in particular the world's stock markets, are the new invisible hand. The strengths and failings of the old invisible hand are well known. Will the new one be better? There are reasons for opti-

---

* In March 2000, the Buenos Aires newspaper *Clarin* ran ads offering free Internet access, and there were similar offers in Brazil at the same time.

mism. First, the stock market is more responsive to events happening a long distance away. In that sense it treats the world as a closed system. Adam Smith's traders could view the world as infinitely large and did not need to pay much attention to what was happening outside a particular zone, or outside a particular industry sector.

The second major distinctive feature of the new invisible hand is that it does not condone types of government corruption that impair financial wealth creation. In Nigeria, Pakistan, Zaire, the Philippines, and Mexico, the middle class had to struggle to save anything, and then had to move its savings out of the country. International pressure on the governments of these countries was too weak to protect middle-class savings if they were deposited in local financial institutions. Now there is intensifying pressure on these governments to treat local savers better. Rates of return are now more realistic. Taxation of local savings has been reduced, or deferred via pension schemes like the AFOREs in Mexico.* Governments have also been strongly advised not to confiscate these savings via hyperinflation, massive devaluation, or outright expropriation.

Savers Needed in Emerging Countries

Why are middle-class savers now being protected in countries where they previously were left to the tender mercies of kleptocracy? The reason is that those middle-class savers are needed. They will be the buyers of the securities that the Boomers are buying now. The Boomers will be trying to sell their accumulated financial assets from 2006 onward, and their selling will intensify after 2012. Who will be saving for retirement at that time? In the United States, births declined after 1957, and did not recover until the 1980s, so there will not be enough Americans saving for retirement in 2006 to 2012 to buy all the securities that the Boomers will be selling. If fewer people are buying in 2006, and they are then devoting less money than the amount that Boomers are trying to sell, the market prices of securities will have to fall. So the Boomers are facing the prospect of paying high prices for securities today and selling them at low prices from 2006 onward.

---

* AFORE is a Spanish acronym that stands for Administrators of Funds for Retirement. Mexico has had a private pension scheme in effect since 1996. Employer and employee put money into an account at a brokerage firm; the money is invested in bonds and belongs to the employee. The account is similar to Chile's pension accounts or U.S. 401(k) accounts.

Will not Euroland and Japanese investors remedy the shortfall and add their buying power? The demographics of other industrial countries do not offer much encouragement. The people who will be buying at that time have already been born, and there are simply not enough of them in the industrial countries. Middle-class savers do not save very much until they turn 40, and they save more from age 50 until they retire. So the people who will be steady buyers of securities in 2006 or 2012 were born in 1956 to 1972. The amount of buying power has to be in excess of $6 trillion per year. This figure assumes that Boomers will sell gradually after they retire. If 60 million Boomers sell $100,000 worth of securities per year, that is $6 trillion per year. If there is not a commensurate amount of buying going on at the same time, there could be a selling spiral.

Demographic data show that the middle classes in the emerging countries are numerous enough to buy all the securities the Boomers will be selling. If the middle classes in the emerging countries can be protected, and can be acculturated to buy securities, they will have enough buying power to buy all the securities at high prices. For example, if there were 600 million people buying $10,000 worth of securities per year in 2006, buying would offset selling. In that case the Boomers would realize the high rates of return they need to afford the retirement they are saving for. In the absence of buying from the middle classes of the emerging countries, the outlook for the Boomers' retirement is less opulent.

Middle-class savers in most emerging countries do not yet have the protection they need to invest in their own local financial markets, and most of them do not have easy and cheap ways of investing internationally. Protection for investors is gradually improving, notably in Singapore, Chile, and Taiwan. But there is still much to be done before the middle classes in the most populous emerging countries will be willing to pour their savings into financial markets the way Americans, Japanese, and Europeans do.

The pressure on governments of emerging countries to keep their hands off middle-class savings, and to allow savers to diversify internationally, is already intense and will increase until the goal of complete protection and complete freedom to move money abroad is accomplished. The pressure comes from the financial markets, which transmit signals about the needs of investors. Today's investors need tomorrow's buyers to be protected.

The Invisible Hand Again: Grooming Future Savers

Another distinctive feature of the new invisible hand is that it pushes the middle classes in the emerging countries to reach a higher standard of living. They will have to accomplish that first before they will be ready to be groomed for their future role as buyers of securities. The buyers will have to be wealthy enough to be able to afford securities, they will have to be well educated enough to know what securities are, and they will have to have access to telecommunications so that they can place the orders and track the progress of their investments.

The poor in the emerging countries will also have to be brought up to a high enough level of income to be buyers of securities. They are not needed as buyers until the time frame from 2026 to 2032. At that time they will be buying the securities that the middle classes of the emerging world bought in the years 2006 to 2012.

There is a more immediate reason for bringing the poor in the emerging countries up to an adequate standard of living: to deter them from causing social disturbances. The Chiapas rebellion, which started January 1, 1994, caused investors to downgrade the Mexican stock market. The assassinations later that same year, and the mishandled devaluation at the end of that year, did additional damage, so any estimate of the dollar loss in securities prices attributable to Chiapas alone is arbitrary, but $20 billion would be a conservative figure. This figure is many times larger than the amount that would have been required to deliver an adequate standard of living to the peasants who revolted.

The new invisible hand therefore mandates that the middle classes and the poor in the emerging countries attain higher standards of living. What is different now is that there is a timetable and a deadline, and the need comes not from altruism but from a wellspring lower in the hierarchy of needs: the monetary self-interest of Baby Boomers and Generation Xers in the United States and their age cohort in Euroland and Japan.

Is Everyone in This Together?

Are the newly wealthy savers in rich countries really going to be concerned about poor people who live thousands of miles away? The wealthy people themselves may not pay any more attention than before to people outside their own immediate sphere. There has been no upwelling of charity commensurate with the surge in financial wealth. In the United States, neither political party has made foreign assistance a prominent part of its platform. So how different is the new invisible hand?

The new invisible hand is more caring than the old one in specific ways and for delimited and well-understood reasons. First, the stock market looks beyond current performance, to the point of being obsessed with future earnings and cash flows. This makes stock market investors very careful to weigh the future versus the present. Every buyer of common stock has to think about who is going to buy the stock later. The company needs to be worth more in the future than it is in the present. This fact leads companies to seek markets for their products everywhere, including in countries where most people are poor. This has always been true, but what is different now is that common stock valuations are high and presume that steady growth will continue. Now, if a company hits market saturation its growth slows down, and its stock price immediately falls. In the past this was less true than it is now, and it was less serious when it happened. Prior to the recent bull market, companies could perform cyclically, with 2 or 3 down years out of 5, and investors would accept that. Now investors expect sustained growth. If a company hits a saturation point with one product in one country, it is supposed to have other products and other countries where its sales are growing. So companies now need markets that are stable and growing. In the past, companies needed access to markets but did not need those markets to be stable. Companies were careful not to upset local elites. They feared nationalization or expropriation but tolerated dictatorships. Now companies need more than access. They need the markets they are selling in to grow steadily. They are now less tolerant of volatility, and they have more reason to be in favor of good treatment for the local populace in the countries where they operate.

Second, the stock market is both responsive and vulnerable to conditions in the entire world. The Asian crisis of 1997 to 1998 illustrates the responsiveness. Money moved to the United States following the Thai devaluation of July 1997. Exchange rates of Asian currencies fell, and Asian stock markets crashed along with them. Asian countries needed export revenue, so they marked down their goods and sold them in the United States. Asia's distress fueled the U.S. stock market boom in two ways: Asian money arrived in the U.S. bond market seeking refuge; and

Asian goods were offered at low prices, which kept down U.S. inflation. Investors then bid up prices of U.S. common stocks, because bond prices were already high, and because the spectre of inflation was banished. Years earlier, an event so far away would have made such a difference only if it had affected financial affairs in London, Paris, or Amsterdam. The Russian bond default of 1998 showed that a country that does not have a large capital market can trigger a panic. Years earlier, a country with such a small capital market, and with such weak economic fundamentals, would not have been able to borrow as much.

Third, stock markets need to know who the new buyers are and how much they are going to be able to buy. Until there are enough new buyers to keep the bull market going, the pressure to pull in more players and potential players will remain and intensify. The obvious place to look for new buyers is in countries that have large populations that are nearly in a position to buy securities. Poland and Malaysia get more attention from stock market experts than Mali and Laos do. If too many conditions would have to be met, as in the case of Somalia, there is not much pressure. Also, attention is directed narrowly at issues that will affect the ability of the populations to be buyers. For the typical investor, the AIDS epidemic in Southeast Asia is a higher priority than the AIDS epidemic in Africa. Southeast Asia has stock markets that have delivered high performance and can quickly become large players, surpassing the size they had reached during their glory days. So the new invisible hand will reach out to people who are at the lower fringe of the middle class well before it will reach out to the poorest people in the poorest countries.

The new invisible hand may extend its reach into the future in other ways as well. It would be truly serendipitous if the rapid growth of financial wealth would bring pressure for environmentally friendly policies. Does the stock market look much farther ahead than the market for goods? A look at a discount table shows that cash flows coming more than 50 years in the future have very little present value. So the trade-off of now versus later will be made differently in the stock market, but the differences will be trade-offs within the 50-year horizon. A company would not sell a factory if its future cash flows have a higher present value than the price that is being offered. An individual facing the same decision might sell—for example, if a person wanted to retire and had no successor.

For this reason, the stock market is more forward-looking than is a market for goods, which are sold only for immediate cash settlement. But it cannot look very far beyond 50 years, so issues like storing nuclear waste may need to be resolved outside its framework.

Within the 50-year time frame, happily, there are many environmental problems the stock market can address. The signals that investors send to government of the emerging countries include themes related to the environment. These themes are a minor part of the total message, but they are included. As with the other signals, the investors' motive is self-serving. Emerging countries are urged to deliver an adequate standard of living to the poorest people in rural areas in order to discourage them from migrating to the cities or rebelling. Migration to the cities is bad because it raises the amount that has to be invested in urban infrastructure. Rebelling is bad because it makes asset prices go down. A cheap way to improve living standards for the rural poor is to improve agricultural practices. This will reduce soil erosion and deforestation, improve tropical ecosystems, and raise the oxygen-recycling capacity of the planet. Another way to improve living standards is to present alternative lifestyles to poor rural women. Credible alternatives to early marriage and high fertility are being delivered via telecommunications and opportunities to work outside the home.

In the industrial countries, the stock market's signals reach managers directly and quickly. For example, the market puts pressure on the managers of companies that produce environmentally damaging chemicals. These managers have stock options, or will soon get them. The stock options make the managers sensitive to future costs and penalties for as long as they anticipate remaining with that company. So if a study indicates that a chemical is damaging the environment, these managers will seek to minimize the loss to the firms they work for and partly own. Closing down the plant would not generally be their first response. Instead, their first response might be to try to sell the offending product only where penalties are unlikely to be assessed. This response seems callous but is rational: It avoids having to write off the factory and incur the cost of closing it. If there is a country where the product can profitably be sold without risk of penalty, it is rational to keep selling it until the factory is worn out. The more delayed response, which is to discontinue new investments in factories to produce the offending product, is the constructive response. In the past, some chemical companies have continued to add new capacity even after the damaging effects of a product have become known. In those days, managers' compensation did not come as much from the stock market as it did from current earnings, and the probability of a severe penalty was lower. The constructive response will come sooner if managers have large stock options, and if the probability of a large financial penalty is great enough to offset the profits to be made from the product. The stock market's signals to management are becoming stronger than the goods market's signals.

The environmental problems that the stock market does not address are those that have long time horizons and those on which expert scientific opinion is divided. For example, pressure coming from investors about global warming is no stronger than it has been for the past 25 years. Investors have not further downgraded the stock of companies that might later be ordered to pay penalties for carbon dioxide emissions. The downgrading took place in the 1970s. Automobile companies and electric utilities have underperformed the broad stock market averages during the bull market that began in 1982. Surprisingly, they have done worse than commodity chemical companies, and continued to do worse in calendar year 1999.[10] But no major new signal has been sent to them. So the stock market has the capability of delivering a brutally strong signal, but in some cases one big signal is all it has sent. After that, the subsequent signals are mild by comparison.

Conclusion

The growth path of magnifying the market value of existing assets is new and is a departure from the earlier growth path of increasing the output of goods and services. The new path stemmed from the earlier one, and differs from it in several important ways, but bears some superficial similarity to it. In particular, the new path retains some of the disadvantages of the earlier path, but does not have all of the disadvantages to the same degree.

The world has been on the new growth path for some time already, so this is a good time to assess the virtues and defects of the new path. One must avoid judging it as if it were a supercharged version of the earlier path. It is different enough to be worthy of a fresh look.

The biggest difference is the amount of wealth the new path can call into existence. It has shown that it is able to increase world wealth very rapidly, and raise it to levels that have never been approached before. It produces enough dollar value to lift all the world's poor up to an adequate standard of living. It may produce a magnitude of wealth large enough to pay for a clean environment and to install sustainable technologies of production. It brings pressure on despotic, kleptocratic governments to respect the savings and property rights of their citizens. It abhors wars that destroy the value of productive assets. What it does not do is put very much of this wealth within the reach of people who would take it and redistribute it, or apply it to upgrading the world's environment.

Whatever one's assessment of the new growth path is, its rise has been awesome. The financial force of accumulated stock market gains is so massive, and is growing so rapidly, as to be overwhelming. Derailing it is already out of the question, and channeling it is also becoming impossible. This book attempts to describe its workings and to assess its consequences, but does not suggest channeling it, controlling it, or stopping it. The widening of the income gap is inexorable, and is based on more immutable foundations than the popular financial press customarily acknowledges. Forces that work to bring rich and poor together, like generosity or sense of community, are small players in the drama. More primeval motives, like self-interest and desire for a comfortable retirement, are on center stage. The stock and bond markets are the puppet-master, and the kingpins of the earlier economic system are the puppets. The stock market pulls people and resources into its orbit and ladles out quick wealth to the people that are closest to its inner councils and to individuals who are lucky enough to be in the vicinity.

The widening of the income gap is only one effect among many. It grabs headlines because there is no automatic mechanism that will narrow the gap in the near future. But there is good news, too: Absolute levels of income will rise steadily for most people on Earth. This is happening because they have to be drawn into the financial economy to be developed into buyers of goods, then into buyers of securities. They also have to be treated well enough that they do not rebel or cause damage to the value of financial assets. Another good implication is that people who are now poor have to be reached by telecommunications and education before they will be buyers of securities. Part of the message they will receive will be heightened awareness of the environment.

Chapter 12

Conclusion: $1 Quadrillion Once Again

Many forces have been simultaneously at work to cause financial wealth to accumulate. The wealth-creation mechanism described in this book has many individual generators, motors, pulleys, and subassemblies. There are more forces contributing to wealth accumulation, and those forces contribute in more ways, than casual observers have noted. The components of the mechanism work in tandem with no guiding cabal to bring about the dramatic growth that financial wealth has experienced.

Past Turning Back

The diverse components of financial wealth creation are now working faster, and with more cumulative power. They will keep multiplying world financial wealth until they run up against a physical limit or some other kind of barrier. They are nowhere near any physical limit that will impede their expansion, although their helter-skelter acceleration may take the world past an ecological point of no return. Barriers of other kinds may slow down the wealth-accumulation process from time to time. There may be political backlashes, policy errors, natural disasters, epidemics, terrorist attacks, or wars. There will almost certainly be violent swings in financial markets, particularly stock markets. But there are no impediments on the immediate horizon that will turn back the tide of financial wealth accumulation.

Each of the components of the mechanism that has created so much financial wealth is ordinary and unremarkable on its own terms. Every human actor in the drama is responding to conditions and incentives in reasonable ways. The value-creation processes in companies and in national stock markets are all understandable case by case, and many of them have operated sporadically at times in previous generations.

The wealth-creation process is feeding on itself, but this is certainly not the first time that has happened. There have been credit expansions and bubbles before. What is new about this growth process is its geographical span, its duration, and its sheer immensity. It is larger, has gone on longer, and has drawn in more people than any previous financial expansion. It has now directly touched the lives of hundreds of millions of people and has reached dozens of countries. It is different from the South Sea Bubble, the Tulip Panic, the Roaring Twenties, and the Japanese Bubble Economy of the 1980s. It does not depend on any single anomaly of economic policy, nor on a single technological advance, nor on a single well-kept secret. Its hallmark is that middle-class people, beginning with middle-class Americans, have quickly developed a remarkably strong preference for financial assets over tangible assets. That preference has become self-reinforcing. People who put equal amounts into stocks and gold in 1980 now wonder why they were so cautious. A consequence has been that most new savers put all their money into financial assets, and do not buy collectibles, farmland, or income properties. The more aggressive their investment posture is, the better they do. Even the ones who are wary of buying common stocks put their retirement accounts into money market funds. They wait to make a study of the stock market before putting the money into stocks, or they wait for a dip in the stock market, intending to buy at a timely moment. But their intent is to buy stocks and bonds sooner or later. There are a few who are never going to buy stocks, and who will always feel more secure owning gold coins and precious stones. Nowadays their caution seems almost paranoid. Caution had legitimacy and credibility in bygone days, but now it seems quaint or neurotic. Prior to the 1990s, people felt fatalistic and powerless about the occasional sharp declines in stock prices. Declines were inevitable and damaging, but nothing could be done about them. They were like hurricanes or earthquakes. Now a big decline could occur, but it would be such a calamity that the full force of government intervention would fight desperately to remedy any sustained decline in stock prices.

A big decline in the stock market would throw the retirement plans of tens of millions of voters into turmoil. They would postpone big purchases and start saving more of their current income. This would cause a recession possibly as long and as intractable as the one Japan is now suffering. Many elected officials would be defeated in the next election. It follows that governments in the United States and Euroland will do everything in their power to keep stock prices high and will help stock prices rise further if they can.

This book puts forward the view that the financial wealth-creation process has gone beyond the point where it can be rolled back. It has now generated so much wealth, and acquired so many supporters, that it is not going to be stopped. It has enough influence and enough persuasive power to prevail easily against any groups that seek to slow it down or put it into reverse. Furthermore, the wealth is not merely unrealized gains in the pockets of a few Silicon Valley magnates. It is much more widespread, and tens of millions of middle-class people have tapped it. There are millions more who are counting on further rapid increases in financial wealth. The wealth-creation process is like a snowball rolling down a long, steep hill. The snowball quickly gets big, gathers speed, and then rolls over objects in its path. This one is already big enough to be shaking the entire earth as it rumbles down its trajectory. This snowball has gotten so big, and has so much momentum, that it is going to keep rolling for a long time. This chapter speculates on how much farther it can conceivably roll, what alterations to the landscape it will make, and what objects in its path it might crush.

The preceding chapters show the wealth-creation mechanism piece by piece. They attempt to show each piece of it in enough detail so that one can see how each piece works in isolation. They also attempt to show how commonplace and unremarkable each piece is by itself. The individuals and corporations each act in ordinary self-interested ways. The aggregate of all these individuals, corporations, and managers is on display and is now parading on center stage. The many pieces of the financial wealth-creation and -propagation mechanism are filling up the stage and crowding the other players off. This chapter next calculates a scenario of how large the total pile of financial wealth will become, how far financial wealth will propagate, how deeply into the middle classes it will percolate, and what sort of prosperity it will bring to the world. The scenario is extreme, and it states conditions that have to be met if its extreme value is to be reached. The chapter then queries whether the growth path described here will be worse or better for the environment. It ends by speculating on what some of the side effects and unintended consequences may be. Some of the side effects may be ugly, but they will probably happen regardless of whether they are stated here, so it is better to lay them out where people can see them, debate them, and take remedial action if there is any that would help.

$1 Quadrillion of Financial Wealth

World financial wealth would have to increase by more than 10 times to reach the $1 quadrillion level. This magnitude is $1,000 trillion, about 12 times greater than the $78 trillion that had been reached as of mid-1998. To see what would have to happen for the $1 quadrillion level to be reached, it is useful first to see what would have to happen for the $100 trillion level to be reached.

After reading the arguments and examples in this book, most readers will probably be ready to concede that world financial wealth will soon surpass the $100 trillion level. The descriptions of how financial wealth is being generated have hopefully given some credibility to the wealth-creation process. Although no group is guiding it, the wealth-creation machinery is robust and resilient. Readers who thought that wealth was rising on flimsy and temporary foundations, or was a result of collective mania, hopefully now believe that the underpinnings of the current prosperity are rather more solid. So they may concede that the $100 trillion level is just around the corner. This level is only a bit higher than what the world has already reached. World output is projected to reach $45 trillion by 2002, so world financial wealth of $100 trillion would be only slightly greater than 2 times the annual value of world output.

Whether world financial wealth will continue growing to the $100 trillion level, and then surpass $500 trillion to reach $1 quadrillion, however, depends on many conditions. These have not all been met consistently, and it is not clear that they will be met in the future. Several conditions will have to be satisfied if world wealth is to reach the $100 trillion level, and then a higher degree of compliance will be required if world wealth is to reach levels higher than that. Here is a list of several conditions that have been satisfied recently, and will have to go on being satisfied if world wealth is to keep rising.

- *Inflation in the dollar and euro zones will have to remain low.* There cannot be any increase in inflation, because higher inflation slows down an important part of the wealth-creation machine. Higher inflation frightens some investors away from buying financial assets. It also frightens other investors away from buying long-term bonds; investors who were buying long-term bonds switch to buying short-term bonds. And it frightens many investors away from buying common stocks. Common stocks offer a higher return on average than bonds, but if investors are able to earn enough in bonds, many of them do not take the risk of buying stocks.

  World financial wealth can rise quickly, and reach the levels discussed here, only if stock prices rise quickly. Any deterrent to buying common stocks would slow down or stop the financial wealth-creation machine or put it into reverse. This assertion may sound extreme, but a few minutes of reflection will show that it accurately characterizes the situation. There are other ways that financial wealth can rise, but they will not add as much to the total, and they will work more slowly. For example, there is room for increase via securitization. Many existing businesses and properties are not yet securitized, and an asset is worth more if it is securitized. Therefore, more financial wealth can be created if all income-producing properties are securitized. This path, however, does not have the potential to take world financial wealth as high as $500 trillion or $1 quadrillion. If 100% of the world's income-producing properties were securitized, the total impact would probably not carry world financial wealth much higher than the $150 trillion level. The newly issued securities would be worth more than the underlying assets were worth before they were securitized. The reason is that millions of buyers can buy a security, but only a few large buyers can compete to buy all of a large income-producing asset. So after a large asset is securitized, there is more demand for it; consequently, its market value is higher. This advantage, however, goes only so far. If the large asset is a factory that belongs to a single owner, after it is securitized it is still the same factory, but now it belongs to millions of small investors. The point is that the factory is still the same. Its ownership has been reconfigured so that its market value is greater, but its future profits have not increased. Another reason that securitization cannot quickly carry world wealth to the $1 quadrillion level is that it would take a long time to issue and distribute the new securities. Securitization is too slow, and by itself it does not raise people's expectations about future growth rates enough.

Another way of raising financial wealth is for governments with strong credit ratings to issue more bonds. This, however, will not raise world wealth very far. There is an upper limit to how many more bonds each government can issue without losing its credit rating or having to raise taxes. This way of raising financial wealth would add only $5 or $10 trillion to the total.

The conclusion, therefore, is inescapable. If world financial wealth is to surpass $100 trillion quickly, and then keep rising to the $1 quadrillion level, the total market value of common stocks, about $35 trillion as of the first quarter of 2000, would have to keep rising rapidly. Stocks that have not been issued yet would have to be issued, and then rise above their issue prices; and stocks that already are listed on exchanges would have to keep rising.

Inflation is the enemy of stock prices. When inflation is high, the future profits of a company look less valuable. A profit of $1 million that is to be earned 20 years into the future has a present value of $553,676 when the applicable discount rate is 3% ($1 million/$(1.03)^{20}$ = $553,676). This example uses 3% as the lowest discount rate that investors might normally use. It is the textbook figure for the risk-free opportunity cost of capital. When a higher discount rate, for example 7%, has to be used because of inflation, the present value is only $258,419 ($1 million/$(1.07)^{20}$ = $258,419). You may argue that the comparison is unfair, and if the discount rate is higher because of inflation, then the dollar amount of the payoff coming in the future should also be inflated. This is true, but what hurts the stock price is the uncertainly about inflation. You may argue that it is irrational for stock investors to fear inflation. Conventional wisdom holds that corporations can raise prices enough to defend their profits, but there is still uncertainty. Stock market investors fear inflation because they cannot anticipate how much the price index will rise, and which companies will have a hard time raising their prices. So investors hold back when inflation is rising. They stop buying stock so fearlessly.

A further implication is that if world financial wealth is to rise past $100 trillion, or past $200 trillion, common stocks will have to constitute a larger portion of total financial wealth than they currently do. Bonds and bank deposits have traditionally accounted for two-thirds of financial assets, and common stocks have accounted for the other third. In the future, if financial wealth is to keep rising rapidly, common stocks will have to account for higher and higher proportions of total financial wealth. Bond issuance cannot carry the total to levels that are 5 or 10 times higher than today's level; there is not enough collateral in the world. Common stock does not depend on collateral or cash flows that already exist for its value. Common stock depends on future cash flows for its value. For this reason, its market value is not held in restraint by what already exists. So if there is to be a further rapid rise in the value of world financial wealth, much of the rise will have to come from higher stock prices.

- *There cannot be any wars.*   This condition can operate at two levels of stringency. At the level stringent enough for world wealth to reach $100 trillion or $200 trillion, there cannot be any wars that damage valuable properties or kill people who have skills that the modern economy needs. This level of stringency is not a sweeping prohibition against all wars. All wars are damaging to wealth, but a war that damages an insured building hurts both the building and the insurance company. All wars kill people, but a war that kills a Java programmer hurts the rate of expansion of the World Wide Web. Financial wealth can increase past the $100 trillion level with wars going on in a few underdeveloped countries. The losses and the expense are wasteful, but the $100 trillion level can still be reached because value is being created so rapidly elsewhere. To reach the more demanding level of $500 trillion or $1 quadrillion, however, will take a concerted effort by everyone in the world. All peoples would have to put aside their differences, resolve their disputes, and get to work. Every person and every productive asset would immediately have to be assigned to its best and highest use. Ignorance, weak enforcement of legal rights, discrimination, oppression, and counterproductive incentives would have to be remedied without delay.

- *Governments will have to keep lowering corporate profits tax rates.* Common stock prices would rise quickly if corporate tax rates were reduced to zero. The lost revenue could easily be replaced by altering the income taxes levied on individuals. In the example that follows, a tax levied on individuals will replace the revenues collected from corporations. All forms of personal income, including realized and unrealized capital gains and inheritances, would be sources for tax collections. More types of income that individuals receive would be taxable in this example because corporations no longer would pay income tax. To see the effect that a change in tax policy could have, suppose that the corporate tax rate is 30%. There is a corporation that earned $100 million before tax. Its stock is trading at 25 times earnings. The market value of its shares therefore would be $100 million $\times (1 - 0.30) \times 25 = \$1.75$ billion. The tax collector is getting $30 million a year from the corporation. Now suppose that the corporate tax rate is set at zero. The market capitalization of the company should rise to $100 million $\times 25 = \$2.5$ billion. This is an increase of $750 million. This increase would accrue to the stockholders of the company. The tax collector could get the $30 million that was being raised before by assessing a tax of $30 million/$750 million = 4% on the unrealized gains.

It may seem radical to propose taxing unrealized gains. Tax codes have not levied any rates on paper profits before. In this example the tax is levied on unrealized gains to show how small the tax would be as a percentage of the paper profit. Taxing the paper profit also makes the tax revenue come in as soon as it did when the tax was on the corporation's profits. This is important because tax revenues need to continue so that governments can go on servicing the interest payments they owe on bonds. Taxing the paper profit also focuses attention on the relative magnitudes of income and wealth. The corporation pays 30% of its income in taxes, or its shareholders pay 1.2% of the market value of its common stock, or they pay 4% of the value of their windfall gains when the tax is shifted.

These relative magnitudes apply for the new economic policy contemplated in this book. Suppose that the objective of U.S. economic policy will be to raise the value of financial assets, and suppose that the policy succeeds and wealth grows. For example, U.S.

wealth at market prices could reach $60 trillion, with the U.S. GNP at $10 trillion. For simplicity, suppose that federal tax collections totaled $2 trillion. This is 20% of GNP, but only 3.33% of wealth. The tax burden in dollars is the same but is much lighter as a percentage of wealth. With the economic policy contemplated here wealth would grow much faster than income, so the relative size of the tax burden as a percentage of wealth would shrink.

The purpose of this example is to show that financial wealth might increase faster if taxes are shifted. It is also to show the rapidly changing relative magnitudes of wealth versus income. The example is simple and does not consider secondary effects. The example does not prove that taxes should be assessed only on financial wealth. Nor does it show that tax collections can be increased without distorting the economy. Tax policy is a complicated subject, and incentives are easy to distort or pervert. All this example does is point out that the rapid rise in financial wealth introduces new possibilities into the fiscal debate.

- *The rate of profit on new investments in high technology will have to remain high.*   One of the prime movers of the stock market rise has been the high rate of return on new investments in telecommunications, semiconductors, biotechnology, and software. The current wave of innovation and buildout must continue. Indeed, the current wave must not only continue, it must exceed the growth rate that stock market analysts are using—and it must go on longer than they expect. Otherwise, stock prices will stop rising and begin falling. If stock market analysts revise their growth projections for a company upward, its stock price goes up.

How Quickly Can $1 Quadrillion Be Reached?

What is the shortest time the world might need to reach financial wealth of $1 quadrillion? For discussion purposes, suppose that all the conditions previously stated suddenly hold at a level of stringency that has previously been reached only intermittently. Inflation is zero, there are no wars, corporate profit taxes have been cut to zero, and the rate of profit on new investments in high technology has stayed high and has kept rising. Let us now construct an example using a set of macroeconomic aggregates that might prevail in a future year, and that would support world financial wealth of $1 quadrillion.

In this hypothetical future year, the annual value of world output is $80 trillion. This is 2 times the level of 1999. The entire increase is real. There has been no inflation whatsoever since 1999. All human activity has been directed toward producing goods and services. Discrimination has ceased. All humans are now producing what they are most qualified to produce, and selling their output in the market that will pay the most. Added value has been maximized for the human population. All land, buildings, and equipment have been put to their most highly valued use. All productive assets are held in the legal form that makes them most valuable. For most assets, this is a corporation with bonds and shares listed on stock exchanges.

This example ignores how much investment would be required to double world output. This example presumes that a doubling of world output occurs from the 1999 level. It then examines whether this doubling would be enough to support financial wealth more than 10 times the level of 1999.

With world output at the $80 trillion level, a hypothetical mix of financial assets worth $1 quadrillion might be composed of the following:

Assets	Worth
Cash and bank deposits	$10 trillion
Government bonds	$165 trillion
Corporate bonds	$125 trillion
Common stocks	$700 trillion

These assets would be worth more than 12 times the value of annual output. This multiple is unprecedented. When the market value of claims on an economy exceeds 5 times annual output, it usually does not go higher, and often falls back to 3 times annual output. One reason is that the percentage of annual output that has to be paid to the holders of the claims becomes too large, and then the share paid to workers has to be increased.

Let us distribute the $80 trillion of annual output and see if enough of it can be directed to the holders of securities to validate these very high market valuations. First, governments would collect $20 trillion in taxes and spend it all. Of that $20 trillion, $5 trillion would be paid as interest on government bonds. Using 3% as the yield on government bonds, and assuming they are perpetual bonds, their market value would be $165 trillion ($5 trillion/0.03 = $165 trillion). This figure is, of course, more than 4 times higher than the market value of government bonds as of 2000.

After allowing for government, there is annual output of $60 trillion to be allocated. Let us assign $40 trillion to wages and $20 trillion to payments to corporate bondholders and stockholders. These are extreme figures. The percentage for wages and salaries would normally be higher, and the percentage to corporate interest payments and earnings would normally be lower. But let us use these extreme percentages to see if the total value of financial wealth can come to $1 quadrillion.

The $20 trillion of corporate interest payments and earnings would have to support bonds and stocks worth more than $800 trillion. If corporate interest payments were $5 trillion, and the applicable yield on corporate bonds were 4%, and the bonds were perpetual, corporate bonds would have a market value of $125 trillion.

There would remain $15 trillion of corporate profits. In this example these are not taxed, so all $15 trillion would support the market value of common stock. If the market value of common stock were $700 trillion, the price/earnings (P/E) ratio of the average common stock would have to be 700/15 = 46.

This P/E ratio is high but not unprecedented. It implies a high expected growth rate of corporate earnings, but not an impossibly high rate. For example, suppose that the average investor requires an expected rate of return of 8% in order to be willing to hold common stock instead of corporate bonds that yield 4% or government bonds that yield 3%. In this case, the growth rate of the average company would have to be slightly less than 6%, around 5.82% [46 = 1/(0.08 − 0.0582)].

Real growth of almost 6% a year! This is slightly more than twice the rate the world has achieved since the end of World War II. Could the average investor possibly believe that the world would grow that fast into the future, when it has rarely exceeded annual growth of 3%?

Investors do not need to believe this. Instead, they could believe something much easier to imagine: They could believe that half the companies will grow at 3% and the other half will grow at 9%. Or they could believe that one-third of the companies will not grow, another third will grow at 3%, and the remaining third will grow at 15%. Any combination that averages 6% will do, and if investors believe that forecast, they will pay high prices for common stocks.

Investors will believe a high-growth forecast for a company if both the company and the economy have done very well in the recent past. This numerical illustration shows how pivotal investor confidence is. Further increases in financial wealth depend on investors' believing an optimistic forecast of future prosperity. In this example, common stocks account for 70% of the total hypothetical $1 quadrillion of financial wealth—a much higher proportion than has ever occurred.

The main point that these calculations illustrate is that world financial wealth can increase so much more than annual output. In the numerical illustration, world output doubles and world financial wealth increases by more than 10 times! Of course, the numerical illustration makes many extreme assumptions to arrive at this result. This startling outcome would never happen in real life. Something would surely go wrong. But if nothing did go wrong, the outcome could be an inconceivably high level of financial wealth.

Moreover, if nothing went wrong, the result would happen in a little over 12 years! Beginning with world output of $40 trillion in 2000, world output would reach $80 trillion by 2012 if growth were 6% a year. After 12 years of growth at 6% a year, investors might believe that 6% annual growth is normal. It would then be reasonable for them to pay 46 times earnings for the average common stock.

Table 12.1 shows this scenario of 6% output growth paired with financial wealth reaching $1 quadrillion. This would be an extreme outcome, but if financial wealth increased even half as fast as the projection, the effect would be epochal.

Note that from 2007 onward in this hypothetical forecast, the annual increase in world financial wealth is larger than the value of world output for the year. And for 2012 and 2013, the annual increase in world financial wealth is more than twice the value of world output for the year.

The calculations in this numerical example are rough, and they skip over many important factors. The purpose of this bare-bones example is to show that there is no absolute upper limit to financial wealth. There is no obvious impediment preventing it from reaching $1 quadrillion. There is

Table 12.1   Scenario of World Output and World
Financial Wealth, $ Trillions

Year	World Output	World Financial Wealth
2000	40.0	85
2001	42.3	104
2002	44.8	127
2003	47.4	156
2004	50.2	190
2005	53.0	233
2006	56.2	285
2007	59.4	348
2008	62.9	426
2009	66.6	521
2010	70.4	637
2011	74.5	779
2012	78.9	953
2013	83.5	1,165

no law of physics that prevents world financial wealth from reaching $1 quadrillion by 2012 and surpassing that level by 2013. A human cannot run a mile in 30 seconds, and an automobile cannot go 5,000 miles an hour on land. Those feats are physically impossible. The feat discussed here, in contrast, is improbable but not impossible.

If world wealth does reach $1 quadrillion, the level of wealth would be difficult to imagine. There could be 1 billion millionaires, for example. Assuming that world population had reached 7 billion by that time, 1 person in 7 would be a millionaire. Or there could be 1 million billionaires. Of course for either of those outcomes to occur, the rest of the population would have to have no financial assets at all.

Effect on the Environment

If raising the value of financial assets is now society's main objective, other objectives have lost their previous priority. Old priorities were creating jobs, raising output in all sectors of the economy, narrowing regional disparities, and broadening access to career opportunities. The top priority now is to foster growth that will drive common stock prices higher.

Common stock prices respond to higher forecasts of growth for companies' sales and earnings. The beginning amount of earnings does not matter as much, and neither does the beginning amount of sales revenue. Companies start small. What separates the stars from the mediocrities is how fast they become large. If the objective of economic policy is to raise the market value of financial wealth, growth companies take on more importance than they used to have. In the days when creating jobs was the top priority, growth companies were treated well because they created jobs quickly and because those new jobs replaced the ones that were being lost elsewhere in the economy. Now growth companies have taken on an even greater importance. They are the motors of the stock market boom. Policymakers strive to find ways of helping them, and seek to spur their growth rates. Every politician understands the need for constant renewal in the private sector. Today's big companies will be tomorrow's has-beens. The new giants will be companies that were small just a short time earlier.

Among stock market people there has always been a cult of growth. Other parts of the polity did not have the same unreservedly positive attitude toward growth. In government and in the judiciary there was skepticism about size and growth rates. This skepticism has now been set aside. A new conventional wisdom has taken root in government. Growth, and particularly growth in high tech, is now essential. The checks and balances that used to mediate market power versus labor are now weaker.

If the new reality is that financial wealth will decide more of society's decisions about the future, what does this imply for protecting the environment? There are reasons for concern and reasons for optimism. The concern is that citizens' groups will have less influence. Arguing against growth will be less effective. Antigrowth advocates would be asking people to make a bigger sacrifice than before. When economic magnitudes were given in terms of annual flow variables, activists asked companies to give up $1 of annual earnings. Now economic magnitudes are in terms of stock variables like market capitalization, so activists are still asking companies to give up $1 of annual earnings, but that $1 of earnings is supporting $25 to $50 of stock market value.

Another reason for concern is the fact that faster growth leads to more fossil fuel use. Rising financial wealth supports higher consumption and fuels faster growth, which in turn supports higher prices for financial assets. This self-reinforcing cycle would imply more demand for cars, buses, and electric power. The amount of carbon dioxide that will be released is a cause for concern, and is higher than the absorption capability of forests, even including reforestation schemes.

The main reason for optimism is that publicly listed companies are very sensitive to public opinion, bad publicity, and lawsuits. Their stock prices can fall suddenly if investors think that a lawsuit or a consumer boycott is going to hurt future profits. Companies are now judged according to their future prospects, and more and more of their total market value is determined by their future earnings. Any question mark hanging over those future earnings does more damage now than it did previously.

Manna and Fallout Raining Down

If world financial wealth continues to accumulate as fast as it has recently done, there will be many winners who will bask in unexpected luxury as riches pile up in their retirement accounts. There will also be losers and side effects. Everyone on earth, even primitive people in remote areas, will be affected.

The most obvious losers will be people in rich countries who do not own common stocks. They have already fallen behind and will fall farther behind. They have jobs, and some of them earn good hourly wages, and they will get raises, but the gap between them and the rich will continue to widen.

A bigger category of losers will be people in poor countries who cannot migrate across national boundaries. If they are educated they will find work, but they will earn less than they could make if they could migrate. And uneducated people in poor countries will be the biggest losers of all. Some of them may get jobs working directly or indirectly for the beneficiaries of the new financial wealth. They may be absolutely better off, or no worse off, but their relative position will be unambiguously worse.

There will be side effects too numerous to mention. One is already happening—namely, business elites in each country are losing their national homogeneity. Cross-border acquisitions and mergers create stock market value, and that is why there are so many of them. They have the side effect of putting foreign managers into companies where top managers were previously all of the same nationality. This trend has been going on for a long time, but it may now be accelerating. The underlying reasons for companies to merge are getting stronger in some industry sectors, so the pace of mergers may intensify.

To end on a speculative and optimistic note, there may be another important side effect: Economic isolationism may lose the support and legitimacy that it still retains.

Notes

Chapter 2

1. *Los Angeles Times,* 28 June 1992, p. 1.
2. Data from DRI Global Economics and National Income and Product Accounts.

Chapter 3

1. Data from "Current Yield," *Barrons,* 27 December 1999, 21–22, MW 74 [table].
2. Data from "Round Table," *Barrons,* 18 January 1999, 32 [table].
3. Data from "Round Table," *Barrons,* 12 January 1999, 32 [table].
4. Fernand Braudel, *The Wheels of Commerce* (Berkeley: University of California Press, 1992), 535.
5. *New York Times,* 4 January 2000, p. B-1.
6. Data from Bloomberg News Service, 22 January 2000.

Chapter 5

1. *IMF International Financial Statistics,* November 1997, p. 720, line 791cd.
2. *IMF International Financial Statistics,* November 1997, p. 722, line 93eec.

Chapter 6

1. Concept from the Capital Asset Pricing Model. For a discussion of this model, see a general finance text, for example, Robert C. Higgins, *Analysis for Financial Management,* 5th ed. (Boston: Irwin/McGraw-Hill, 1998), Chapter 8.
2. Figures for market capitalization from Value Line; figure for market capitalization of the emerging country stock markets quoted in *IFC*

Indexes, July 1999 Emerging Markets Data Base (Washington, DC: International Finance Corporation, 1999).

3. U.S. stock market capitalization cited in *Barrons*, 8 May 2000, MW 74 [table]; *The Economist*, 13 November 1999, 85; and "Emerging Stockmarkets," *The Economist*, 5 August 2000, 100.

4. Data from "Mutual Funds and the Retirement Market," *Investment Company Institute Research in Brief* 8, no. 4 (Washington, DC: Investment Company Institute, July 1999), and the U.S. Census Bureau.

5. Data from *IFC Indexes*, July 1999 Emerging Markets Data Base (Washington, DC: International Finance Corporation, 1999).

6. Figure computed from 12-month rolling cumulative return figures provided by DRI Global Economics.

Chapter 11

1. William K. Stevens, "Conservationists Win Battles but Fear War Is Lost," *New York Times*, 11 January 2000, p. D-5.

2. Information from Kimberly Blanton, "Prosperity Is Slow to Trickle Down," *Boston Sunday Globe*, 6 February 2000, p. A-39.

3. Information from the Federal Reserve Bank of St. Louis Data Bank.

4. Data for emerging market performance compiled by Morgan Stanley Capital Markets and reported weekly in *Barrons*.

5. Data from "Lipper Mutual Funds Quarterly," *Barrons*, 10 January 2000, F 45 [table].

6. Data from "Dow Jones U.S. Total Market Industry Groups," showing stock market performance of each industry group for selected time periods, in *Barrons*, 10 January 2000, MW 67 [table].

7. Data from illustration of stock market performance of health care industry subgroups for 1999 in *Barrons*, 10 January 2000, 13 [table].

8. Data from "Dow Jones U.S. Total Market Industry Groups," showing stock market performance of each industry group for selected time periods, in *Barrons*, 10 January 2000, MW 67 [table].

9. Data from "Dow Jones U.S. Total Market Industry Groups," showing stock market performance of each industry group for selected time periods, in *Barrons*, 10 January 2000, MW 67 [table].

10. Data from "Dow Jones U.S. Total Market Industry Groups," showing stock market performance of each industry group for selected time periods, in *Barrons*, 10 January 2000, MW 67 [table].

Index

About the Author

JOHN EDMUNDS is chairman of the finance faculty at Babson College and is faculty advisor to the Cutler Investment Management Center and the Babson College Fund. His areas of interest are capital markets, international finance, derivatives, and emerging markets. He is also on the faculty of the Arthur D. Little School of Management. Prior to 1993 he was professor of capital markets at Instituto de Empresa in Madrid, Spain, where he was the first holder of a chair funded by Asesores Bursatiles, a leading Spanish securities firm. He has taught at other schools in the Boston area, including Harvard, the Fletcher School of Law and Diplomacy, Northeastern University, and Boston University. He has also taught at INCAE in Costa Rica and La Universidad Catolica Madre y Maestra in the Dominican Republic. At Arthur D. Little he was voted Professor of the Year in 1994. He has lived in six countries and has spent a total of 18 years abroad. His international experience is in Latin America and Europe, and he has also worked in Asia and Africa. He holds a DBA in international business from the Harvard Business School, an MBA in finance and quantitative methods with honors from Boston University, an MA in economics from Northeastern University, and an AB in economics cum laude from Harvard College. He has been a consultant for the Harvard Institute for International Development, the Rockefeller Foundation, Stanford Research Institute, and numerous private companies. He is the author of more than 70 articles and cases, published both in academic and practitioner journals, including *The European Management Journal* and *New Economy*. He is fluent in Spanish and also speaks French.